C. WRITING THAT ARGUES OR PERSUADES

Begin with the writing situation:

- What are you writing about? (p. 3)
- Who is going to read your writing? (p. 4)
- How should you talk about this topic for your readers? (p. 4)
- What is the required length, deadline, and format, as well as the background for your assignment? (pp. 3–4)

Compose using writing processes:

- See Chapter 4. (pp. 11–19)
- What strategies can help you organize your writing? (p. 15)

Think critically about using sources:

- Does your argument require research? (Chapters 7–11)
- If yes, how many and what kind of sources are needed to persuade your readers? (p. 55)
- What resources are appropriate for your course and available? (Discipline-Specific Resources)
- Should you use tables, graphs, or images? Audio or video? (pp. 38–41)

Think carefully about your final steps:

- What citation style, if any, should you use? (Parts 3–5)
- Did you cite all your sources correctly? (Parts 3–5)
- Did you carefully edit and proofread your writing? (Parts 6–8)
- What design conventions are appropriate for this type of writing? (pp. 32–34)

Writing Intensive

Essentials for College Writers
Second Edition

Elaine P. Maimon
Governors State University

Janice H. Peritz
*The City University of New York,
Queen's College*

Kathleen Blake Yancey
Florida State University

Mc Graw Hill

Connect
Learn
Succeed™

Published by McGraw-Hill, an imprint of The McGraw-Hill Companies, Inc., 1221 Avenue of the Americas, New York, NY 10020. Copyright © 2013, 2009, 2007 by the McGraw-Hill Companies, Inc. All rights reserved. Printed in the United States of America. No part of this publication may be reproduced or distributed in any form or by any means, or stored in a database or retrieval system, without the prior written consent of The McGraw-Hill Companies, Inc., including, but not limited to, in any network or other electronic storage or transmission, or broadcast for distance learning.

This book is printed on acid-free paper.

1 2 3 4 5 6 7 8 9 0 DOC/DOC 1 0 9 8 7 6 5 4 3 2

ISBN: 978-0-07-338405-4
MHID: 0-07-338405-4

Executive Sponsoring Editor:
  Christopher Bennem
Senior Marketing Manager:
  Kevin Colleary
Senior Development Editor:
  Carla Kay Samodulski
Managing Editor: *Anne Fuzellier*
Production Editor:
  Margaret Young
Interior and Cover Designer:
  Preston Thomas, Cadence Design
Buyer II: *Louis Swaim*
Production Service: *Alma Bell, Thompson Type*

Composition: *Thompson Type*
Printing: *45# New Era Thin Plus*

Vice President Editorial:
  Michael Ryan
Publisher: *David S. Patterson*
Senior Director of Development:
  Dawn Groundwater

Cover image: © Le Do,
  iStockphoto

Credits: *The credits section for this book is on page C-1 and is considered an extension of the copyright page.*

Library of Congress Cataloging-in-Publication Data
Maimon, Elaine P.
    Writing intensive / Elaine Maimon, Janice Peritz.—2nd ed.
       p. cm.
    Includes bibliographical references and index.
    Previous ed.: 2007.
    ISBN-13: 978-0-07-338405-4 (acid-free paper)
    ISBN-10: 0-07-338405-4 (acid-free paper)
  1. English language—Rhetoric.   2. Interdisciplinary approach in education.   3. Academic writing.   4. Report writing.   I. Peritz, Janice. II. Title.
    PE1408.M3368 2011
    808'.042—dc23

                                                    2011025111

The Internet addresses listed in the text were accurate at the time of publication. The inclusion of a website does not indicate an endorsement by the authors or McGraw-Hill, and McGraw-Hill does not guarantee the accuracy of the information presented at these sites.

www.mhhe.com

How to Find the Help You Need in *Writing Intensive*

Writing Intensive is a reference for all writers and researchers. When writing in any situation, you are bound to come across questions about writing and research. *Writing Intensive* provides you with answers to your questions.

Begin with "Start Smart." If you are responding to an assignment, go to the Start Smart gatefold on the inside front cover to determine the type of writing the assignment requires, along with the steps involved in constructing it. The gatefold gives you an easy means of accessing the many resources available to you within *Writing Intensive,* from help with finding a thesis to advice on documenting your sources.

Check the table of contents. If you know the topic you are looking for, try scanning the brief contents on the front cover flap or the detailed contents on the inside back cover. The brief contents lists all part and chapter titles in the book. The complete contents includes the part and chapter numbers and titles as well as each section number and title. If you are looking for specific information within a general topic (how to correct an unclear pronoun reference, for example), scanning the detailed table of contents on the inside back cover will help you find the section you need.

Look up your topic in the index. The comprehensive index at the end of *Writing Intensive* (beginning on page I-1) includes all of the topics covered in the book. For example, if you are not sure whether to use *I* or *me* in a sentence, you can look up "*I* vs. *me*" in the index.

In the List of Discipline-Specific Resources. At the end of the book (pp. D-1–D-5), you will find a comprehensive list of sources that have already been checked for relevance and credibility.

Check the documentation flowcharts. By answering the questions posed in the charts on pages 100–3 (for the MLA documentation style) and 160–62 (for the APA documentation style), you can usually find the model that you are looking for.

Look up a word in the Glossary of Usage or a term in the Glossary of Grammatical Terms. If you are not sure that you are using a particular word such as *farther* or *further* correctly, try looking it up in the Glossary of Usage on pages 266–78. If you need the definition for a grammatical term such as *linking verb,* consult the Glossary of Grammatical Terms on pages G-1–G-12.

Refer to Chapter 43 if you are a multilingual student. Chapter 43 provides help with the use of articles, helping verbs, and other problem areas for multilingual students.

Use the reference tools on each page. The reference features shown on page vii, most of which appear throughout *Writing Intensive,* will help you find the advice you need:

>   The **chapter number and title** give the topic of the chapter.
>
>   The **running head** gives the topic covered on the page.
>
>   The **main heading** includes the chapter number and section letter (for example, 25a) as well as the title of the section.
>
>   **Examples,** many of them with hand corrections, illustrate typical errors and how to correct them.
>
>   **Thumb tabs,** each containing the number and letter of the last section on the page (for example, 25b on page 230) and, usually, an abbreviation or symbol for that section, help you find the topic you are looking for.
>
>   The **"Identify and Edit" boxes** in a number of the chapters in Parts 6-8 help you recognize and correct errors.

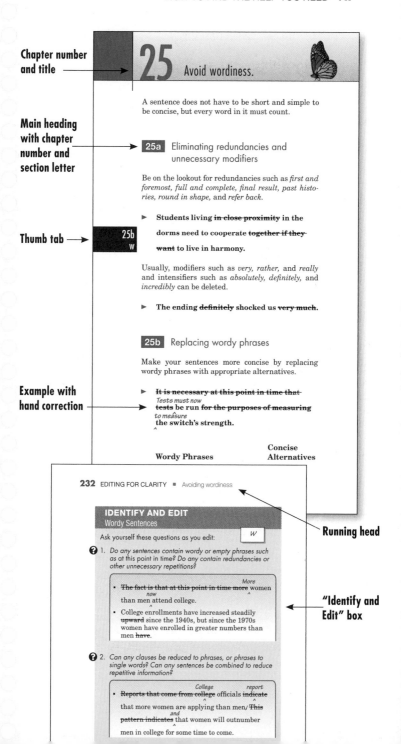

Chapter number and title

25 Avoid wordiness.

A sentence does not have to be short and simple to be concise, but every word in it must count.

Main heading with chapter number and section letter

25a Eliminating redundancies and unnecessary modifiers

Be on the lookout for redundancies such as *first and foremost, full and complete, final result, past histories, round in shape,* and *refer back.*

Thumb tab

25b
w

▶ Students living ~~in close proximity~~ in the dorms need to cooperate ~~together if they want~~ to live in harmony.

Usually, modifiers such as *very, rather,* and *really* and intensifiers such as *absolutely, definitely,* and *incredibly* can be deleted.

▶ The ending ~~definitely~~ shocked us ~~very much~~.

25b Replacing wordy phrases

Make your sentences more concise by replacing wordy phrases with appropriate alternatives.

Example with hand correction

▶ ~~It is necessary at this point in time that~~
Tests must now
tests be run ~~for the purposes of measuring~~
to measure
the switch's strength.

Wordy Phrases	Concise Alternatives

232 EDITING FOR CLARITY ■ Avoiding wordiness

Running head

IDENTIFY AND EDIT
Wordy Sentences

Ask yourself these questions as you edit: [W]

❷ 1. *Do any sentences contain wordy or empty phrases such as at this point in time? Do any contain redundancies or other unnecessary repetitions?*

- ~~The fact is that at this point in time more~~ women
  More
  now
  than men attend college.

- College enrollments have increased steadily
  ~~upward~~ since the 1940s, but since the 1970s
  women have enrolled in greater numbers than
  men ~~have~~.

"Identify and Edit" box

❷ 2. *Can any clauses be reduced to phrases, or phrases to single words? Can any sentences be combined to reduce repetitive information?*

- ~~Reports that come from college~~ officials ~~indicate~~
  College   *report*
  that more women are applying than men~~.~~ ~~This~~
  and
  pattern ~~indicates~~ that women will outnumber
  men in college for some time to come.

> Anybody who is involved in working across the disciplines is much more likely to have a lively mind and a lively life.
>
> —MARY FIELD BELENKY

PART 1

Common Assignments across the Curriculum

1

Writing in college

Most college courses require at least some writing, including one or more formal papers. Your writing projects might be case studies in the social sciences, lab reports in the hard sciences, texts for oral presentations in business studies, and analyses in the humanities, to name a few possibilities. Writing is a way to learn about the conventions of different disciplines and to make sense of your intellectual experiences.

1a Learning about common college assignments

No matter what your course of study, writing will be an important part of your college experience. Understanding what is being asked of you as a writer is a critical ingredient of your success.

Although writing assignments can differ, all writing has elements in common. There are also common writing assignments—types of writing required by courses in many different disciplines. The three most common types of papers are informative reports, interpretive analyses, and arguments:

- **Informative reports** occur in all disciplines. In an informative report, the writer passes on what he or she has learned about a topic or issue.

- **Interpretive analyses** explore the meaning of written documents, cultural artifacts, social situations, and natural events.

- **Arguments** are valued in all fields of study. These types of papers support a point or justify an opinion through logic and concrete evidence.

1b Learning how to understand assignments

From a journal entry to an essay exam to a research report, college writing assignments aim to enhance your knowledge while stimulating your creativity. Even when an instructor provides explicit and specific directions, you still need to make the assignment your own to write an effective response to it.

The following questions and suggestions will help you begin figuring out your assignments:

- **What has the professor said in class about the purpose of the assignment?** Check your notes, and consult with classmates. *(See also the next section on exploring the writing situation.)*

- **What are some key terms in the assignment that might give you a clue about what is being asked of you?** Terms like *comment, consider,* and *discuss* do not point to a particular purpose. *Classify, illustrate, report,* and *survey* are frequently associated with the task of **informing.** *Analyze, compare, explain,* and *reflect* are often associated with **interpreting.** *Agree, assess, defend,* and *refute* go with the task of **arguing.**

- **What type of project are you being asked to write?** Is it one of the common assignments, or is it particular to a discipline?

- **How long is the paper supposed to be, and when is it due?** Many topics must be narrowed to be completed on time and within the specified number of pages. Some instructors may note due dates for progress reports or first drafts.

- **What format is required for the assignment?** Some assignments, like a laboratory report, must follow a conventional form. When research is assigned, instructors generally will prefer a particular style of documentation. Check with your instructor. *(See the documentation sections, Parts 3–5.)*

1c   Exploring the writing situation

As a writer, in college and beyond, it is important to consider the situation in which you are writing. Also known as the **rhetorical situation,** the **writing situation** refers to the considerations that all writers take into account as they write. When writers think about their situation, they reflect on the following:

- The primary **purpose** of their writing
- Which **audience(s)** to address
- The **context** for their writing
- What **stance,** or authorial tone, to take
- Which **genre** and **medium** are most appropriate for the purpose, audience, and writing task

All writing tasks are framed by a rhetorical situation. A writer's context includes the means of communication, current events, and the environment in which the communication takes place. To manage a writing situation successfully, writers must consider their purpose, audience, and context, both before writing and as they compose. By keeping their rhetorical situation in mind, writers find the writing process easier to manage, and the project that results will be stronger and more effective.

2a Understanding the assignment

An **informative report** passes on what someone has learned about a topic or issue; it teaches. An informative report gives you a chance to do the following:

- Learn more about an issue that interests you
- Make sense of what you have read, heard, and seen
- Teach others what you have learned

Note: Instructors sometimes assign a special kind of informative report called a *review of the literature.* Here the term *literature* refers to published research reports, and the term *review* means that you need to present an organized account of the current state of knowledge in a specific area, not refute the research or argue for your opinion.

2b Approaching writing an informative report as a process

- **Select a topic that interests you.** The major challenge of writing informative reports is engaging the reader's interest. Selecting a

KNOW the SITUATION

Informative Reports

Purpose: To inform

Audience: Classmates and instructor, representing the general public

Stance: Reasonable, informed, objective

Genre: Informative report

Medium: Print, text attachment, Web page, video, audio, poster

Commonly used: In most disciplines, the workplace, and public life

topic that interests you makes it more likely that your report will interest your readers.

- **Consider what your readers know about the topic.** Assume that your readers have some general familiarity with your topic area but that most do not have clear, specific knowledge of your particular topic.

- **Develop an objective stance.** A commitment to objectivity gives your report its authority. Present differing views fairly, and do not take sides in a debate.

- **Compose a thesis that summarizes your knowledge of the topic.** An informative thesis typically reports the results of the writer's study. Before you decide on a thesis, review the information you have collected. Compose a thesis statement that presents the goal of your paper and forecasts its content. In an informative report on the work of the group Sisters in Islam (SIS), you might have the following thesis.

    > Based in Malaysia, SIS has developed three key ways to promote women's rights within the context of the Muslim religion and its holy book, the Qur'an.

- **Provide context in your introduction.** Informative reports usually begin with a simple introduction to the topic and a straightforward statement of the thesis. Provide some context or background, but get to your specific topic as quickly as possible, and keep it in the foreground.

- **Organize your paper by classifying and dividing information, describing a process, or using a comparison.** Clarity matters. Develop ideas in an organized way by classifying and dividing information into categories, subtopics, or the stages of a process. Consider using a comparison to clarify ideas.

- **Illustrate key ideas with examples.** Use specific examples to help readers understand your most important ideas. Examples make reports interesting as well as educational.

- **Define specialized terms, and spell out unfamiliar abbreviations.** Specialized terms will probably not be familiar to most readers. Explain these terms with a synonym (a word with the same meaning) or a brief definition—as we have just done. Spell out unfamiliar abbreviations the first time you use them, with the abbreviation in parentheses: *In September, the union will present its case to the National Labor Relations Board (NLRB).*

- **Conclude by answering "So what?"** Conclude with an image that suggests the information's value or sums it all up. The conclusion reminds readers of the topic stated in the introduction and answers the question "So what?"

3a writing

3
Interpretive analyses and writing about literature

3a   Understanding the assignment

Interpretation means working to understand a written document, literary work, cultural artifact, social situation, or natural event and then explaining what you understand in a meaningful and convincing way to readers. When an assignment asks you to compare, explain, analyze, discuss, or do a reading of something, you are expected to study that subject closely. An interpretive analysis moves beyond description, however, and examines or compares particular items for a reason: to answer a

**3b
writing**

Interpretive Analyses

Purpose: To enhance understanding
Audience: Classmates and instructor, representing the general public
Stance: Thoughtful, inquisitive, open-minded
Genres: Review, critique, blog
Medium: Print, text attachment, Web page, video, audio
Commonly used: In the arts, humanities, and many other disciplines

critical question in ways that enhance your readers' understanding of people's conditions, actions, beliefs, or desires.

3b Approaching writing an interpretive analysis as a process

▪ **Discover an aspect of the subject that is meaningful to you.** Think about your own feelings and experiences while you read, listen, or observe. Connecting your feelings and experiences with what you are studying can help you develop new ideas and fresh interpretations.

▪ **Develop a thoughtful stance.** Think of yourself as an explorer. Be thoughtful, inquisitive, and open-minded. When you write your analysis, invite your readers to join you on an intellectual journey, saying, in effect, "Come, think this through with me."

▪ **Use an intellectual framework.** To understand your subject, use a relevant perspective or an intellectual framework. For example, the basic elements of fiction, such as plot, character, and setting, are often used to analyze stories. Sigmund Freud's theory of conscious and unconscious forces in conflict has been applied to various subjects, including people, poems, and historical periods.

No matter what framework you use, analysis entails figuring out how the parts make up a meaningful whole. Treat the whole as more than the sum of its parts, and recognize that interpreting meaning is a complex problem with multiple solutions.

■ **List, compare, classify, and question to discover your thesis.** To figure out a thesis, explore separate features of your subject. Try one or more of the following strategies:
  ■ Take notes about what you see or read; if it helps, write a summary.
  ■ Look for and list points of likeness and difference.
  ■ Name the class of things to which the item you are analyzing belongs (for example, memoirs), and then identify important features of that class (for example, scene, point of view, friends, turning points).
  ■ Ask yourself questions about the subject you are analyzing, and write down any interesting answers. Imagine what kinds of questions your professor or classmates might ask about the artifact, document, or performance.

■ **Make your thesis focused and purposeful.** To make a point about your subject, focus on one or two questions. Resist the temptation to describe or comment on everything you see.

> In the first section of Schubert's *Der Atlas,* both the tempo and the harmonic progression express the sorrow of the hero's eternal plight.

Although you want your point to be clear, you also want to make sure that your thesis anticipates the "So what?" question and sets up an interesting context for your interpretation. Unless you relate your specific thesis to some more general issue, idea, or problem, your interpretive analysis may seem pointless to readers.

- **Introduce the general issue, a clear thesis or question, and relevant context.** In interpretive analyses, an introduction needs to do the following (often in more than one paragraph):
  - Identify the general issue, concept, or problem at stake. You can also present the intellectual framework that you are applying.
  - Provide relevant background information.
  - Name the specific item or items you will focus on.
  - State the thesis or pose the main question(s) your analysis will address.

  Even though you may begin with a provocative statement or a stimulating example, make sure that your introduction does the four things listed above.

- **Plan your analysis so that each point supports your thesis.** After you pose a key question or state your thesis, you need to organize your points to answer the question or support your interpretive thesis. Readers must be able to follow your train of thought and see how each point you make is related to your thesis.

- **Conclude by answering "So what?"** The conclusion of an interpretive analysis needs to answer the "So what?" question by saying why your thesis—as well as the analysis that supports and develops it—is relevant to the larger issue identified in the introduction or to our understanding of people's conditions, actions, beliefs, or desires.

4 Arguments

In college, opinions based on personal feelings have less weight than reasoned positions expressed as written arguments. When you write an argument, your purpose is to take part in the debate by stating and supporting your position on an issue. In addition to position papers, written arguments appear in other forms, including critiques, reviews, and proposals.

- **Critiques** focus on a position someone has taken on an issue. The critique fairly summarizes that position and either refutes or defends it. *Refutations* present contradictory evidence or expose inadequate reasoning. *Defenses* clarify the author's reasoning, present new arguments to support the position, and show that criticisms of the position are unreasonable or unconvincing. Critiques address the question "What is true?"

- **Reviews** evaluate an event, artifact, practice, or institution. Judgments in reviews should be principled; that is, they should be determined by reasonable criteria. Reviews address the question "What is good?"

- **Proposals,** sometimes called **policy papers,** are designed to cause change in the world. Proposals ask readers to see a situation and to act on that situation in a certain way. Proposals address the question "What should be done?"

4b Approaching writing your own argument as a process

Figure out what is at issue. Before you can take a position on a topic like air pollution or cyberbullying, you must figure out what is at issue. Ask questions about your topic. Do you see indications that

11

4b writing

KNOW the SITUATION

Arguments

Purpose: To persuade

Audience: Audience members can be close to a writer (for example, classmates) or distant from him or her (for example, citizens of an unfamiliar country); in either case, keying in on members of that audience is important because reasons, examples, and stories should speak to them.

Stance: Reasonable

Genres: Arguments appear as stand-alone genres and inside other genres like reviews, critiques, and proposals.

Medium: Print, digital, or networked depending on the audience and the topic. (A proposal for a new bridge might be more compelling in a visual medium, for example.)

Commonly used: In most disciplines, the workplace, and public life

all is not as it should be? Have things always been this way, or have they changed for the worse? From what different perspectives—economic, social, political, cultural, medical, geographic—can problems be understood? Do people interested in the topic disagree about what is true, what is good, or what should be done?

Based on your answers to such questions, identify the issues your topic raises, and decide which of these issues you think is most important, interesting, and appropriate for you to write about.

Develop a reasonable stance that negotiates differences. You want your readers to respect your intelligence and trust your judgment. Conducting research on an issue can make you well informed; reading other people's views can enhance your thoughtfulness. Pay attention to the places where you disagree with the opinions of others, but also note what you have in common—topical interests, key questions, or underlying values.

Avoid language that may promote prejudice or fear. Misrepresentations of other people's ideas are out of place, as are personal attacks. Write arguments to open minds, not slam doors shut.

Trying out different perspectives can also help you figure out where you stand on an issue. *(Also see the next paragraph, on stating your position.)* Make a list of the arguments for and against a specific position; then compare the lists, and decide where you stand, perhaps on one side or the other or somewhere in the middle. Does one set of arguments seem stronger than the other? Do you want to change or qualify your initial position?

Compose a thesis that states your position. A strong, debatable thesis, or claim, on a topic of public interest is a key ingredient of an effective written argument. Without debate, there can be no argument and no reason to assert your position. Personal feelings and accepted facts are not debatable and therefore cannot serve as an argument's thesis.

PERSONAL FEELING, NOT A DEBATABLE THESIS

I feel that developing nations should not suffer food shortages.

ACCEPTED FACT, NOT A DEBATABLE THESIS

Food shortages are a fact of life in many developing nations.

DEBATABLE THESIS

Current food shortages in developing nations are in large part caused by climate change and the use of food crops in biofuels.

In proposals and policy papers, the thesis presents a solution in terms of the writer's definition of the problem. Because this kind of thesis is both complex and qualified, you will often need more than one sentence to state it clearly. You will also need numerous well-supported arguments to make it credible.

Identify key points to support and develop your thesis. A strong, debatable thesis should be supported and developed with sound reasoning and carefully documented evidence. You can think of an argument as a dialogue between the writer and readers. Anticipate questions, and answer them by presenting reasons that are substantiated with evidence and by refuting opposing views. Define any abstract terms, such as *freedom,* that figure importantly in your arguments.

Usually an argument includes more than one type of claim and more than one kind of evidence. Employ generalizations based on empirical data or statistics, authoritative claims based on the opinions of experts, and ethical reasons based on the application of principle.

As you conduct research for your paper, note evidence—facts, examples, and expert testimony—that can be used to support each argument for or against your position. Demonstrate your trustworthiness by properly quoting and documenting the information you have gathered from your sources. Also build your credibility by paying attention to **counterarguments,** substantiated claims that do not support your position. Consider whether a reader could reasonably draw different conclusions from your evidence or disagree with your assumptions. Use one of the following strategies to address potential counterarguments:

- Qualify your thesis in light of the counterargument by including a word such as *most, some, usually,* and *likely:* "Students with credit cards *usually* have trouble with debt" recognizes that some do not.

- Add to the thesis a statement of the conditions for or exceptions to your position: "Businesses *with over five hundred employees* saved money using the new process."

- Choose one or two counterarguments, and refute their truth or their importance. Introduce a counterargument with a signal phrase like "Others might contend . . ." *(See Part 2: Researching, p. 94, for a discussion of signal phrases.)* Refute a counterargument's truth by questioning the author's interpretation of the evidence or the author's assumptions.

4b writing

Create an outline, including a linked set of reasons. Begin drafting by writing down your thesis and outlining the way you will support and develop it. Arguments are most effective when they present a chain—a linked set—of reasons. Your outline should include the following parts:

- An introduction to the topic and the debatable issue.

- A thesis stating your position on the issue.

- A point-by-point account of the reasons for your position, including the evidence (facts, examples, authorities) you will use to substantiate each major reason.

- A fair presentation and refutation of one or two key counterarguments.

- A response to the "So what?" question. Why does your argument matter? If appropriate, include a call to action.

Appeal to your audience. You want your readers to see you as *reasonable, ethical,* and *empathetic*—qualities that promote communication among people who have differences. When you read your argument, pay attention to the impression you are making. Ask yourself these questions:

- Would a reasonable person be able to follow my logic and acknowledge the evidence I offer in support of my thesis?

- Have I presented myself as ethical and fair? What would readers who have never met me think of me after reading what I have to say?

- Have I expressed my feelings about the issue? Have I been fair in seeking to arouse the reader's emotions?

Emphasize your commitment to dialogue in the introduction. To promote dialogue with readers, look for common ground—beliefs, concerns, and values you share with those who disagree with you and those who are undecided. Sometimes called **Rogerian argument** after the psychologist Carl Rogers, the common-ground approach is particularly important in your introduction, where it can build bridges with readers who might otherwise become too defensive or annoyed to read further. Keep the dialogue open throughout your essay by maintaining an objective tone and acknowledging opposing views. If possible, return to that common ground at the end of your argument.

Conclude by restating your position and emphasizing its importance. After presenting your reasoning in detail, remind readers of your thesis. To encourage readers to appreciate your argument's importance, the version of your thesis in your conclusion should be more complex and qualified than the one in your introduction. Readers may not agree with you, but they should know why the issue and your argument matter. If you are writing a proposal, readers will finally want to know that the proposed solution will not cause worse problems than it solves; they realize that policy papers and proposals call for actions and that actions have consequences.

Reexamine your reasoning. After you have completed the first draft of your paper, take time to reexamine your reasoning. Ask yourself the following questions:

- Have I given a sufficient number of reasons to support my thesis, or should I add one or two more?
- Have I made any mistakes in logic? *(See the list of Common Logical Fallacies on pp. 17–19.)*

Use visuals in your argument. Consider including visuals that support your argument's purpose.

Each should relate directly to your argument as a whole or to a point within it. Visuals also may provide evidence: a photograph can illustrate an example, and a graph can present statistics that support an argument.

Clearly and adequately develop each claim presented in support of your thesis. Is your supporting evidence accurate, sufficient, and relevant? *(For more on quoting, paraphrasing, and documenting sources, see Part 2: Researching, pp. 85–90 and 93–97, and Parts 3–5.)*

COMMON FALLACIES or MISTAKES in REASONING

Logical Fallacies: These fallacies involve mistakes in reasoning.

Non sequitur: A conclusion that does not logically follow from the evidence presented or one that is based on irrelevant evidence: "Students don't care about responsibility; they often default on their student loans." [*Students who default on loans could be faced with high medical bills or unemployment.*]

False cause or post hoc: An argument that falsely assumes that because one thing happens after another, the first event was a cause of the second event: "I drank green tea, and my headache went away; therefore, green tea cures headaches." [*How do we know that the headache didn't go away for another reason?*]

Self-contradiction: An argument that contradicts itself: "No absolute statement can be true." [*The statement itself is an absolute.*]

Circular reasoning: An argument that restates the point rather than supporting it with reasonable evidence: "The wealthy should pay more taxes because taxes should be higher for people with higher incomes." [*Why should wealthy people pay more taxes? The rest of the statement doesn't answer this question; it just restates the position.*]

COMMON FALLACIES
(continued)

Begging the question: A form of circular reasoning that assumes the truth of a questionable opinion: "The president's poor relationship with the military has weakened the armed forces." [*Does the president really have a poor relationship with the military?*]

Hasty generalization: A conclusion based on inadequate evidence: "It took me over an hour to find a parking spot downtown. Therefore, the city should build a new parking garage." [*Is this evidence enough to prove this very broad conclusion?*]

Sweeping generalization: An overly broad statement made in absolute terms. When made about a group of people, a sweeping generalization is a **stereotype:** "College students are carefree." [*What about the many students who work to put themselves through school? And those who spend long hours studying?*]

Either/or fallacy: The idea that a complicated issue can be resolved by resorting to one of only two options when in reality there are additional choices: "Either the state legislature will raise taxes or our state's economy will suffer." [*Are these really the only two possibilities?*]

Ethical Fallacies: These fallacies undermine a writer's credibility by showing lack of fairness to opposing views and lack of expertise on the subject of the argument.

Ad hominem: A personal attack on someone who disagrees with you rather than on the person's argument: "The district attorney is a lazy political hack, so naturally she opposes streamlining the court system." [*Even if the district attorney usually supports her party's position, does that make her wrong about this issue?*]

Guilt by association: Discrediting a person because of problems with that person's associates, friends, or family. "Smith's friend has been convicted of fraud, so Smith cannot be trusted." [*Is Smith responsible for his friend's actions?*]

False authority: Presenting the testimony of an unqualified person to support a claim. "As the actor who plays Dr. Fine on *The Emergency Room,* I recommend this weight-loss drug because . . ." [*Is an actor qualified to judge the benefits and dangers of a diet drug?*]

Emotional Fallacies: These fallacies stir readers' sympathy at the expense of their reasoning.

False analogy: A comparison in which a surface similarity masks a significant difference: "Governments and businesses both work within a budget to accomplish their goals. Just as business must focus on the bottom line, so should government." [*Is the goal of government to make a profit? Does government instead have different goals?*]

Bandwagon: An argument that depends on going along with the crowd, on the false assumption that truth can be determined by a popularity contest: "Given the sales of that book, its claims must be true." [*Sales volume does not indicate the truth of the claim. How do we know that a popular book presents accurate information?*]

Red herring: An argument that diverts attention from the true issue by concentrating on an irrelevant one: "Hemingway's book *Death in the Afternoon* is not successful because it glorifies the brutal sport of bullfighting." [*Why can't a book about a brutal sport be successful? The statement is irrelevant.*]

5a Personal essays

The personal essay is a literary form. Like a poem, a play, or a story, it should feel meaningful to readers and relevant to their lives. A personal essay should speak in a distinctive voice and be both compelling and memorable.

- **Make connections between your experiences and those of your readers.** When you write a personal essay, you are exploring your experiences, clarifying your values, and composing a public self. The focus, however, does not need to be on you. You might write a personal essay about a tree in autumn or an athletic event, but whatever focus you choose, remember that your readers expect to learn more than the details of your experience. They expect to see connections between your experience and their own.

- **Turn your essay into a conversation.** Personal essayists usually use the first person (*I* and *we*) to create a sense that the writer and reader are engaged in the open-ended give-and-take of conversation. Your rhetorical stance—whether you appear shy, belligerent, or friendly in this conversation, for example—will be determined by the details you include in your essay as well as the connotations of the words you use.

- **Structure your essay like a story.** There are three common ways to narrate events and reflections:
  - **Chronological sequence** uses an order determined by clock time; what happened first, followed by what happened second, then third, and so on.
  - **Emphatic sequence** uses an order determined by the point you want to make; for emphasis, events and reflections are ar-

ranged either from least to most important or from most to least important.

- **Suspenseful sequence** uses an order determined by the emotional effect the writer wants the essay to have on readers. To keep readers hanging, the essay may begin with a puzzling event, then flash back or go forward. Some essays may even begin with the end and then flash back to recount how the writer came to that insight.

■ **Let details tell your story.** Details shape a story. The details you emphasize, the words you choose, and the characters you create communicate the point of your essay. Often it is not even necessary to state your thesis.

Details also control the pace of your essay. To emphasize a particular moment or reflection, provide numerous details to slow the reader down. As an alternative, use details sparingly to surprise the reader, especially in a context otherwise filled with rich detail.

■ **Connect your experience to a larger issue.** To demonstrate the significance of a personal essay to its readers, writers usually connect their individual experience to a larger issue. A personal essay about the interaction between a mother and her daughter might be connected to the larger issue of mothers working and to the psychology of family relationships.

5b Lab reports in the experimental sciences

Scientists form hypotheses and plan new experiments as they observe, read, and write. When they work in the laboratory, they keep well-organized and detailed notebooks. They also write and publish lab reports to share their discoveries with other scientists.

Lab reports usually include the following sections: Abstract, Introduction, Methods and Materials, Results, Discussion, Acknowledgments, and References. Begin drafting the report, section by section, while your experiences in the lab are still fresh in your mind.

Follow the scientific conventions for abbreviations, symbols, and numbers (often listed in your textbook). Use numerals for dates, time, pages, figures, tables, and standard units of measurement. Spell out numbers between one and nine that are not part of a series of larger numbers.

Revise to make sure that each part of your lab report does what it is expected to do.

- **Abstract.** An abstract is a one-paragraph summary of what your lab report covers. It answers these questions:
  - What methods were used in the experiment?
  - What variables were measured?
  - What were the findings?
  - What do the findings imply?

- **Introduction.** In the introduction, state your topic, summarize prior research, and present your hypothesis.

  Employ precise scientific terminology *(α-amylase),* and spell out the terms that you will later abbreviate *(gibbelleric acid [GA]).* Use the passive voice when describing objects of study, which are more important than the experimenter. *(For a discussion of active and passive voices, see Part 6: Editing for Clarity, pp. 256–57.)* Use the present tense to state established knowledge ("the rye seed *produces*"); use the past tense to summarize the work of prior researchers ("Haberlandt *reported*").

- **Methods and materials.** Select the details that other scientists will need to know to replicate the experiment. Using the past tense, recount in chronological order what was done with specific materials.

5b writing

▪ **Results.** In this section, tell readers about the results that are relevant to your hypothesis, especially those that are statistically significant. Results may be relevant even if they are different from what you expected.

You might summarize results in a table or graph. Every table and figure you include in a lab report must be referred to in the text. Point out relevant patterns the table or figure reveals. If you run statistical tests on your findings, do not make the tests themselves the focus of your writing. Reserve interpretations for the Discussion section.

Note: Like the terms *correlated* and *random,* the term *significant* has a specific statistical meaning for scientists and should therefore be used in a lab report only in relation to the appropriate statistical test.

▪ **Discussion.** In discussing your results, interpret your major findings by explaining how and why each finding does or does not confirm the original hypothesis. Connect your work with prior scientific research, and look ahead to potential future research.

▪ **Acknowledgments.** In professional journals, most reports of experimental findings include a brief statement acknowledging those who assisted the author(s).

▪ **References.** Include at the end of your report a listing of all manuals, books, and journal articles you consulted during your research and writing process. Use one of the citation formats developed by the Council of Science Editors (CSE style), unless your instructor prefers another format. *(See Part 5: Other Documentation Styles.)*

5c Case studies in the social sciences

Social scientists are trained observers and record-ers of individual and group behavior. They write to see clearly and remember precisely what they ob-serve and then to interpret its meaning.

- **Choose a topic that raises a question.**
  When doing a case study, your purpose is to connect what you see and hear with issues and concepts in the social sciences. Choose a topic, and turn it into a research question. Write down your hypothesis—a tentative answer to your research question. Record types of behavior and other categories (for example, appearances) to guide your re-search in the field.

- **Collect data.** Make a detailed and accurate record of what you observe and when and how you observe it. Whenever you can, count or measure, and record word-for-word what is said. Use frequency counts—the number of occurrences of specific, narrowly defined instances of behavior. If you are observing a classroom, for example, you might count the number of teacher-directed questions asked by several children. Your research methodologies course will cover many ways to quantify data.

- **Assume an unbiased stance.** In a case study, you are presenting empirical findings, based on careful observation. Avoid value-laden terms and unsupported generalizations.

- **Discover meaning in your data.** As you review your notes, try to uncover connections, identify inconsistencies, and draw inferences. For example, ask yourself why a subject be-haved in a specific way, and consider different explanations for the behavior. Draw on the techniques for quantitative analysis that you have learned in a statistics course.

■ **Present your findings in an organized way.** There are two basic ways to present your findings in the body of a case study: as stages of a process and in analytic categories. Using stages of a process, a student studying gang initiation organized her observations chronologically into appropriate stages. If you organize your study this way, be sure to transform the minute-by-minute history of your observations into a pattern with distinct stages. Using analytic categories, a student observing the behavior of a preschool child organized his findings according to three categories from his textbook: motor coordination, cognition, and socialization.

5c
writing

■ **Include a review of the literature, a statement of your hypothesis, and a description of your methodology in your introduction.** The introduction presents the framework, background, and rationale for your study. Begin with the topic, and review related research, working your way to the specific question that your study addresses. Follow that with a statement of your hypothesis, accompanied by a description of your **methodology**—how, when, and where you made your observations and how you recorded them.

Note: Develop stages or categories while you are making your observations. In your analysis, be sure to illustrate your stages or categories with material drawn from your observations—with descriptions of people, places, and behavior, as well as with well-chosen quotations.

■ **In the conclusion, discuss your findings.** The conclusion of your case study should answer these three questions: (1) Did you find what you expected? (2) What do your findings show, or what is the bigger picture? and (3) What should researchers explore further?

5d ▪ Essay exams

Essay exams can be stressful because you are writing under the pressure of the clock. Thinking strategically as you prepare for the test will reduce the stress and may even transform the exam into a learning experience.

- **Prepare with the course and your instructor in mind.** Consider the specific course as your writing context and the course's instructor as your audience:
  - What questions or problems did your instructor explicitly or implicitly address? What frameworks did your instructor use to analyze topics?
  - What key terms did your instructor repeatedly use during lectures and discussions?
- **Understand your assignment.** Essay exams are designed to test your knowledge and understanding, not just your memory. Make up some essay questions that require you to:
  - **Explain** what you have learned in a clear, well-organized way. *(See question 1 in the box on p. 27.)*
  - **Connect** what you know about one topic with what you know about another topic. *(See question 2 in the box on p. 27.)*
  - **Apply** what you have learned to a new situation. *(See question 3 in the box on p. 27.)*
  - **Interpret** the causes, effects, meanings, value, or potential of something. *(See question 4 in the box on p. 27.)*
  - **Argue** for or against some controversial statement about what you have learned. *(See question 5 in the box on p. 27.)*

  Almost all these directions require you to synthesize what you have learned from your reading, class notes, and projects.

NAVIGATING THROUGH COLLEGE AND BEYOND

Essay Exam Questions across the Curriculum

During finals week, you may be asked to respond to essay questions like the following:

1. Discuss the power of the contemporary presidency as well as the limits of that power. [*from a political science course*]

2. Compare and contrast the treatment of labor supply decisions in the economic models proposed by Greg Lewis and Gary Becker. [*from an economics course*]

3. Describe the observations that would be made in an alpha-particle scattering experiment if (a) the nucleus of an atom were negatively charged and the protons occupied the empty space outside the nucleus and (b) the electrons were embedded in a positively charged sphere. [*from a chemistry course*]

4. Examine the uses of caesura and enjambment in the following poem, and analyze their effect on the poem's rhythm. [*from a literature course*]

5. In 1800, was Thomas Jefferson a dangerous radical, as the Federalists claimed? Define key terms, and support your position with evidence from specific events and documents. [*from an American history course*]

- **Plan your time.** Quickly look through the whole exam, and determine how much time you will spend on each part. You will want to move as quickly as possible through the questions with lower point values and spend the bulk of your time responding to those that are worth the greatest number of points.

- **Respond to short identification questions by showing the significance of the**

information. The most common type of short-answer question is the identification question: Who or what is *X?* In answering questions of this sort, present just enough information to show that you understand *X*'s significance within the context of the course.

- **Be tactical in responding to essay questions.** Keep in mind that essay questions usually ask you to do something specific with a topic. Begin by determining precisely what you are being asked to do. Before you write anything, read the question—all of it—and circle key words.

  > (Explain)(two) ways in which Picasso's *Guernica* evokes war's terrifying (destructiveness.)

  To answer this question, you need to focus on two of the painting's features, such as color and composition, not on Picasso's life.

- **Use the essay question to structure your response.** Usually, you can transform the question itself into the thesis of your answer. If you are asked to agree or disagree with the Federalists' characterization of Thomas Jefferson in the election of 1800, you might begin with the following thesis:

  > **In the election of 1800, the Federalists characterized Jefferson as a dangerous radical. Although Jefferson's ideas were radical for the times, they were not dangerous to the republic.**

  Take a minute or two to list evidence for each of your main points, and then write the essay.

- **Check your work.** Save a few minutes to read through your completed answer, looking for words you might have omitted or key sentences that make no sense. Make corrections neatly.

5e Oral presentations

When we write, we imagine the presence of absent strangers. When we speak, the strangers are there in front of us, expecting us to connect with them. To do so, prepare a speech that is appropriate, clear, and memorable.

- **Consider the interests, background knowledge, and attitudes of your audience.** An oral presentation should suit the occasion. Find out as much as you can about your listeners before you prepare the speech. What does the audience already think about your topic? If you are addressing an unfamiliar audience, ask the people who invited you to speak to fill you in on the audience's interests and expectations. You also can adjust your speech once you get in front of the actual audience, making your language more or less technical, for example, or offering additional examples to illustrate points.

- **Decide on the purpose of your presentation.** Do you want to intensify your audience's commitment to what they already think, provide new and clarifying information, provoke more analysis and understanding of the issue, or change what the audience believes about something?

- **Make your opening interesting.** A strong opening puts the speaker at ease and gains the audience's confidence and attention. Stories, brief quotations, striking statistics, and surprising statements are good attention getters. Try crafting an introduction that lets your listeners know what they have to gain from your presentation—for example, new information or new perspectives on a subject of common interest.

- **Make the focus of your presentation explicit and the organization clear-cut.** Select two or three ideas that you most want your audience to hear—and to remember. Make these ideas the focus of your presentation, and tell your audience what to expect by previewing the content of your presentation—"I will make three points about fraternities on campus"—and then listing the three points.

■ **Be direct.** For clarity, speak in basic sentence structures, repeat key terms, and pay attention to the pace and rhythm of your speech.

■ **Use visual aids.** Slides, posters, objects, video clips, and music help make your focus explicit. Avoid oversimplifying your ideas to fit them on a slide. Make sure the images, videos, or music fit your purpose and audience. Presentation software such as PowerPoint can help you stay focused while you are speaking.

■ **Make eye contact and keep your audience interested.** When giving your talk, make eye contact with your listeners to monitor their responses, and adjust your message accordingly. For most occasions, it is inappropriate to write out everything you want to say and then read it word for word; nor do you want to read from the slides. Instead, speak from an outline or bullet points, and write out only those parts of your presentation where precise wording counts, such as quotations.

In some scholarly or formal settings, precise wording may be necessary, especially if your remarks are to be published or if your remarks will be quoted by others. If a script feels necessary, triple-space the typescript of your text; avoid carrying sentences over from one page to another; and mark your manuscript for pauses, emphasis, and the pronunciation of proper names. You should also practice your delivery. It should take about seventy-five seconds to deliver one triple-spaced page of text.

- **Conclude in a memorable way.** Your final comments will be the part of your speech that your audience remembers most.

- **Rehearse.** Whether you are using an outline or a script, practice with a clock, and leave yourself time to insert occasional remarks during the actual performance.

5f writing

5f Coauthored projects

A project is coauthored when more than one person is responsible for producing it. In many fields, working collaboratively is essential. Here are some suggestions to help you make the most of this challenge:

- Working with your partners, decide on some ground rules, including meeting times, deadlines, and ways of reconciling differences. Will the majority rule, or will some other principle prevail? Is there an interested and respected third party who can be consulted if the group's dynamics break down?

- Will the group meet primarily online or in person?

- Divide the work fairly so that everyone has a part to contribute to the project. Keep in mind that each group member should do some researching, drafting, revising, and editing. Responsibility for taking notes at meetings should rotate.

- In your personal journal, record, analyze, and evaluate the intellectual and interpersonal workings of the group as you see and experience them. If the group's dynamics begin to break down, seek the assistance of a third party.

- After each group member has completed his or her assigned part or subtopic, gather the whole group to weave the parts together and create a focused piece of writing with a consistent voice. At this point group members usually need to negotiate with one another. Although healthy debate is good for a project, tact is essential.

5g Portfolios

A **portfolio** is an ordered selection of your work. The principles that guide selection and order depend on the occasion, purpose, and audience.

As soon as you select a major, you should consider keeping an organized folder of your work in that area. The folder can be organized chronologically, by field or subfield, or by issue. Each year, it is a good idea to create a portfolio that reflects what you have learned and how you learned it. Successful job candidates often prepare well-organized portfolios of carefully selected materials to take with them to job interviews.

6 Design academic texts.

A crucial writing task is to format your text so that readers can "see" your ideas clearly. In this chapter, we focus on designing responses to academic writing assignments. Like writing decisions, design decisions must be purposeful to be effective. Consider your writing situation, including your purpose for writing as well as the needs of your audience. Your goal is to enhance the content of your text, not just decorate it.

6a Considering audience and purpose

As you plan your document, consider your purpose and the needs of your audience. If you are writing an informative project for a psychology class, your

NAVIGATING THROUGH COLLEGE AND BEYOND

The Basics: Margins, Spacing, Fonts, and Page Numbers

Here are a few basic guidelines for formatting academic texts:

- **First page:** In an assignment under five pages, you can usually place a header with your name, your professor's name, your course and section number, and the date on the first page, above the text. If your text exceeds five pages, page 1 is usually a title page.

- **Font:** Select a common font and choose the ten- or twelve-point size.

- **Margins:** Use one-inch margins on all four sides of your text. Adequate margins make your document easier to read and give your instructor room to write comments and suggestions.

- **Margin justification:** Line up, or justify, the lines of your document along the left margin but not along the right margin. Leaving a "ragged right"—or uneven—right margin, as in this box, enables you to avoid odd spacing between words.

- **Spacing:** Double-space unless you are instructed to do otherwise, and indent the first line of each paragraph five spaces. (Many business documents are single-spaced, with an extra line space between paragraphs, which are not indented.)

- **Page numbers:** Place page numbers in the upper or lower right-hand corner of the page. Some documentation styles require a header next to the page number. *(See Parts 3–5.)*

**6b
design**

instructor—your primary audience—will probably prefer that you follow the guidelines provided by the American Psychological Association (APA). If you are writing a lab report for a biology or chemistry course, you will likely need to follow a well-established format and use the documentation style recommended by the Council of Science Editors (CSE) to cite sources. A history review might call for the use of the Chicago style. Interpretive analyses for language and literature courses usually use the style recommended by the Modern Language Association (MLA). *(For help with the MLA, APA, and Chicago documentation styles, see Parts 3–5.)*

6b Using the tools available in your word-processing program

Most word-processing programs provide a range of options for editing, sharing, and, especially, designing your document. For example, if you are using Microsoft Word 2010, you can access groups of commands by clicking on the various tabs at the top of the screen. Figure 6.1 shows the Home tab, which contains basic formatting and editing commands. You can choose different fonts and sizes; add bold, italic, or underlined type; insert numbered or bulleted lists; and so on. Other tabs allow you to add boxes and drawings, make comments, and change the page layout.

Word-processing programs vary in their arrangement of options. Some include menus of commands on toolbars instead of on tabs. Take some time to learn the different formatting options available in your program.

FIGURE 6.1 The Home tab in Microsoft Word 2010.

6c   Thinking intentionally about design

For any document that you create in print or online, whether for an academic course or for a purpose and an audience beyond college, apply the same basic design principles.

- **Organize information for readers.** You can organize information visually and topically by grouping related items, using boxes, indents, headings, spacing, and lists. These variations in text appearance help readers scan, locate important information, and dive in when they need to know more about a topic. If a color printer is available to you and your instructor allows you to use color, you have another tool for organizing information. Choose colors that display well for all readers.

  White space, areas of a document that do not contain type or graphics, can also help you organize information. Generous margins and plenty of white space above headings and around other elements make the text easier to read. You should also introduce visuals within your text and position them so that they appear near—but never before—the text reference. Balance your visuals and other text elements; for example, don't try to cram too many visuals onto one page.

- **Use font style and lists to make your text readable and to emphasize key elements.** Fonts, or *typefaces,* are designs that have been established by printers for the letters in the alphabet, numbers, punctuation marks, and special characters. For most academic texts, choose a standard, easy-to-read font and a ten- or twelve-point size. You can manipulate fonts for effect: for example, twelve-point Times New Roman can be **boldfaced,** *italicized,* and <u>underlined</u>. Serif fonts have tiny lines at the ends of letters such as *n* and *y;* sans serif fonts do not have these lines. Standard serif fonts such as the following have traditionally been used for basic printed text because they are easy to read:

Times New Roman

Courier

Bookman Old Style

Palatino

Numbered or bulleted lists help you cluster large amounts of information, making the information easier for readers to reference and understand. Format text as a numbered or bulleted list by choosing the option you want from your word-processing program's formatting commands. Introduce the list with a complete sentence followed by a colon (:), use parallel structure in your list items, and put a period at the end of each item only if the entries are complete sentences.

Putting information in a box provides emphasis and makes it easy to locate for future reference. Most word-processing programs offer several ways to enclose text within a border or box.

▪ **Format related design elements consistently.** In design, the key words are simplicity, contrast, and consistency. If you emphasize an item by putting it in italic or bold type or in color, or if you use a graphic element such as a box to set it off, consider repeating this effect for similar items so that your document has a unified look. Even a simple horizontal line can be a purposeful element in a long document when used consistently for organization.

▪ **Use headings to organize long documents.** In short texts, headings can be disruptive and unnecessary. In longer texts, though, they can help organize complex information. (For headings in APA style, see Chapter 21.) Effective headings are brief, descriptive, and consistent in grammatical structure and formatting. For example, they can be phrases beginning with -*ing* words *(Fielding Inquiries, Handling Complaints)* or nouns and noun phrases *(Customer Inquiries, Complaints)*.

6c design

Headings at different levels can be in different forms. Place and highlight headings consistently throughout the text. You might center all first-level headings, which correspond to the main points in your outline. If you have second-level headings—your supporting points—you might align them at the left margin and underline them. Third-level headings, if you have them, could be aligned at the left margin and set in plain type:

First-Level Heading

<u>Second-Level Heading</u>

Third-Level Heading

- **Using design elements sparingly and intentionally.** If you use too many graphics, headings, bullets, boxes, or other elements in a document, you risk making it as "noisy" as a loud radio. Standard fonts have become standard because they are easy on the eye. Bold type, italic type, underlining, and other graphic effects should not continue for more than one sentence at a time.

- **Meet the needs of readers with disabilities.** If your potential audience might include the visually or hearing impaired, use a large, easily readable sans serif font (fourteen points or larger), ample spacing between lines, and appropriate high-contrast colors. Include narrative descriptions of all visuals; if you include audio or video files in an electronic document, provide transcripts as well as a narrative description of what is happening in the video. For further information, consult the American Council of the Blind (<http://acb.org/accessible-formats.html>),

Lighthouse International (<www.lighthouse
.org/accessibility/design/accessible-print
-design/making-text-legible>), and the
American Printing House for the Blind
(<www.aph.org/edresearch/lpguide.htm>).

6d Using and integrating visuals, audio, and video

Technology makes it easy to go beyond words to
pictures, graphs, sounds, and videos—all with the
goal of improving a specific project. An important
question in deciding whether to include multimedia
materials is, What do they contribute to the project?

When you use data, visuals, audio files, or
videos created by someone else, always credit
your source. These sources are often protected by
copyright, and you will need permission from the
copyright holder to use this material in your own
work, including on the Web. *(For information about
finding visuals, see Part 2: Researching, pp. 70–74.)*

1. Using Visuals Effectively
Visuals such as tables, charts, and graphs can clarify complex data or ideas. Effective visuals are used
for specific purposes, not for decoration, and each
type of visual illustrates some kinds of material
better than others. For example, compare the table
and the line graph on page 40. Both present data
that show changes over time, but does one strike
you as clearer or more powerful than the other?

2. Integrating visuals into documents
If you decide to use a table, chart, or diagram, keep
this general advice in mind:

1. **Number tables and other figures** consecutively throughout your paper, and label
   them appropriately: Table 1, Table 2, and so

on. Do not abbreviate *Table*. *Figure* may be abbreviated as *Fig*.

6d
visuals

2. **Refer to the visual element in your text** before it appears, placing the visual as close as possible to this reference. Always refer to a visual by its label: for example, "See Figure 1."

3. **Give each visual a title and, if necessary, a caption** that clearly explains what the visual shows.

4. **Include explanatory notes below the visuals,** and use the word *Note* followed by a colon to introduce explanations of the visual as a whole. To explain a specific element within the visual, use a superscript *letter* (not a number) both after the specific element and before the note. This footnote should appear directly beneath the graphic, not at the foot of the page or at the end of your paper.

5. **Credit sources for visuals.** Use the word *Source,* followed by a colon and complete documentation, including the author, title, publication information, and page number if applicable.

Note: The Modern Language Association (MLA) and the American Psychological Association (APA) provide other guidelines for figure captions and crediting sources of visuals. *(See Part 3: MLA Documentation Style, pp. 152–53, and Part 4: APA Documentation Style, p. 195.)*

3. Using audio and video effectively

You might use audio elements such as music, interviews, or speeches to present or illustrate your major points. Video elements—clips from films, TV, YouTube, or your personal archive—are likewise valuable for clear explanation or powerful argument. No matter how entertaining, audio and video should not be used as mere decoration.

TYPES of VISUALS and THEIR USES

Tables

Tables organize precise data for readers. Because the measurements in the example include decimals, it would be difficult to plot them on a graph.

Emissions from Waste (Tg CO_2 Eq.)

Gas/Source	1990	1995	2000	2001	2002	2003	2004	2005
CH_4	185.8	182.2	158.3	153.5	156.2	160.5	157.8	157.4
Landfills	161.0	157.1	131.9	127.6	130.4	134.9	132.1	132.0
Wastewater treatment	24.8	25.1	26.4	25.9	25.8	25.6	25.7	25.4
N_2O	6.4	6.9	7.6	7.6	7.7	7.8	7.9	8.0
Domestic wastewater treatment	6.4	6.9	7.6	7.6	7.7	7.8	7.9	8.0
Total	192.2	189.1	165.9	161.1	163.9	168.4	165.7	165.4

Note: Totals may not sum due to independent rounding.
SOURCE: U.S. Environmental Protection Agency. *Inventory of U.S. Greenhouse Gas Emissions and Sinks: 1996–2006*. U.S. Environmental Protection Agency, Apr. 2008. Web. 9 June 2008. p. 8-1.

Bar graphs

Bar graphs highlight comparisons between two or more variables, such as the percentage of men and women employed in various jobs in the nation's newsrooms. They allow readers to see relative sizes quickly.

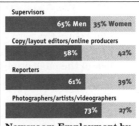

Newsroom Employment by Gender, 2009

Pie charts

Pie charts show the size of parts in relation to the whole. The segments must add up to 100 percent of something, differences in segment size must be noticeable, and there should not be too many segments.

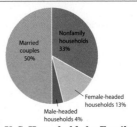

U. S. Households by Family Type, 2010

Line graphs

Line graphs show changes in one or more variables over time. The example shows how the life goals of U.S. college students have changed over a span of forty-three years.

Life Goals of First-Year College Students in the United States, 1966–2009.

Diagrams

Diagrams show processes or structures visually. Common in technical writing, they include timelines, organization charts, and decision trees. The example shows the factors involved in the decision to commit a burglary.

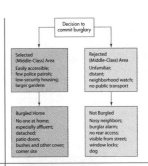

Photographs

Photos can reinforce your point by showing readers what your subject actually looks like or how it has been affected. This image could support a portrayal of Eminem as a talented but controversial artist.

Eminem

Maps

Maps highlight locations and spatial relationships, and they show relationships between ideas. This one shows the routes followed by slaves escaping to freedom in the nineteenth century, prior to the Civil War.

Routes to Freedom on the Underground Railroad

Illustrations

Like photographs, illustrations make a point dramatically.

Adbusters Public-Service Advertisement.

6e design

6e Designing pages for the Web

Thanks to Web editing software, it is now almost as easy to create a Web site and post it on the Internet as it is to write a print text using word-processing software. Many Web-based businesses like Google provide free server space for hosting sites and offer tools for creating Web pages. Many schools also make server space available for student Web sites.

To be effective, a Web site must be well designed and serve a well-defined purpose for its audience. In creating a Web site, plan the site, draft its content, and select its visuals; then revise and edit as you would for any other composition. The following guidelines will help you compose a Web site.

1. Planning a structure for your site

Like most print documents, a Web site can have a hierarchical, linear structure, where one page leads to the next. Because of the hyperlinked nature of this medium, however, a site can also be organized in a hub-and-spoke structure, with a central page leading to other pages. To choose the structure that will work best for your site, consider how users will want to access information or opinion on the site.

To determine your site's structure, try mapping the connections among its pages by arranging them

 For MULTILINGUAL WRITERS

Designing a Web Site Collaboratively

If you are asked to create a Web site as part of a class assignment, try to make arrangements to work with a partner or a small group. The kind of interaction involved in writing the content and designing the site will provide you with beneficial language support. At the same time, you will be able to provide the project with the benefit of your unique multicultural viewpoint.

in a storyboard. Represent each page with an index card, and rearrange the pages on a flat surface, experimenting with different possible arrangements. Alternatively, use sticky notes on a whiteboard, and draw arrows connecting them. Also begin planning the visual design of your site. For consistency, establish a template page, including background color and fonts. Choose a uniform location (for example, at the top, in the middle) for material that will appear on each page, such as site title, page title, navigation links, and your contact information. *(See pp. 44–45 on designing a site with a unified look.)*

6e design

2. Gathering content for your site

The content for a Web site will usually consist of written work along with links and graphics. Depending on your situation, you might also provide audio files, video files, and even animation.

Follow these special requirements for written content on a Web site:

- Usually readers neither expect nor want lengthy text explanations; they expect chunks of information—short paragraphs—delivered quickly.

- Chunks for each topic or point should fit on one screen. Avoid long passages that require readers to use the scroll bar.

- Use links to connect your interests with those of others and to provide extra sources of credible and relevant information. Make links part of your text, and give them descriptive names. Place links at the end of a paragraph so readers do not navigate away in the middle.

As you prepare your written text, gather any graphics, photographs, and audio and video files that you plan to include. Some sites allow you to download images, and some images, including many of the historical photographs available through the Library of Congress, are in the public domain. Always cite any material that you do not generate yourself. If your Web text will be public, request permission for use of any material not in the public domain unless the site says permission is not needed. Check for a credit in the source, and if the contact information of the creator is not apparent, e-mail the sponsor of the site and ask for it. *(For citation formats see Parts 3–5.)*

3. Designing Web pages to capture and hold interest

On good Web sites, you will find such easy-to-follow links as "what you'll find here," FAQs (frequently asked questions), or "list of those involved." In planning the structure and content of your site, keep your readers' convenience in mind.

4. Designing a readable site with a unified look

The design of your site should suit its writing situation, in the context of its purpose and intended audience: a government site to inform users about copyright law will present a basic, uncluttered design that focuses attention on the text. A university's home page might feature photographs of young people and sun-drenched lawns to entice prospective students. Readers generally appreciate a site with a unified look. "Sets" or "themes" are readily available at free graphics sites offering banners, navigation buttons, and other design elements. You also can create visuals with a graphics program, scan your own art, and scan or upload personal photographs. Design your home page to complement your other pages, or your readers may lose track of where they are in the site—and lose interest in staying:

- Use a design template to keep elements of page layout consistent across the site.
- Align items such as text and images.
- Consider including a site map—a Web page that serves as a table of contents for your entire site.

- Select elements such as buttons, signs, and backgrounds with a consistent design suited to your purpose and audience. Use animations and sounds sparingly.

- Use colors that provide adequate contrast, white space, and sans serif fonts to make text easy to read. Pages that are too busy are not visually compelling. *(For more on design, see pp. 35–37.)*

- Limit the width of your text; readers find wide lines of text difficult to process.

- Leave time to find appropriate image, audio, and video files created by others and to obtain permission to use them.

- Always check your Web site to be sure all the pages and links load as planned.

5. Designing a Web site that is easy to access and navigate

Help readers find their way to the areas of the site they want to visit. Make it easy for them to take interesting side trips if they would like to without wasting their time or losing their way:

- **Identify your Web site on each page, and provide a link to the home page.** Remember that readers will not always enter your Web site through the home page. Give the title of the site on each page, and provide an easy-to-spot link to your home page.

- **Provide a navigation bar on each page.** A **navigation bar** can be a simple line of links that you copy and paste at the top or bottom of each page. A navigation bar on each page makes it easy for visitors to move from the site's home page to other pages and back again.

- **Use graphics that load quickly.** Limit the size of your images to no more than forty kilobytes so that they will load faster.

- **Use graphics judiciously.** Your Web site should not depend on graphics alone to make its message clear and interesting. Graphics should reinforce your purpose. Avoid clip art, which often looks unprofessional.

- **Be aware of the needs of visitors with disabilities.** Provide alternate ways of accessing visual and auditory information. Include text descriptions of visuals, media files, and tables (for users of screen-reader software or text-only **browsers**). All audio files should have captions and full transcriptions. *(See pp. 37–38.)*

6. Using peer feedback to revise your Web site

Before publishing your site, to be read by anyone in the world, proofread your text carefully, and ask friends to look at your site in different browsers and share their responses with you. Make sure your site reflects favorably on your abilities.

6f Creating and interacting with blogs and wikis

Weblogs or **blogs** are Web sites that can be continually updated. They often invite readers to post comments on entries. Some blogs provide a space where a group of writers can discuss one another's work and ideas. In schools, classes have used blogs to discuss issues, organize work, develop sources, compile portfolios, and gather and store material and commentary. Figure 6.2 depicts a blog for a writing class.

Blogs have become important as vehicles for public discussion and commentary. Most presidential campaigns in 2008 maintained blogs on their Web sites, and many conventional news sources, like the *New York Times,* link to their own blogs. Compared to other types of publications and academic writing, blogs have an informal tone that

FIGURE 6.2 The blog for a writing course.

combines information, entertainment, and personal opinion.

A **wiki** is another kind of Web-interfaced database that can be updated easily. One well-known wiki is the online encyclopedia *Wikipedia*. Many instructors do not consider *Wikipedia* a credible source for research because almost anyone can create or edit its content. Although changes are reviewed before appearing on the site, the reviewers may not have the requisite expertise. Verify that the information provided is correct by confirming it with another source. Some other wikis, such as *Citizendium,* rely on experts in a discipline to write and edit articles.

1. Creating your own blog

To begin blogging, set up a blog site with a server such as blogger.com or wordpress.com. Be sure about your writing situation, especially regarding purpose, which may be very specifically focused on a single issue or, alternatively, provide space for a range of opinions.

Some social networking sites such as *NING* will, for a charge, allow users to create blogs. These blogs can sometimes be used to explore a topic or find an expert on a particular subject. For example, if school policy permits it, you might informally survey your friends on a campus issue or set up a group to discuss the topic.

> *Caution:* Blogs and profiles on social networking sites are more or less public depending on the level of access they allow. Do not post anything (including photographs and videos) that you would not want family members, teachers, and prospective employers to view.

2. Setting up a wiki

A wiki is an updateable Web site for sharing and coauthoring content. In addition to using wikis to conduct research together, students often use them simply to share their writing and various kinds of information—for instance relevant videos or Web sites related to a common research topic. Coauthors and peer reviewers find wikis useful because they provide a history of the revisions in any document. To create a wiki, begin by identifying the platform you will use, probably one like wikispaces.com that provides set-up tools and direction, and the writing situation for your wiki.

Like blogs, wikis can have a limited number of participants or be open to the world.

For all knowledge and wonder (which is the seed of knowledge) is an impression of pleasure in itself.

—FRANCIS BACON

Researching

7 Understand the purpose of research projects.

College faculty in all fields are researchers. Besides searching out existing information about a particular subject in their specialty, they do research to create new knowledge about that topic. Joining the academic community means becoming a researcher.

7a Understanding primary and secondary research

Primary research means working in a laboratory, in the field, or with an archive of raw data, original documents, and authentic artifacts to make first-hand discoveries.

Secondary research means looking to see what other people have learned and written about a topic. Knowing how to identify facts, interpretations, and evaluations is key to good secondary research:

- **Facts** are objective. Like your body weight, facts can be measured, observed, and independently verified.

- **Interpretations** spell out the implications of facts. Are you as thin as you are because of your genes—or because you exercise every day? The answer to this question is an interpretation.

- **Evaluations** are debatable judgments about a set of facts or a situation. Attributing a person's thinness to genes is an interpretation, but the assertion that "one can never be too rich or too thin" is an evaluation.

Once you are up-to-date on the facts, interpretations, and evaluations in a particular area, you will be able to design a research project that adds to this knowledge. Usually, what you will add is your *perspective* on the sources you have found and read:

- Given all that you have learned about the topic, what strikes you as important or interesting?

- What patterns do you see, or what connections can you make between one person's work and another's?
- Where is the research going, and what problems still need to be explored?

7b Recognizing the connection between research and writing in college and beyond

In one way or another, research informs all college writing. But some assignments require more rigorous and systematic research than others. These **research projects** offer you a chance to go beyond your course texts—to find and read both classic and current material.

Classic sources are respected older works that made such an important contribution to a particular area of research that contemporary researchers use them as touchstones for further research. In many fields, sources published within the past five years are considered current. A research paper constitutes your contribution to the ongoing conversation.

7c Understanding the research assignment

Consider the rhetorical situation of the research project. Think about your project's audience, purpose, voice/tone/stance, genre, context, and scope.

1. Audience
Thinking critically about the needs and expectations of practitioners of the discipline will help you to plan a research strategy and create a schedule for writing your project.

2. Purpose
Your *purpose* for writing a research project depends on both the specifics of the assignment as set by

your instructor and your own interest in the topic. Your purpose might be one of the following:

- **Informative:** Explain, describe, define, review
- **Interpretive:** Analyze, compare, explain, interpret
- **Persuasive:** Assess, justify, defend, refute, determine

3. Voice/tone/stance
Your voice and tone in a research paper should be that of a well-informed, helpful individual. Remember that you are sharing with others who want to be informed.

4. Genre/medium
Research projects prepared for different purposes will reflect characteristics of various genres and may be expressed in different media.

5. Context
The overall situation will affect the presentation of your projects.

6. Scope
A project's scope includes the expected length of the paper, the deadline, and any other requirements such as number and type of sources.

7d Choosing an interesting research question

If you choose an interesting question, your research is likely to be more meaningful.

1. Choose a question with personal significance.
Get personally involved in your work. Begin with the wording of the assignment, analyzing the proj-

ect's required scope, purpose, and audience *(see Part 1: Common Assignments across the Curriculum, pp. 3–4)*. Then browse through the course texts and your class notes, looking for a match between your interests and topics, issues, or problems in the subject area.

7d
research

2. Make your question specific.

The more specific your question, the more your research will have direction and focus. Make a question more specific by asking one of the reporter's questions: the *who, what, why, when, where,* or *how* of a topic.

After you have compiled a list of possible research questions, choose one that is relatively specific or rewrite a broad one to make it more specific and answerable. For example, a student could

NAVIGATING THROUGH COLLEGE AND BEYOND

Typical Lines of Inquiry in Different Disciplines

Research topics and questions differ from one discipline to another, as the following examples show:

- **History:** How important were volunteers in the creation of lending libraries in nineteenth-century America?

- **Marketing:** What marketing strategies have successfully persuaded busy adults that they should volunteer?

- **Political science:** What role did volunteers play in the election of local and national political candidates in the late twentieth century?

- **Anthropology:** How have volunteers contributed to the creation of archives?

rewrite the following broad question about volunteerism to make it answerable:

TOO BROAD | How has the volunteerism of young people affected the United States?

ANSWERABLE | Why do today's college students choose to volunteer?

3. Find a challenging question.

To be interesting, a research question must be challenging. If a question can be answered with a simple yes or no, a dictionary-like definition, or a textbook presentation of information, choose another question, or rework the simple one to make it more challenging.

NOT CHALLENGING | Do college students volunteer?

CHALLENGING | What motivates college students to give of their "time and treasure" when they get no material reward for such efforts?

4. Speculate about answers.

Sometimes it can be useful to develop a **hypothesis**—an answer to your research question—to work with during the research process. Keep an open mind as you work, and be aware of the assumptions embedded in your research question or hypothesis. Consider, for example, the following hypothesis:

HYPOTHESIS | College students volunteer for more than one reason.

This hypothesis assumes that because college students differ from one another in many ways, they have more than one reason for volunteering. However, assumptions are always open to question. Researchers must be willing to adjust their ideas as they learn more about a topic.

7e Creating a research plan

Take some time at the beginning to outline a research plan. Even though you will probably modify your plan later, your work will go more smoothly if you have definite goals from the beginning. As a starting point, use the schedule shown in the following box.

7e research

SCHEDULING YOUR RESEARCH PROJECT

Task	Date
Phase I	
Complete general plan for research.	_____
Decide on topic and research question.	_____
Consult reference works and reference librarians.	_____
Make a list of relevant keywords for online searching *(see Chapter 8, pp. 58–59)*.	_____
Compile a **working bibliography** *(see Chapter 12, p. 79)*.	_____
Sample some items in bibliography.	_____
Make arrangements for primary research (if necessary).	_____
Phase II	
Locate, read, and evaluate selected sources.	_____
Take notes, write summaries and paraphrases.	_____
Cross-check notes with working bibliography.	_____
Conduct primary research (if necessary).	_____

SCHEDULING YOUR RESEARCH PROJECT *(continued)*

Task	Date
Find and create visuals.	_____
Confer with instructor or writing center (optional).	_____
Develop thesis and outline or plan organization of paper.	_____
Phase III	
Write first draft, deciding which primary and secondary source materials to include.	_____
Have peer review (optional).	_____
Revise draft.	_____
Confer with instructor or writing center (optional).	_____
Do final revision and editing.	_____
Create works-cited or references page.	_____
Proofread and check spelling.	_____
Due date	_____

8 Find and manage print and online sources.

To conduct a meaningful search through the vast amount of available information, focus on the following three activities:

- Collecting keywords from reference works
- Using library databases
- Finding material in the library and on the World Wide Web

For MULTILINGUAL WRITERS

Researching a Full Range of Sources

Your mastery of a language other than English can sometimes give you access to important sources. Do not limit yourself to sources in your first language, however. Even if you find researching in English challenging, it is important to broaden your search as soon as you can to include a range of print and Internet resources written in English.

**8a
research**

8a Consulting various kinds of sources

You should always consult more than one source, and usually more than one *kind* of source. Here are some of the available resources:

- **General reference works**
  Encyclopedias, annuals, and almanacs
  Computer databases, bibliographies, and
      abstracts

- **Specialized reference works
  (for overview and keywords)**
  Discipline-specific encyclopedias, almanacs,
      and dictionaries

- **Books and electronic texts**

- **Periodical articles**
  In newspapers
  In magazines
  In scholarly and technical journals
  On the Web

- **Web sites**

- **Other online sources**

- **Virtual communities**
  MUDs (multiuser dimensions)
  MOOs (multiuser object-oriented
      dimensions)

- **Government documents, pamphlets, and census data**

- **Primary sources**
  Original documents like literary works, art objects, performances, manuscripts, letters, and personal journals
  Museum collections, maps, and photo, film, sound, and music archives
  Field notes, surveys, and interviews
  Results of observation and lab experiments

8b Searching with keywords

Most online research—whether conducted in your library's catalog, in a specialized database, or on the Web—requires an understanding of **keyword searches.** In this context, a **keyword** is a term (or terms) you enter into a **search engine** (searching software) to find sources that have information about a particular subject.

Many search engines allow you to refine a keyword search by using these strategies:

- **Group words together.** Put quotation marks or parentheses around the phrase you are looking for—for example, "traditional news media."

- **Use Boolean operators.**

  AND (+) Use AND or + when words must appear together in a document: New York Times + blogs.

  OR Use OR if one of two or more terms must appear in your results: blogs OR "online journalism."

  NOT (–) Use NOT or – in front of words that you do not want to appear together in your results: Cass NOT John.

- **Use truncation plus a wildcard.** For more results, combine part of a keyword with an asterisk (*) used as a wildcard: blog* (for "blogger," "blogging," "blogs," and so forth).

■ **Search the fields.** Some search engines enable searching within fields, such as the title field of Web pages or the author field of a library catalog. Thus, TITLE + "News media" will give you all pages that have "News Media" in their title.

8c
library

8c Using the library in person and online

Librarians know what is available in your library and how to get material from other libraries. They can also show you how to access the library's computerized book catalog, periodical databases, and electronic resources or how to use the Internet to find information relevant to your research project.

Discipline-specific **help sheets,** found at most college libraries, list the location of relevant periodicals and noncirculating reference books, along with information about special databases, indexes, and sources of information on the Internet.

1. Reference works

Reference works provide an overview of a subject area and are less up to date than the specialized knowledge found in academic journals and scholarly books. If your instructor approves, you may start your research by consulting a general or discipline-specific encyclopedia, but for college research, you must explore your topic in more depth. Often, the list of references at the end of an encyclopedia article can lead you to useful sources on your topic.

Reference books do not circulate, so plan to take notes or make photocopies of the pages you may need to consult later. Check your college library's home page for access to online encyclopedias.

Here is a list of some other reference materials available in print, on the Internet, or both:

**8c
library**

ALMANACS

Almanac of American Politics

Information Please Almanac

World Almanac

BIBLIOGRAPHIES

Bibliographic Index

Bibliography of Asian Studies

MLA International Bibliography

BIOGRAPHIES

African American Biographical Database

American Men and Women of Science

Dictionary of American Biography

Dictionary of National Biography

Webster's New Biographical Dictionary

Who's Who

DICTIONARIES

American Heritage Dictionary of the English Language

Concise Oxford Dictionary of Literary Terms

Dictionary of American History

Dictionary of Philosophy

Dictionary of the Social Sciences

Oxford English Dictionary (OED)

2. Periodicals

Newspapers, magazines, and scholarly journals that are published at regular intervals are classified as **periodicals.** Scholarly and technical journals, which publish articles written by experts and based on up-to-date research and information, are more reliable than articles written by journalists for newspapers and magazines. Ask your instructor or librarian which periodicals are considered important in the discipline you are studying.

Articles published in periodicals are cataloged in general and specialized indexes, many of which are available in electronic formats, known as **databases,** as well as in print volumes shelved in the library's reference section. Many databases provide abstracts of the works they list. If you are searching for articles that are more than twenty years old, use printed indexes. Otherwise, see what your library has available through an online subscription service or on CD-ROM. *(For help with search terms, see pp. 58 and 59.)* The following list includes many of the most popular online indexes to periodical articles:

■ *ABC-CLIO:* This service offers access to numerous history-related databases including *American History* and *American Government* as well as databases on African American, American Indian, and Latino American experience, pop culture, war, and social and world history.

■ *Lexis-Nexis Academic:* Updated daily, this online service provides full-text access to around six thousand newspapers, professional publications, legal references, and congressional sources.

■ *EBSCOhost:* The Academic Search Premier database provides full-text coverage for more than eight thousand scholarly publications, and indexes articles in all academic subject areas.

■ *ERIC:* This database lists publications in the area of education.

■ *Factiva:* This database offers access to the Dow Jones and Reuters news agencies, including newspapers, magazines, journals, newsletters, and Web sites.

■ *FirstSearch:* Offering a common interface for access to general databases such as NetFirst and WorldCat, this service also permits searches of such subject-specific bibliographic databases as ERIC, *Medline,* and the *MLA Bibliography.*

- *General Science Index:* This index is general rather than specialized. It lists scholarly and popular articles by biologists, chemists, and other scientists.

- *Catalog of U.S. Government Publications (CGP):* Updated daily, the online catalog contains records of all publications printed by the U.S. Government Printing Office since 1976. For publications prior to 1976, consult the printed catalog, which was discontinued in 2004.

- *Humanities Index:* This index lists articles from journals in language and literature, history, philosophy, and similar areas.

- *InfoTrac Web:* This service searches bibliographic and other databases such as the *General Reference Center Gold, General Business File ASAP,* and *Health Reference Center.*

- *JSTOR:* This archive provides full-text access to recent issues of journals in the humanities, social sciences, and natural sciences, typically from two to five years before the current date.

- *MLA Bibliography:* Covering from 1963 to the present, the *MLA Bibliography* indexes journals, essay collections, proceedings, and series published worldwide in the fields of modern languages, literature, literary criticism, linguistics, and folklore.

- *Periodical Abstracts:* This database indexes more than two thousand general and academic journals covering business, current affairs, economics, literature, religion, psychology, and women's studies from 1987 to the present.

- *New York Times Index:* This index lists major articles published by the *Times* since 1913.

- *Newspaper Abstracts:* This database provides an index to twenty-five national and regional newspapers.

- *PAIS International:* Produced by the Public Affairs Information Service, this database indexes literature on public policy, social policy, and the general social sciences from 1972 to the present.

- *ProQuest:* This database offers access to dissertations; newspapers and journals; information on sources in business, general reference, the social sciences, and humanities; and historical sources dating back to the nineteenth century.

- *PsycInfo:* Sponsored by the American Psychological Association (APA), this database indexes and abstracts books, scholarly articles, technical reports, and dissertations in psychology and related disciplines such as psychiatry, medicine, nursing, and education.

- *PubMed:* The National Library of Medicine publishes this database, which indexes and abstracts fifteen million journal articles in biomedicine and provides links to related databases.

- *Sociological Abstracts:* This database indexes and abstracts more than 2,600 journal articles, as well as books, conference papers, and dissertations in the area of sociology.

- *Social Science Index:* This index lists articles from journals in such fields as economics, psychology, political science, and sociology.

3. Books

A search of the library's catalog will provide you with a list composed mostly of books. Online library catalogs can be searched by author, title, or keyword or by a subject term listed in the *Library of Congress Subject Headings (LCSH)*. The *LCSH* provides a set of key terms that can be used in your search for sources. Record the **call number** of each book that might prove useful so that you will know where to look for the book on the shelves. Your library's online catalog may list books available in affiliated libraries. A librarian can help you obtain books that are not in your college's library through an interlibrary loan process. This process can take time, however. Consult your librarian.

8d Searching the Internet

The **Internet** is a global network of computers. The easiest and most familiar way to gain access to the Internet is through the **World Wide Web,** which uses hypertext links. Besides providing access to online databases, reference works, and periodicals, the Internet can bring you closer to primary materials that were once difficult to examine firsthand. It can also put you in touch with a research community through e-mail, chat rooms, online class discussions, MOOs (multiuser dimensions, object-oriented), MUDs (multiuser dimensions), discussion lists, news groups, and blogs (continuously updated, often topical Web sites).

Resources that you find on the Web must be critically evaluated for their reliability because, unlike most books and articles, Web sites usually do not go through peer review and evaluation before publication. *(For help with evaluating Web sources critically, see pp. 69–70.)*

Learn how to use search engines and keywords to find useful Web sites, as well as how to gain access to and use other Internet resources such as discussion groups, Usenet news groups, MOOs and MUDs, and blogs.

1. Search engines

To find information that has been published in Web pages, use more than one Internet search engine, since each searches the Web in its own way. Each search engine's home page provides a link to advice on efficient use as well as help in refining a search. Look for a link labeled "search help," "about us," or something similar in any search engine you use.

Simple search engines, or *directories,* use hierarchical indexes to categorize information. These directories are easy to use and selective in the results they return:

- *Yahoo!* <www.yahoo.com>
- *Google* <www.google.com>

Standard search engines send "robots" or "spiders" to all points on the Web to return results, putting the most relevant items at the top of the list:

- *AltaVista* <www.altavista.com>
- *Go.com* <infoseek.go.com>
- *HotBot* <www.hotbot.com>

Other search engines allow users to ask for information in different ways:

- *Ask* <www.ask.com>: Supports natural language searching. Type a question, and click on "ask."
- *Bing* <www.bing.com>: Functions like other search engines, answers questions, and helps in decision-making.

Meta search engines return results by searching other search engines. They provide more sites than a simple search engine, but they are not as selective:

- *Dogpile* <www.dogpile.com>
- *MetaCrawler* <www.metacrawler.com>

2. Online government documents

The U.S. government publishes an enormous amount of information and research every year, most of which is available online. The *Catalog of U.S. Government Publications (CGP)* and the *U.S. Government Periodicals Index* are available as online databases (the periodicals index is available through LexisNexis). The Government Printing Office's own Web site, *The Federal Digital System* <www.gpo.gov/fdsys//> is an excellent resource for identifying and locating federal government publications. Other on-line government resources include the following:

■ *FedWorld Information Network* (maintained by the National Technical Information Service)

■ *FirstGov* (the U.S. government's "Official Web Portal") <http://firstgov.gov/>

■ *The National Institutes of Health* <www.nih .gov>

■ *U.S. Census Bureau* <www.census.gov>

3. Online communication

Usenet news groups, electronic mailing lists, blogs, and social networking offer opportunities to converse regularly with people who have common interests. Participants will have different levels of expertise—or possibly no expertise at all—so carefully evaluate information from these sources:

■ **Discussion lists (electronic mailing lists)** are networked e-mail conversations on particular topics. Lists can be open (anyone can join) or closed (only certain people, such as members of a particular class or group, can join). If the list is open, you can subscribe by sending a message.

■ Unlike lists, **Usenet news groups** are posted to a **news server**—a computer that hosts the news group and distributes postings to participating servers. You must subscribe to read postings since they are not automatically distributed by e-mail.

■ **Podcasts** are downloadable digital audio or video recordings, updated regularly.

■ **RSS** (Really Simple Syndication) **feeds** deliver the latest content from continuously updated Web sites to your browser or home page.

■ **Synchronous communication** includes **chat rooms** organized by topic, where people can carry on real-time discussions.

Instant messaging (IM) links only those who have agreed to form a conversing group. Other formats include virtual worlds such as *Second Life,* MUDs, and MOOs. These can be used for collaborative projects.

**9a
research**

- **Blogs** are Web-based journals that offer information and commentary on a variety of topics. They can be designed to allow readers to post their own comments and questions on a wide range of views on a topic under debate.

9 Evaluate your sources.

Never before in the history of the planet has information been more readily available. The catch is that a good deal of this information is misleading or downright false. Your major task is to evaluate the information that you find for credibility, accuracy, reasonableness, and support (CARS).

Digital technologies give you fast access to a tremendous variety of sources, but it is up to you to pose questions. Is the source relevant: does it pertain to your research topic? Is the source **trustworthy:** does it provide credibility, accuracy, reasonableness, and support?

9a Questioning all sources

Just because something is in print (or on the Web) does not make it relevant or true. How can you determine whether a source is likely to be both **credible** (authoritative, dependable) and useful? Before assessing a source's **credibility,** make sure it is relevant to your topic. Relevance can be a tricky matter and requires careful analysis of the writing situation. What sources will be particularly meaningful or persuasive to your anticipated audience? Relevance is also associated with the academic discipline that forms the context for your work. Your sociology instructor will expect you to give special preference to sociological sources in a project on the organization of the workplace. Your business management instructor will expect you to use material from that field in a project on the same topic.

Here are some questions to ask about any source you are considering:

Reliability

- **What information can you find about the writer's credentials?**

- **Who is the publisher?** University presses and academic publishers are considered more scholarly and therefore more credible than the popular press.

- **Does the work include a bibliography of works consulted or cited?** Trustworthy writers cite a variety of sources and document their citations properly.

- **Does the work argue reasonably for its position and treat opposing views fairly?**

Relevance

- **Do the source's title and subtitle indicate that it addresses your specific research question?**

- **What is the publication date?** Is the material up to date, classic, or historically pertinent?

- **Does the table of contents of a book indicate that it covers useful information?**

- **If the source is an article, does it have an abstract at the beginning? Is there a summary at the end?**

- **Does the work contain headings?** Skim the subheadings to see whether they indicate that the source contains useful information.

- **If the source is a book, does the index include keywords related to your topic?** Be prepared to find that some promising sources turn out to be less relevant than you first thought.

9b Questioning Internet sources

The Internet is a free-for-all. You will find up-to-the-minute material there, but you must carefully question every source you find on the Internet. Consider the following questions when determining whether online information is reliable:

- Who is hosting the site? Is the site hosted by a university or by a government agency?

- Who is speaking on the site? If you cannot identify the author, who is the editor or compiler?

- What links does the site provide? If it is networked to sites with obviously unreasonable or inaccurate content, question the credibility of the original site.

- Is the information on the site supported with documentation from scholarly or otherwise credible sources (for example, government reports)?

Here are some points to keep in mind:

- **Authority and credibility:** Look for information about the individual or organization sponsoring the site. The following extensions in the Web address, or uniform resource locator (URL), can help you determine the type of site (which often tells you something about its purpose):

.com	commercial (business)	**.mil**	military
.edu	educational	**.net**	network
.gov	U.S. government	**.org**	nonprofit organization

A tilde (~) followed by a name in a URL usually means the site is a personal home page not affiliated with any organization.

▪ **Audience and purpose:** A site's purpose influences its presentation of information and the credibility of that information. Is the site's main purpose to promote a cause, advertise a product or service, deliver factual information, present research results, provide news, share personal information, or offer entertainment?

▪ **Context:** Search engines retrieve individual Web pages *out of context*. Always return to the site's home page to determine the source and to complete your citation.

▪ **Timeliness:** Reliable sites usually post the date an item was published or loaded onto the Web or tell you when the information was last updated.

▪ **Objectivity and reasonableness (bias):** Look carefully at the purpose and tone of the text. Clues that indicate a lack of reasonableness include an intemperate tone, broad claims, exaggerated statements of significance, conflicts of interest, no recognition of opposing views, and strident attacks on opposing views.

▪ **Relevance and timeliness:** Is the information appropriate for your research? Consider the intended audience of the site based on its purpose, content, depth of coverage, tone, and style.

9c Evaluating a source's arguments

As you read the sources you have selected, you should continue to assess their reliability. Look for arguments that are qualified, supported with evidence, and well documented. Avoid sources that appeal to emotions unfairly or promote one-sided agendas. A fair-minded researcher needs to read and evaluate sources on both sides of issues, including the relevant primary sources that are available.

10 Find and create effective visuals.

Visuals often serve as support for a writer's thesis. Sometimes they enhance an argument, and other times they constitute the complete argument. In some writing situations, you will be able to prepare or provide your own visuals. You may, for example, make your own sketch of an experiment or create bar graphs from data that you collected. In other situations, however, you may decide to create a visual from data that you found in a source or to search in your library or on the Internet for a visual to use.

10a Finding quantitative data and displaying it visually

Research writing in many disciplines—especially in the sciences, social sciences, business, math, engineering, and other technical fields—almost always requires reference to quantitative information. That information generally has more impact when it is displayed visually in a chart, graph, or map than as raw numbers alone. *(For examples of different types of visuals, see pp. 40–41.)*

- **Finding existing graphs, charts, and maps:** As you search for print and online sources *(see Chapter 8),* take notes on useful graphs, charts, or maps that you might incorporate (with proper acknowledgment) into your text. If your source is available in print only, you may be able to use a scanner to capture and digitize it.

- **Creating visuals from quantitative data:** Sometimes you may find data presented in writing or in tables that would be more effective as a chart or graph. Using the graphics tool available in spreadsheet or other software, you can create your own visual.

- **Displaying the data accurately:** Display data in a way that is consistent with your purpose and not misleading to viewers. Avoid intentionally or unintentionally distorting data. Do not use photo-editing software to alter photographs. Plot the axes of line and bar graphs so that they do not misrepresent data. For example, Nancy Kaplan has pointed out distortions in a graph from a National Endowment for the Arts report on reading practices (Figure 10.1, below). The NEA graph presents the years 1988 to 2004, showing a sharp decline in reading. However, the source for the graph, the National Center for Educational Statistics (NCES), presents a less alarming picture in Figure 10.2 (below). Here, reading levels are plotted over a longer period of time, from 1971 to 2004. In addition, the NEA graph is not consistent in its

FIGURE 10.1 **A distorted display of reading practices indicates a decline.**

FIGURE 10.2 **An accurate display of reading practices shows only mild fluctuations.**

units: the four-year period from 1984 to 1988 takes up the same amount of space as the two-year period from 1988 to 1990. In selectively displaying and distorting data, the NEA graph stacks the deck to argue for the reality of a reading crisis.

Caution: Whether you are using data from a source to create an image or incorporating an image made by someone else, you must give credit to the source of the data or image. Furthermore, if you plan to publish this visual on a Web site or in another medium, you must obtain permission to use it from the copyright holder unless the source specifically states that such use is allowed.

10b Searching for appropriate images in online and print sources

Photographs, pictures of artwork, drawings, diagrams, and maps can provide visual support for many kinds of texts, particularly in subjects like history, English and other languages, philosophy, music, theater, and other performing arts. As with the display of quantitative data, you might *choose* an image from another source, or you might *create* one. When using an image from another source, be sure to cite it correctly. If the image will appear on a public Web site, consult the copyright holder for permission.

The following are three sources of images that you can draw on:

- **Online library and museum image collections and subscription databases:** Several libraries and other archives maintain collections of images online. Follow the guidelines for usage posted on these sites. Your library also may subscribe to an image database such as the Associated Press *AP Multimedia Archive.*

▪ **Images on the Internet:** Many search engines have the ability to search the Web for images. You can conduct an image search on *Google,* for example, by clicking on the "images" option, entering the key term, and then clicking "search." Image- and media-sharing sites such as *Flickr* and *YouTube* can serve as sources as well. Read the information on the site carefully to see what uses of the material are permitted. The Creative Commons site (www.creativecommons.org) lets you search for material with a Creative Commons license. Assume that copyright applies to material on the Web unless the site says otherwise. If your project will be published or placed on a public Web site, you must obtain permission to use this material.

▪ **Images scanned from a book or journal:** You can use a scanner to scan some images from books and journals into a paper, but, as always, only if you are sure your situation is within fair-use guidelines. Also, be sure to credit the source.

Caution: The results of Internet image searches, like those of any Internet search, must be carefully evaluated for relevance and reliability. *(See Chapter 9: Evaluating Sources, pp. 67–71.)* Make sure you have proper source information for any images you use that you find in this way.

11 Conduct research in the archive, field, and lab.

Often research involves more than finding answers to questions in books and other printed or online material (secondary research). When you conduct **primary research**—examining authentic documents and original records in an archive, observing behavior and other phenomena in the field, and experimenting in the laboratory—you participate in the discovery of knowledge.

11a Adhering to ethical principles

In the archive, field, or lab, you are working directly with something precious and immediate: an original record, a group of people, or special materials. An ethical researcher shows respect for materials, experimental subjects, fellow researchers, and readers. Here are some guidelines to follow:

- Handle original documents and materials with great care, always leaving sources and data available for other researchers.
- Accurately report your sources and results.
- Follow proper procedures when working with human participants.

Researchers who work with human participants should also adhere to the following basic principles:

- **Confidentiality:** People who fill out surveys, participate in focus groups, or respond to interviews should be assured that their names will not be used without their permission.
- **Informed consent:** Before participating in an experiment, participants must sign a statement affirming that they understand the general purpose of the research.
- **Minimal risk:** Participants in experiments should not incur any risks greater than they do in everyday life.

75

■ **Protection of vulnerable groups:** Researchers must be held strictly accountable for research done with the physically disabled, prisoners, those who are mentally incompetent, minors, the elderly, and pregnant women.

11b Preparing yourself for archival research

Archives of specialized or rare books, manuscripts, and documents are accessible in libraries, in other institutions, in private collections, and in video and audio format. The more you know about your area of study, the more likely you will be to see the significance of an item in an archival collection.

Some archival collections are accessible in video and audio formats as well as sites on the Internet such as *American Memory* <http://memory.loc.gov> and the *U.S. National Archives and Record Administration (NARA)* <www.archives.gov/index.html>. Others you must visit in person. If you intend to do research in a rare-books library, you will need references, a letter of introduction, or other qualifying papers. Archives often will not allow you to browse; instead, use finding aids (often available online) to determine which records you need to see.

11c Planning your field research carefully

Field research involves recording observations, conducting interviews, or administering surveys.

1. Observing and writing field notes
College assignments offer opportunities to conduct systematic observations. When you use direct observation, keep careful records in order to retain the information you gather. *(For advice on conducting and*

recording direct observation, see Part 1: Common Assignments across the Curriculum, pp. 24–26.)

11c research

2. Conducting interviews

Interviews are useful in a wide variety of writing situations. To be useful as research tools, interviews require systematic preparation and implementation:

- Identify appropriate people for your interviews.
- Do background research, and plan a list of open-ended questions.
- Take careful notes; if possible, record the interview. (Be sure to obtain your subject's permission if you use recording equipment.) Verify quotations.
- Follow up on vague responses with questions that get at specific information. Do not rush interviewees.
- Probe inconsistencies and contradictions politely.
- Write thank-you notes to interviewees, and later send them copies of your report.

3. Taking surveys

Surveys are useful when it is important to go beyond individual impressions to a more systematic basis for forming conclusions. Conducted either orally or in writing, **surveys** are made up of structured questions. Written surveys are called **questionnaires.** The following suggestions will help you prepare informal surveys:

- Define your purpose and your target population—the people who are relevant to the purpose of your interview. Are you trying to gauge attitudes, learn about typical behaviors, or both?
- Write clear directions and questions. For example, if you are asking multiple-choice

questions, make sure that you cover all possible options and that none of your options overlap.

- Make sure that your questions do not suggest a preference for one answer over another.
- Make the survey brief and easy to complete.

11d Keeping a notebook when doing lab research

To provide a complete and accurate account of your laboratory work, keep careful records in a notebook. The following guidelines will help you take accurate notes on your research:

- **Recording immediate, on-the-spot, accurate notes on what happens in the lab:** Write down as much detail as possible. Measure precisely; do not estimate. Identify major pieces of apparatus, unusual chemicals, and laboratory animals in detail. Use drawings, when appropriate, to illustrate complicated equipment setups.

- **Following a basic format:** Present your results in a format that allows you to communicate all the major features of an experiment. The five basic sections that must be included are title, purpose, materials and methods, results, and conclusions. Include tables, when useful, to present results. *(For more advice on preparing a lab report, see Part 1: Common Assignments across the Curriculum, pp. 21–23.)*

- **Writing in complete sentences, even if you are filling in answers to questions in a lab manual:** Resist the temptation to use shorthand to record your notes. Later, the complete sentences will provide a clear, unambiguous record of your procedures and results. Highlight cause-effect relationships in your sentences by using the following transitions: *then, next, consequently, because,* and *therefore.*

■ **Revising and correcting your laboratory notebook in visible ways when necessary:** If you make a mistake in recording laboratory results, correct it clearly by erasing or by crossing out and rewriting on the original sheet. If you make an uncorrectable mistake in your lab notebook, simply fold the sheet lengthwise, and mark *omit* on the face side.

If you add sheets to your notebook, paste them permanently to the appropriate pages. Unanticipated results often occur in the lab, and you may find yourself jotting down notes on a convenient scrap of paper. Attach these notes to your laboratory notebook.

12 Work with sources and avoid plagiarism.

Once you have a research question to answer, an idea about what the library and Internet have to offer, and some reliable, appropriate sources in hand, you are ready to begin working with your sources. If you pay attention to detail and keep careful records at this stage, you will stay organized, save time, and credit sources appropriately.

12a Maintaining a working bibliography

As you research, compile a **working bibliography**—a list of those books, articles, pamphlets, Web sites, and other sources that seem most likely to help you answer your research question. Maintain an accurate, complete record of all sources you consult so that you can find sources again and cite them accurately.

While the exact bibliographic information you will need depends on your documentation style, the following list includes the major elements of most systems. *(See Parts 3–5 for the requirements of specific documentation styles.)*

12a research

Book

- Call number (so you can find the source again; not required for documentation)
- Names of all authors, editors, and translators
- Title of chapter
- Title and subtitle of book
- Edition (if not the first), volume number (if applicable)
- Publication information (city, publisher, date)
- Medium (print)

Periodical article

- Names of authors
- Title and subtitle of article
- Title and subtitle of periodical
- Date, edition or volume number, issue number
- Page numbers
- Medium (print)

Article from database (in addition to the preceding)

- Name of database
- Date you retrieved source
- URL of database's home page (if online)
- Medium (Web, CD-ROM, or DVD-ROM)

Internet source (including visual, audio, video)

- Names of all authors, editors, or creators

- Title and subtitle of source
- Title of larger site, project, or database (if applicable)
- Version or edition, if any
- Publication information, if available, including any about a version in another medium (such as print, radio, or film)
- Date of electronic publication or latest update, if available
- Sponsor of site
- Date you accessed site
- URL of site
- Any other identifying numbers, such as a Digital Object Identifier (DOI)

Other sources

- Name of author or creator
- Title
- Format (for example, photograph or lecture)
- Title of larger publication, if any
- Publisher, sponsor, or institution housing the source
- Date of creation or publication
- Any identifying numbers

There are various ways to record bibliographic information for later use. *(See pp. 117, 128, and 135 for examples of bibliographic information in a book, an article, and an online source in MLA style and pp. 171, 179, and 190 for examples in APA style.)*

1. Using note cards or a word processor

One classic method for taking notes is still useful: using three-by-five-inch or four-by-six-inch note cards to compile the working bibliography, with each potential source getting a separate card. You can also use the cards to include all information necessary for documentation, to record brief quotations, and to note your own comments (carefully marked as yours). Because each source has its own card, this method can help you rearrange information when you are deciding how to organize your paper, and it then can help you create your list of citations. Instead of handwriting on cards, you can record bibliographic information in a computer file.

2. Printouts

The results of searches in online or library indexes and databases usually include bibliographic information about the sources they list. You can print these results directly from your browser or, in some cases, save them to disk and transfer them to a Word file. Be sure also to record the name of the database and the date of your search.

3. Photocopies and printouts from Web sites

If you photocopy articles, essays, or pages of reference works from a print or a microfilm source, take time to note the bibliographic information on the photocopy. Similarly, if you print out a source you found on a Web site or copy it to your computer, be sure to note the site's author, name, sponsor, date of publication, complete URL, and the date you visited it.

12b Creating an annotated bibliography

An annotated bibliography includes full citation details, correctly formatted, which you will need for your works-cited or references list. The annotation provides a summary of major points for each source, including your own reactions and ideas about where this material might fit in your project. Also record your evaluation of the source's relevance and reliability *(see Chapter 9, pp. 68–69)*. An annotated bibliography helps you remember what you have found in your search, as well as helping you organize your findings.

12c Taking notes on your sources

Take notes on your sources by annotating photo-copies of your source material or by noting useful quotations and ideas on paper, on cards, or in a computer file. Make note of useful ideas and powerful quotations. See whether categories emerge that can help you organize your project.

1. Annotating

One way to take notes is to annotate photocopied articles and printouts. (Do this for sources you save to your computer by using the Comments feature in your word processor.) As you read, do the following:

- On the first page, write down complete bib-liographic information for the source.

- Record your questions, reactions, and ideas in the margins.

- Comment on ideas that agree with or differ from those you have already learned about.

- Put important and difficult passages into your own words by paraphrasing or summarizing them in the margin. *(For help with paraphras-ing and summarizing, see pp. 85–89.)*

- Use a highlighter to mark statements that are key to understanding an issue or are especially well expressed.

2. Taking notes in a research journal or log

A **research journal** or **research log** can be a spi-ral or loose-leaf notebook, a box of note cards, or a word-processing document on a laptop computer, or a blog—whatever form you are most comfort-able with. Use the journal to write down leads for sources and to record ideas and observations about your topic as they occur to you.

When you have finished annotating a photo-copy, printout, or electronic version of an article, use your research journal to explore some of the comments, connections, and questions you recorded. If you do not have a copy of the material to annotate, take notes directly in your research journal.

**12d
research**

Enclose in quotation marks any exact words from a source. Label the passage a "quotation," and note the page number. Unless you think you might use a particular quotation in your paper, express the author's ideas in your own words by using a paraphrase or a summary.

12d Taking stock and synthesizing as you paraphrase, summarize, and quote your sources

When you take stock, remember your writing situation. As you synthesize what you have learned from the sources you are consulting, think about how these sources relate to one another:

■ Where do they agree, and where do they disagree?

■ Where do you stand relative to these sources?

■ Which do you agree with, which do you disagree with, and why?

■ Did anything you read surprise or disturb you, and how will it affect your audience?

Writing down your responses to such questions can help you clarify what you have learned from working with sources and decide whether and how you want to use them as you develop your own claim.

The credibility of your work depends on the relevance and reliability of your sources as well as the scope and depth of your reading and observation. College research projects tend to require multiple sources and viewpoints. As a general rule you should consult more than two sources and use only sources that are both reliable and respected by people working in the field. To determine whether you have located appropriate and sufficient sources, ask yourself the following questions:

- Are your sources trustworthy? *(See Chapter 9, pp. 67–71, for more on evaluating sources.)*
- If you have developed a tentative answer to your research question, have your sources provided you with sufficient facts, examples, and ideas to support that answer?
- Have you used sources that examine the issues from several different perspectives?

12d research

1. Paraphrasing information from sources

When you **paraphrase,** you put someone else's statements into your words and sentence structures. A paraphrase is not a word-for-word translation. Paraphrase when a passage's details are important to your topic but its exact words are not memorable or when you need to reorder a source's ideas or clarify complicated information. Here are guidelines for writing a paraphrase:

- **Read the passage carefully.** Focus on its sequence of ideas and important details.
- **Be sure you understand the material.** Look up any unfamiliar words.
- **Imagine addressing an audience that has not read the material.**
- **Without looking at the original passage, write down its main ideas and key details.**
- **Use clear, direct language.** Express complicated ideas as a series of simple ones.
- **Check your paraphrase against the original.** Make sure your text conveys the source's ideas accurately without copying its words or sentence structures. Add quotation marks around any phrases from the source or rewrite them.
- **Note the citation information.** List author and page number after every important point.

In the unacceptable paraphrase that follows, the writer has used synonyms for some terms but retained the phrasing of the original. The writer also failed to enclose all borrowed expressions—highlighted here—in quotation marks. The acceptable paraphrase, by contrast, is more concise than the original, and although it quotes a few words from the source, the writer has expressed the definition in a new and different way.

12d
research

SOURCE

The media used to work in a one-to-many pattern—that is, by broadcasting. The Internet, though it can be used for one-to-many transmission, is just as well suited for few-to-few, one-to-one, and many-to-many patterns. Traditionally, the media connected audiences "up" to centers of power, people of influence, and national spectacles. The Internet does all that, but it is equally good at connecting us laterally—to peers, to colleagues, and to strangers who share our interests. When experts and power players had something to communicate to the attentive publics they wished to address, they once had to go through the media. Now they can go direct.

—J. ROSEN, "The New News"

The unacceptable paraphrase (following) alters the sentence structure of the source but plagiarizes by using some of the original wording (highlighted in the example) without quotation marks.

UNACCEPTABLE PARAPHRASE: PLAGIARISM

The news was previously transmitted from one to many. Online media, although they can function in this way, can also follow a few-to-few, one-to-one, and many-to-many pattern. In the past, traditional news outlets connected audiences up to those in a position of power. Online media can do that as well, but they also succeed in connecting us laterally to others who share our interests. If those in a position of power wanted

> to reach their attentive publics, traditional news outlets used to be their only method. Currently, they can communicate directly with their audiences (Rosen).

In contrast, the acceptable paraphrase expresses all ideas from the original using different words and phrasing. Although it quotes a few words from the source, the writer has used quotation marks and indicates where the paraphrase begins.

ACCEPTABLE PARAPHRASE

According to Rosen, the shift away from expert reporting to citizen journalism has opened doors for those who both produce and consume the news. No longer at the mercy of those in a position to seek out and select what makes the news, citizens now have more authority, through the power of blogging, to investigate and publicize the events that matter to us. As a result, we are linked to other informed citizens like never before.

2. Summarizing information from sources

When you **summarize,** you state the main point of a piece, condensing paragraphs into sentences, pages into paragraphs, or a book into a few pages. Summarizing works best for very long passages and when the central idea of a passage is important but the details are not. Here are guidelines for writing a summary:

- **Read the material carefully.** Locate relevant sections.
- **If the text is longer than a few paragraphs, divide it into sections, and in one or two sentences sum up each section.** Compose a topic sentence for each of these sections.
- **Be sure you understand the material.**
- **Imagine explaining the points to an audience that has not read the material.**

- **Identify the main point of the source, in your words.** Compose a sentence that names the text, the writer, what the writer does (reports, argues), and the most important point.

- **Note any other points that relate to your topic.** State each one (in your own words) in one sentence or less. Simplify complex language.

- **Combine your sentence stating the writer's main point with your sentences about secondary points or those summarizing the text's sections.**

- **Check your summary against the original** to see whether it makes sense, expresses the source's meaning, and does not copy any wording or sentence structure.

- **Note all the citation information for the source.**

Here are two summaries of a passage on journalism by Clay Shirky, which is reprinted first. The unacceptable summary is simply a restatement of Shirky's thesis using much of his phrasing (highlighted).

SOURCE

For the next few decades, journalism will be made up of overlapping special cases. Many of these models will rely on amateurs as researchers and writers. Many of these models will rely on sponsorship or grants or endowments instead of revenues. Many of these models will rely on excitable 14-year-olds distributing the results. Many of these models will fail. No one experiment is going to replace what we are now losing with the demise of news on paper, but over time, the collection of new experiments that do work might give us the journalism we need.

– CLAY SHIRKY, "Newspapers and Thinking the Unthinkable"

UNACCEPTABLE SUMMARY: PLAGIARISM

The journalism of the future will be made up of overlapping special cases, some of which will rely on novice reporters and new revenue models. Although many of these models will fail, they will, collectively, help to give us the journalism we need.

The acceptable summary states Shirky's main point in the writer's own words. Note that the acceptable summary still requires a citation.

ACCEPTABLE SUMMARY

According to Shirky, partnerships between traditional and citizen journalism will take several forms. Although many wonder if blogs can offer information that is as reliable as traditionally and expertly researched news, they have undeniably helped to usher in a new era of journalism in which more people have a say in what is reported and how it is delivered ("Newspapers" 29).

3. Quoting your sources directly

Sometimes the writer of a source will say something so eloquently and perceptively that you will want to include that writer's words as a **direct quotation** in your work.

In general, quote these types of sources:

- Primary sources (for example, in a text about Rita Dove, a direct quotation from her, or an associate)
- Sources containing very technical language that cannot be paraphrased
- Literary or historical sources, when you analyze the wording
- An authority in the field whose words support your thesis
- Debaters explaining their different positions on an issue

To avoid inadvertent plagiarism, be careful to indicate that the content is a direct quotation when you copy it onto your note cards or into your research notebook. Try to keep quotations short, and always place quotation marks around them. You might also use a special color to indicate direct quotations or deliberately make quotation marks oversized.

12e Avoiding plagiarism and copyright infringement

Knowledge develops in a give-and-take process akin to conversation. In this kind of situation, it is a matter of integrity and honesty to acknowledge others, especially when you use their words or ideas. The failure to acknowledge sources correctly—either intentionally or inadvertently—is **plagiarism.** Writers who unfairly use copyrighted material found on the World Wide Web or in print are legally liable for their acts.

To avoid plagiarism, adhere to these guidelines:

■ Do not rely too much on one source, or you may slip into using that person's thoughts as your own.

■ Keep accurate records while doing research and taking notes. If you do not know where you got an idea or a piece of information, do not use it in your paper until you find out. *(See 12c, pp. 83–84.)*

■ When you take notes, be sure to put quotation marks around words, phrases, or sentences taken verbatim from a source. If you use any of those words, phrases, or sentences when summarizing or paraphrasing the source, put them in quotation marks. Changing a word here and there while keeping a source's sentence structure or phrasing constitutes plagiarism, even if you credit the source for the ideas. *(See 12d, pp. 86–87 for an example.)*

■ Cite the source of all ideas, opinions, facts, and statistics that are not common knowledge: information that readers in a field would know about from a wide range of general resources.

**12e
research**

■ Choose an appropriate documentation style, and use it consistently and properly. *(See 13c, pp. 97–98.)*

All written materials, including student projects, letters, and e-mail, are covered by copyright, even if they do not bear an official copyright symbol. A copyright grants its owner exclusive rights to the use of a protected work, including reproducing, distributing, and displaying the work. Determine that you have used copyrighted material fairly by considering the following four questions:

■ **What is the purpose of the use?** Educational, nonprofit, and personal use are more likely to be considered fair than commercial use.

■ **What is the nature of the work being used?** In most cases, imaginative and unpublished materials can be used only if you have the permission of the copyright holder.

■ **How much of the copyrighted work is being used?** The use of a small portion of a text for academic purposes is more likely to be considered fair than the use of a whole work for commercial purposes.

■ **What effect would this use have on the market for the original?** The use of a work is usually considered unfair if it would hurt sales of the original.

13 Write the paper.

You have chosen a research question and have located, read, and evaluated a variety of sources. It is now time to develop a thesis that will allow you to share your perspective on the issue and make use of all that you have learned.

13a writing

13a Planning and drafting your paper

Whether your research project is primarily informative, interpretive, or argumentative, keep your overall situation in mind—purpose, audience, and context—as you decide on a thesis to support and develop:

- **Decide on a thesis.** Consider the question that guided your research as well as others provoked by what you have learned during the process. Revise the wording of these questions, and summarize them in a central question that is interesting and relevant to your audience *(see Chapter 7, pp. 52–54)*. Compose an answer that you can use as your tentative thesis.

- **Outline a plan for supporting and developing your thesis.** Guided by your tentative thesis, outline a plan that uses your sources in a purposeful way. Decide on the kind of structure you will use—explanatory, exploratory, or persuasive—and choose facts, examples, and ideas drawn from a variety of sources to support your thesis. *(See Chapters 2–4 in Part 1 for more on explanatory, exploratory, and argumentative structures.)*

- **Write a draft that you can revise, share, and edit.** When you have a tentative thesis and a plan, you are ready to write a draft. Many writers present their thesis or focal question at the end of an introductory, context-setting paragraph or two. The introduction should interest readers.

As you write beyond the introduction, be prepared to reexamine and refine your thesis. When drawing on ideas from your sources, be sure to quote and paraphrase properly. *(For advice on quoting and paraphrasing, see Chapter 12, pp. 89–90 and 85–87.)*

13b writing

Make your conclusion as memorable as possible. You may need to review the paper as a whole before writing the conclusion. Often writers will come up with fresh ideas for their introduction, body paragraphs, or conclusion as they revise and edit their first draft, which is one reason it is important to spend time revising and editing your paper. *(For help with editing, see Parts 6–8.)*

■ **Integrate visuals.** Well-chosen visuals like photographs, drawings, charts, graphs, and maps can sometimes help illustrate your argument. In some cases, a visual might itself be a subject of your analysis. When integrating visuals, be sure to give careful attention to figure numbers and captions. *(See Chapter 17, pp. 152–53, for the requirements in MLA style and Chapter 21, p. 195, for the requirements in APA style.)*

13b Integrating quotations

To integrate quotations properly and effectively, follow these guidelines.

1. Integrating brief quotations

Use quotations when a source's exact words are important and make your writing more memorable, fair, or authoritative. Quotations should be short, enclosed in quotation marks, and well integrated into your sentence structure, as in the following example from a research report on the impact of blogging.

According to Stephen Cass, *we media* is "a term that encompasses a wide range of mostly amateur activities—including blogging and commentary in online forums—that have been made possible by an array of technologies" (62).

The quotation is effective because it provides a concise, memorable definition of "we media." The writer integrates the quotation effectively by introducing the name of the source *(Stephen Cass)* using a **signal phrase** *(according to)* and then blending the quotation into the structure of her own sentence. You may also include the title of the work for context: "Gary Goldhammer tackles this question in his book *The Last Newspaper* . . ."

By contrast, the following poorly integrated quotation is not set up for the reader in any way:

POORLY INTEGRATED QUOTATION

If the blogging machine makes traditional news outlets defunct, how can we be certain that the news we consume is credible and reliable? "Every citizen can be a reporter, but not every citizen should or will. Every person will get news, but not in the same way, not at the same time, and not with the same perspective" (Goldhammer 13).

When you introduce a brief quotation with a signal phrase, you have three basic options:

- You can use a complete sentence followed by a colon.
- You can use a phrase.
- You can make the source's words part of your own sentence structure.

The option you choose depends in part on the length of the quotation and the point you are making with it:

- **A complete sentence followed by a colon:** Introducing a quotation with a complete sentence allows you to provide context for the quote. Use a colon (:) at the end of this introductory sentence, not a semicolon or a comma.

COMPLETE SENTENCE

New York University professor and media consultant Clay Shirky explains how this aspect of blogging is affecting news: "The change isn't a shift from one kind of news institution to another, but rather in the definition of news" (*Here Comes Everybody* 65-66.)

More than one work by Shirky is being cited, so a shortened version of the title is included in MLA style.

- ▪ **An introductory or explanatory phrase, followed by a comma:** Phrases move the reader efficiently to the quotation.

    PHRASE

    As New York University Professor Clay Shirky explains, "The change isn't a shift from one kind of news institution to another, but rather in the definition of news" (*Here Comes Everybody* 65-66.)

    Instead of introducing a quotation, the signal phrase can follow or interrupt it.

- ▪ **Part of your sentence structure:** When you can, integrate the quotation as part of your own sentence structure without any punctuation between your words and the words you are quoting. By doing so, you will clearly connect the quoted material with your own ideas.

    QUOTATION INTEGRATED

    New York University Professor Clay Shirky notes that this transformation "isn't a shift from one kind of news institution to another, but rather in the definition of news" (*Here Comes Everybody* 65-66).

13b
writing

2. Using brackets within quotations

Sentences that include quotations must make sense grammatically. Sometimes you may have to adjust a quotation to make it fit properly into your sentence. Use brackets to indicate any minor adjustments you have made. For example, *over* has been changed to *Over* to make the quotation fit in the following sentence.

> "[O]ver time," Shirky writes, "the collection of new experiments that do work might give us the journalism we need" ("Newspapers" 29).

3. Using ellipses within quotations

Use ellipses to indicate that words have been omitted from the body of a quotation, but be sure that what you omit does not significantly alter the source's meaning. *(For more on using ellipses, see Part 8: Editing for Correctness, pp. 370–71.)*

> The Pew Research Center explains, "One concept that will get more attention is . . . what some call a 'pro-am' (professional and amateur) model for news."

4. Using block format for longer quotations

If you use a verse quotation longer than three lines or a prose quotation longer than four typed lines, set the quotation off on a new line and indent each line one inch (ten spaces) from the left margin *(see Part 8: Editing for Correctness, p. 362)*. (This is MLA style; APA and Chicago have different conventions.) Double-space above and below the quotation. If the quotation is more than one paragraph, indent the first line of each new paragraph a quarter inch. Do not use quotation marks. Writers often introduce a block quotation with a sentence ending in a colon.

Be careful to integrate the block quotation into your paper: tell your readers why you want them to read it; afterwards, comment on it.

13c Documenting your sources

Whenever you use information, ideas, or words from someone else's work, you must acknowledge that person. The only exception to this principle is when you use information that is common knowledge, such as the chemical composition of water or the names of the thirteen original states.

How sources are documented varies by field and discipline. Use the documentation style that is appropriate for the particular discipline you are contributing to. If you are not sure which of the styles covered in this handbook to use, ask your instructor. If you are required to use an alternative style, consult the list of manuals in the box on pages 97–98.

13c sources

NAVIGATING THROUGH COLLEGE AND BEYOND

Style Manuals for Specific Disciplines

DISCIPLINE	POSSIBLE STYLE MANUAL
Chemistry	Coghill, Anne M. and Lorrin R. Garson, eds. *The ACS Style Guide: A Manual for Authors and Editors.* 3rd ed. Washington: American Chemical Society, 2006.
Geology	Bates, Robert L., Rex Buchanan, and Marla Adkins-Heljeson, eds. *Geowriting: A Guide to Writing, Editing, and Printing in Earth Science.* 5th ed. Alexandria, VA: American Geological Institute, 1995.
Government and Law	Garner, Diane L., and Diane H. Smith, eds. *The Complete Guide to Citing Government Information Resources: A Manual for*

(continued)

13c
sources

NAVIGATING *(continued)*

DISCIPLINE	POSSIBLE STYLE MANUAL
Government and Law *(continued)*	*Writers and Librarians.* Rev. ed. Bethesda, MD: Congressional Information Service, 1993.
	Harvard Law Review et al. *The Bluebook: A Uniform System of Citation.* 18th ed. Cambridge: Harvard Law Review Assn., 2005.
Journalism	*Associated Press Stylebook, 2011.* Revised and updated ed. New York: Basic Books, 2011.
Linguistics	Linguistic Society of America. "LSA Style Sheet." *LSA Bulletin.* Published annually in the December issue.
Mathematics	American Mathematical Society. *AMS Author Handbook: General Instructions for Preparing Manuscripts.* Providence: AMS, 2007.
Medicine	Iverson, Cheryl, ed. *American Medical Association Manual of Style: A Guide for Authors and Editors.* 10th ed. New York: Oxford University Press, 2007.
Political Science	American Political Science Association. *Style Manual for Political Science.* Rev. ed. Washington: APSA, 2006.

Next to the originator of a good sentence is the first quoter of it.

—Ralph Waldo Emerson

PART 3

MLA Documentation Style

The charts on pages 100–03 can help you locate the right example of a works-cited list entry for a particular kind of source. Answering the questions provided will usually lead you to the sample entry you need. You can also use the directory on pages 118–20 in Chapter 15.

MLA

Entries in a Works-Cited List:
BOOKS (116–26)

❓ *Is your source a complete book or part of a book?*

No **Yes**
↓

		Go to this entry (or these entries) on page(s)
Is it a complete book with one named author?		
Is it the only book by this author that you are citing?	**1**	*116*
Are you citing more than one book by this author?	**2**	*116*
Is it a published doctoral dissertation?	**27**	*130*
Is it a complete book with more than one named author?	**3**	*120*
Is it a complete book without a named author?		
Is the author an organization?	**4**	*121*
Is the author anonymous or unknown?	**16**	*126*
Is it a complete book with an editor or a translator?		
Is there an editor only or an editor and an author?	**5, 6**	*121*
Is it an anthology?	**7**	*121*
Is it a translation?	**10**	*124*
Is it the published proceedings of an academic conference?	**26**	*130*
Is it a complete book with an edition, a volume, or a series number?		
Does it have an edition number (for example, Second Edition)?	**11**	*125*
Is it one or more volumes of a multivolume work (for example, Volume 3)?	**13**	*125*
Is it one in a series?	**14**	*125*
Is it a complete book but not the only version?		
Is your book a sacred work (such as the Bible)?	**12**	*125*
Is your book a republished work (for example, a classic novel)?	**15**	*126*
Does the book's title include the title of another book?	**5**	*121*
Is your source part of an edited book?		
Is it a work in an anthology or a chapter in an edited book?	**7**	*121*
Are you citing two or more items from the same anthology?	**7**	*121*
Is it a published letter (that is, part of a published collection)?	**33**	*132*
Is it an article in a reference work (such as an encyclopedia)?	**8**	*124*
Is it a preface, an introduction, a foreword, or an afterword?	**9**	*124*
Is it a graphic novel or comic book?	**17**	*126*

Check the next page or the directory on pages 118–20, or consult your instructor.

Entries in a Works-Cited List:
PRINT PERIODICALS OR OTHER PRINT SOURCES (127–33)

❓ *Is your source from a journal, a magazine, or a newspaper?*

No   Yes
↓

	Go to this entry (or these entries) on page(s)	
Is it from an academic journal?	**18**	*127*
Is it from a magazine?	**19**	*127*
Is it an article?	**20**	*128*
Is your source a letter to the editor?	**23**	*129*
Is it a review (such as a review of a book or film)?	**21**	*129*
Is it an interview?	**29**	*131*
Is it from a newspaper?		
Is it an article?	**20**	*128*
Is it a review (such as a review of a book or film)?	**21**	*129*
Is it an editorial?	**22**	*129*
Is it a letter to the editor?	**23**	*129*
Is it an interview?	**29**	*131*

❓ *Is it a print source but not a book or a periodical article?*

No   Yes
↓

	Go to this entry (or these entries) on page(s)	
Is it published by the government or by a nongovernment organization?	**24, 25**	*130*
Is it a statute or law case (print or online)?	**35**	*133*
Is it an unpublished dissertation or an abstract of a dissertation?	**27, 28**	*130, 131*
Is it a personal letter or a letter from an archive?	**34**	*133*
Is it a map, a chart, a cartoon, or an advertisement?	**30–32**	*131, 132*

Check the next page or the directory on pages 118–20, or consult your instructor.

Entries in a Works-Cited List:
ELECTRONIC OR OTHER NONPRINT SOURCES (134–50)

❓ *Did you find your nonprint source online?*

No   Yes
↓

Go to this entry (or these entries) on page(s)

Is it a professional or personal Web site?	**36**	*134*
Is it a page, selection, or part of a Web site or larger online work?	**37**	*134*
Is it part of a wiki or another reference work?	**42, 43**	*138*
Is it from an online scholarly journal?		
Is it an article?	**59**	*142*
Is it an editorial or a letter to the editor?	**60**	*143*
Is it an article you found through a subscription database service (such as EBSCO or ProQuest)?	**61, 62**	*144*
Is it from an online magazine or newspaper?	**39**	*136*
Is it an editorial or a letter to the editor?	**40, 41**	*136*
Does your online source also exist in print or in another medium?		
Is it a book or part of a book?	**50, 51**	*140, 141*
Is it a doctoral dissertation?	**52**	*141*
Is it a pamphlet or brochure?	**53**	*141*
Is it a map or chart?	**54**	*141*
Is it a work of art (such as a painting, drawing, or photograph)?	**55**	*142*
Is it a video or film?	**56**	*142*
Is it a radio or television program?	**57**	*142*
Is it archival material?	**58**	*142*
Is your source sponsored by or related to the government?	**48, 49**	*139, 140*
Is it an online communication?		
Is it a blog or blog entry?	**38**	*136*
Is it a posting to a news group or other type of online forum?	**47**	*139*
Is it an e-mail communication?	**63**	*144*
Is your source an online graphic, audio, or video file or podcast?	**44–46**	*138, 139*

MLA

❓ *Is your source a computer-based source that is not found online?*

No Yes

Go to this entry (or these entries) on page(s)

Is it a digital file stored on your computer?		
Is it an audio file (for example, an MP3)?	**64**	*146*
Is it an image?	**65**	*146*
Is your source stored on film, CD-ROM, DVD, or Blu-ray?	**66, 67, 70, 71**	*146, 147*
Is it computer software?	**68**	*147*
Is it a video game?	**69**	*147*

❓ *Is it another nonprint source?*

No Yes

Go to this entry (or these entries) on page(s)

Is it a television or radio program?	**72**	*148*
Is it a broadcast interview?	**73**	*148*
Is it a personal, a telephone, or an e-mail interview?	**77**	*149*
Is it a sound recording, musical composition, or work of art?	**74–76**	*149*
Is it a lecture, speech, or performance?	**78, 79**	*149, 150*

Check the directory on pages 118–20 or consult your instructor.

The documentation style developed by the Modern Language Association (MLA) is used by many researchers in the arts and humanities, especially by those who write about language and literature. The guidelines presented here are based on the seventh edition of the *MLA Handbook for Writers of Research Papers* (New York: MLA, 2009).

College texts include information, ideas, and quotations from sources that must be accurately documented. Documentation allows others to see the path you have taken in researching and writing your project. *(For more on what to document, see Part 2: Researching, pp. 90–91.)*

The MLA documentation style has three parts:

- In-text citations
- List of works cited
- Explanatory notes and acknowledgments

In-text citations and a list of works cited are mandatory; explanatory notes are optional.

14 MLA style: In-text citations

In-text citations let readers know that they can find full bibliographical information about your sources in the list of works cited at the end of your paper.

1. Author named in sentence In your first reference, give the author's full name as the source presents it. Afterward, use the last name only, unless two or more of your sources have the same last name *(see no. 6)* or unless two or more works by the same author appear in your works-cited list *(no. 3)*.

> signal phrase
> ⌐New York University professor and media
> consultant Clay Shirky explains¬ how this aspect
> of blogging is affecting news: "The change isn't a
> shift from one kind of news institution to another,
> but rather in the definition of news" (65).

The parenthetical page citation comes after the closing quotation mark but before the period.

2. Author named in parentheses If you do not name the source's author in your sentence, then you must provide the name in the parentheses. (Give the full name if the author of another source has the same last name.)

> For many, the term *we media* aptly characterizes
> the kind of citizen journalism that blogging
> represents; it is "a term that encompasses a wide
> range of mostly amateur activities—including
> blogging and commentary in online forums—
> that have been made possible by an array of
> no comma after author's name
> technologies" (Cass 62).

There is no comma between the author's name and the page number. If you cite two or more distinct pages, however, separate the numbers with a comma: (Cass 62, 70).

3. Two or more works by the same author   MLA

If you use two or more works by the same author, you must identify which work you are citing, either in your sentence or in an abbreviated form in parentheses: (Shirky, *Here Comes Everybody* 66).

book title is italicized
In *Here Comes Everybody: The Power of Organizing*

without Organizations, Shirky compares new forms of

media, like blogging, to fundamental advances in

human literacy, such as the printing press (66).

MLA In-Text Citations: Directory to Sample Types
(See pp. 116–50 for works-cited examples.)

4. Two or three authors of the same work   If a source has up to three authors, you should name them all either in your text, as the next example shows, or in parentheses: (Perlmutter and McDaniel 60).

> Mass communication experts David D. Perlmutter and Misti McDaniel argue that bloggers are exceptionally good at reporting on issues in a way that creates mass appeal (60).

5. More than three authors   If a source has more than three authors, either list all the authors, or give the first author's last name followed by *et al.* (not italicized), meaning "and others" (note that *et,* which means "and," is fine as is, but *al.,* which is an abbreviation for *alia,* needs a period). Do the same in your works-cited list.

> Changes in social regulations are bound to produce new forms of subjectivity (Henriques et al. 275).

MLA IN-TEXT CITATIONS

- Name the author, either in a signal phrase such as "Shirky compares" or in a parenthetical citation.
- Include a page reference in parentheses. No "p." precedes the page number; if the author is named in the parentheses, there is no punctuation between the author's name and the page number.
- Place the citation as close to the material being cited as possible and before any punctuation marks that divide or end the sentence except in a block quotation, where the citation comes one space after the period or final punctuation mark. See no. 12 for quotations ending with a question mark or an exclamation point.
- Italicize the titles of books, magazines, and plays. Place quotation marks around the titles of articles and short poems.
- For Internet sources, follow the same general guidelines as for print sources. Keep the parenthetical citation simple, providing enough information for your reader to find the full citation in your works-cited list. Cite either the author's name or the title of the site or article. Begin the parenthetical citation with the first word of the corresponding works-cited list entry.
- For works without page or paragraph numbers, give the author or title only. Often it is best to mention them in your sentence, in which case no parenthetical citation is needed.

6. Authors with the same last name   If the authors of two or more of your sources have the same last name, include the first initial of the author you are citing (R. Campbell 63); if the first initial is also shared, use the full first name, as shown in the following example.

> In the late nineteenth century, the sale of sheet
> music spread rapidly in a Manhattan area along
> Broadway known as Tin Pan Alley (Richard
> Campbell 63).

7. Organization as author   Treat the organization as the author. If the name is long, put it in a signal phrase.

> The Centre for Contemporary Cultural Studies
> claims that "there is nothing inherently concrete
> about historiography" (10).

8. Unknown author   When no author is given, cite a work by its title, using either the full title in a signal phrase or an abbreviated version in the parentheses. When abbreviating the title, begin with the word by which it is alphabetized in your works-cited list.

> title of article
> "Squaresville, USA vs. Beatsville" makes the
> Midwestern small-town home seem boring
> compared with the West Coast artist's "pad" (31).

> The Midwestern small-town home seems boring
> compared with the West Coast artist's "pad"
> ("Squaresville" 31).

9. Entire work   Acknowledge an entire work in your text, not in a parenthetical citation. Include the work in your list of works cited, and include in the text the word by which the entry is alphabetized.

> Sidney J. Furie's film *Lady Sings the Blues* presents
> Billie Holiday as a beautiful woman in pain rather
> than as the great jazz artist she was.

10. Paraphrased or summarized source If you include the author's name in your paraphrase or summary, include only the page number or numbers in your parenthetical citation. Signal phrases clarify that you are paraphrasing or summarizing.

signal phrase
Shirky cites an example from 2002, when it was the bloggers, not the mainstream reporters, who first publicized former Mississippi senator Trent Lott's controversial remarks at Strom Thurmond's hundredth birthday party, resulting in Lott's decision to step down from his position as majority leader (61).

11. Source of a long quotation For a quotation of more than four typed lines of prose or three of poetry, do not use quotation marks. Instead, indent the material you are quoting by one inch. Following the final punctuation mark of the quotation, allow one space before the parenthetical information.

Shirky describes what this trend toward "pro-am" reporting might look like:

> For the next few decades, journalism will be made up of overlapping special cases. Many of these models will rely on amateurs as researchers and writers. Many of these models will rely on sponsorship or grants or endowments instead of revenues. Many of these models will rely on excitable 14-year-olds distributing the results. Many of these models will fail. . . . [O]ver time, the collection of new experiments that

ellipses and brackets indicate an omission from the quotation

MLA

> do work might give us the journalism we
>
> need. ("Newspapers" 29)

12. Source of a short quotation Close the quotation before the parenthetical citation. If the quotation concludes with an exclamation point or a question mark, place the closing quotation mark after that punctuation mark, and place the sentence period after the parenthetical citation.

> *Encyclopaedia Britannica* defines a *blog,* short for
>
> *Web log,* as an "online journal where an individual,
>
> group, or corporation presents a record of
>
> activities, thoughts, or beliefs" ("Blog").

> Shakespeare's Sonnet XVIII asks, "Shall I compare
>
> thee to a summer's day?" (line 1).

13. One-page source You need not include a page number in the parenthetical citation for a one-page printed source.

14. Government publication To avoid an overly long parenthetical citation, name within your text the government agency that published the source.

> According to a report issued by the Bureau of
>
> National Affairs, many employers in 1964 needed
>
> guidance to apply new workplace rules that
>
> ensured fairness and complied with the Civil Rights
>
> Act of 1964 (32).

15. Photograph, map, graph, chart, or other visual

VISUAL APPEARS IN YOUR PAPER

> An aerial photograph of Manhattan (Fig. 3), taken
>
> by the U.S. Geological Survey, demonstrates

how creative city planning can introduce parks

and green spaces within even the most densely

populated urban areas.

If the caption you write for the image includes all the information found in a works-cited list entry, you need not include it in your list.

VISUAL DOES NOT APPEAR IN YOUR PAPER

An aerial photograph of Manhattan taken by the

U.S. Geological Survey demonstrates how creative

city planning can introduce parks and green spaces

within even the most densely populated urban

areas (TerraServer-USA).

Provide a parenthetical citation that directs your reader to information about the source of the image in your works-cited list.

16. Web site or other online electronic source

If you cannot find the author of an online source, then identify the source by title or sponsor, either in your text or in a parenthetical citation. Because most online sources do not have set page, section, or paragraph numbers, they must usually be cited as entire works.

organization cited as author
The Pew Research Center argues that one model

in the future will involve partnerships between

traditional and newer forms of media and, in

particular, that one type of relationship will be a

concept known as a "pro-am" (for "professional
page number not provided
and amateur") approach to news.

17. Work with numbered paragraphs or sections instead of pages

To distinguish them from page numbers, use the abbreviation *par(s).* or the type of division such as *section(s)* or *screen(s).*

> Rothstein suggests that many German Romantic
> musical techniques may have originated in Italian
> opera (par. 9).

Give the paragraph or section number(s) after the author's name and a comma in a parenthetical citation: (Rothstein, par. 9).

18. Work with no page or paragraph numbers When citing an electronic or print source without page, paragraph, or other reference numbers, try to include the author's name in your text instead of in a parenthetical citation.

> author's name
> Mathew Ingram, a technology journalist and
> blogger, notes that "I think the more people there
> are writing, and the easier it is to publish writing
> of all kinds, the more likely we are to find the
> information we need."

19. Multivolume work When citing more than one volume of a multivolume work in your paper, include with each citation the volume number, followed by a colon, a space, and the page number.

> Scott argues that today people tend to solve
> problems "by turning to the Web" (2: 5).

If you consult only one volume of a multivolume work, then specify that volume in the works-cited list *(see p. 125)* but not in the parenthetical citation.

20. Literary works

Novels and literary nonfiction books Include the relevant page number, followed by a semicolon, a space, and the chapter number.

> Jenkins states that because Harry Potter's
> fandom involves both adults and children, it's a

> "space where conversations could occur across
> generations" (216; ch. 5).

If the author is not named in your sentence, add the name in front of the page number: (Jenkins 216; ch. 5).

Poems Use line numbers, not page numbers.

> In "Trumpet Player," Hughes says that the music
> "Is honey / Mixed with liquid fire" (lines 19-20).
> This image returns at the end of the poem, when
> Hughes concludes that "Trouble / Mellows to a
> golden note" (43-44).

Note that the word *lines* (not italicized), rather than *l.* or *ll.*, is used in the first citation to establish what the numbers in parentheses refer to; subsequent citations need not use the word *lines*.

Plays and long, multisection poems Use division (act, scene, canto, book, part) and lines, not page numbers. In the following example, notice that Arabic numerals are used for act and scene divisions as well as for line numbers: (*Ham.* 2.3.22-27). The same is true for canto, verse, and lines in the following citation of Byron's *Don Juan:* (*DJ* 1.37.4-8). (The *MLA Handbook* lists abbreviations for titles of certain literary works.)

21. Religious text Cite material in the Bible, Upanishads, or Koran by book, chapter, and verse, using an appropriate abbreviation when the name of the book is in the parentheses rather than in your sentence. Name the edition from which you are citing.

> As the Bible says, "The wise man knows there will
> be a time of judgment" (*Holy Bible, Rev. Stand. Vers.,*
> Eccles. 8.5).

Note that titles of biblical books are not italicized.

22. Historical document For familiar documents such as the Constitution and the Declaration of Independence, provide the document's name and the numbers of the parts you are citing.

> Judges are allowed to remain in office "during good
>
> behavior," a vague standard that has had various
>
> interpretations (US Const., art. 3, sec. 1).

23. Indirect source When you quote or paraphrase a quotation you found in someone else's work, put *qtd. in* (not italicized, meaning "quoted in," with a period after the abbreviation) before the name of your source.

> Advertising agencies try to come up with ways to
>
> "interrupt" people so that "they pay attention to
>
> one-way message[s]" (qtd. in Scott 7).

In your list of works cited, list only the work you consulted, in this case the indirect source by Scott.

24. Two or more sources in one citation When you credit two or more sources, use a semicolon to separate the citations.

> The impact of blogging on human knowledge,
>
> communication, and interactions has led to
>
> improvements in our daily lives. We are not only
>
> more up to date on the latest goings-on in the
>
> world but are also connected to other informed
>
> citizens like never before (Ingram; Shirky).

25. Two or more sources in one sentence Include a parenthetical reference after each idea or quotation you have borrowed.

Ironically, Americans lavish more money each

year on their pets than they spend on children's

toys (Merkins 21), but the feral cat population—

consisting of abandoned pets and their offspring—

is at an estimated 70 million and growing (Mott).

26. Work in an anthology   When citing a work in a collection, give the name of the specific work's author, not the name of the editor of the whole collection.

"Exile marks us like a talisman or tattoo. It teaches

us how to endure long nights and short days"

(Agosin 273).

Here, Agosin is cited as the source, even though his work appears in a collection edited by Ringoberto Gonzalez. Note that the list of works cited must include an entry for Agosin.

27. E-mail, letter, or personal interview   Cite by name the person you communicated with, using either a signal phrase or parentheses.

Blogging is a beneficial tool to use in the classroom

because it allows students to keep up with new

media trends (Carter).

In the works-cited list, after giving the person's last name you will need to identify the kind of communication and its date *(see pp. 133, 144, and 149).*

15 MLA style: List of works cited

MLA documentation style requires a works-cited page with full bibliographic information about your sources. The list of works cited should appear at the end of your research project, beginning on a new page entitled "Works Cited." Include only those sources you cite, unless your instructor tells you to prepare a "Works Consulted" list.

Books

Figure 15.1 shows where the elements of a works-cited entry for a book can be found.

1. Book with one author   Italicize the book's title. Generally only the city, not the state, is included in the publication data. Conclude with the medium (Print). In MLA style, abbreviations are suggested for most publishers, for instance, *Wayne State UP* for *Wayne State University Press,* and *Random* for *Random House.*

> Shirky, Clay. *Here Comes Everybody: The Power of*
>
> *Organizing without Organizations.* New York:
>
> Penguin, 2008. Print.

2. Two or more works by the same author(s)
Give the author's name in the first entry only. For subsequent works authored by that person, replace the name with three hyphens and a period. Alphabetize by title.

> Shirky, Clay. *Here Comes Everybody: The Power of*
>
> *Organizing without Organizations.* New York:
>
> Penguin, 2008. Print.

> ---. "Newspapers and Thinking the Unthinkable."
>
> *Risk Management* May 2009: 24-29. *Academic*
>
> *Search Elite.* Web. 21 Apr. 2010.

MLA

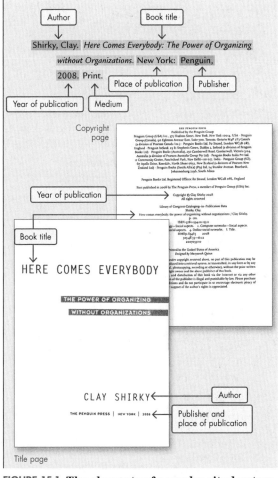

FIGURE 15.1 The elements of a works-cited entry: books. Information for a book citation can be found on the book's title and copyright pages.

MLA

MLA

3. Book with two or more authors Name two or three authors in the order in which they appear on the title page, putting the last name first for the first author only.

> Reeder, Joelle, and Katherine Scoleri. *The IT Girl's*
>
> *Guide to Blogging with Moxie.* Hoboken: Wiley,
>
> 2007. Print.

When a work has more than three authors, you may list them all or use the abbreviation *et al.* (meaning "and others") to replace the names of all authors except the first.

4. Organization as author Consider as an organization any group, commission, association, or corporation whose members are not identified on the title page.

> Centre for Contemporary Cultural Studies. *Making*
>
> *Histories: Studies in History Writing and Politics.*
>
> London: Hutchinson, 1982. Print.

5. Book by an editor or editors If the title page lists an editor instead of an author, begin with the editor's name followed by the abbreviation *ed.* with a period (not italicized). Use *eds.* when more than one editor is listed. Only the first editor's name should appear in reverse order. When a book's title contains the title of another book (as this one does), do not italicize the title-within-a-title (here, *The Invisible Man*).

> title in title not italicized
> O'Meally, Robert, ed. *New Essays on* The Invisible
>
> Man. Cambridge: Cambridge UP, 1988. Print.

6. Book with an author and an editor Put the author and title first, followed by the abbreviation *Ed.* (not italicized, for "edited by") and the name of the editor. However, if you cited something written by the editor, see no. 5.

> James, Henry. *The Portrait of a Lady.* Ed. Robert D.
>
> Bamberg. New York: Norton, 1975. Print.

7. Work in an anthology or textbook or chapter in an edited book List the author and title of the selection, followed by the title of the anthology, *Ed.* (not italicized) and the editor's name, publication data, page numbers of the selection, and medium. The first example cites a reading from a textbook.

MLA

Brodkey, Linda. "On the Subjects of Class and Gender in 'The Literacy Letters.'" *Cross-Talk in Comp Theory*. Ed. Victor Villanueva. Urbana: NCTE Press, 2003. 677-96. Print.

Fisher, Walter R. "Narration, Knowledge, and the Possibility of Wisdom." *Rethinking Knowledge: Reflections across the Disciplines*. Eds. Robert F. Goodman and Walter R. Fisher. Albany: SUNY Press, 1995. 169-92. Print.

When citing two or more items from the same anthology, include a complete entry for the anthology beginning with the name of the editor(s). Each selection should have its own entry in the alphabetical list that includes only the author, title of the selection, editor, and page numbers. When citing the anthology as a whole, begin the entry with just the editor's name, followed by *ed.* (not italicized).

Eggers, Dave, ed. *The Best American Nonrequired Reading 2007*. Boston: Houghton, 2007. Print.

MLA LIST of WORKS CITED

- Begin on a new page with the centered title "Works Cited."
- Include an entry for every source cited in your text.
- Include author, title, publication data, and medium (such as print, Web, radio) for each entry, if available. Use a period to set off each of these elements from the others. Leave one space after the periods.
- Do not number the entries.
- Put entries in alphabetical order by author's or editor's last name. If the work has more than one author, see no. 3 *(p. 120)*. (If the

author is unknown, use the first word of the title, excluding the articles *a, an,* or *the*).

- Italicize titles of books, periodicals, long poems, and plays. Put quotation marks around titles of articles, short stories, and short poems.

- Capitalize the first and last and all important words in all titles and subtitles. Do not capitalize articles, prepositions, coordinating conjunctions, and the *to* in infinitives unless they appear as the first or last word in the title. Place a colon between title and subtitle unless the title ends in a question mark or an exclamation point.

- In the publication data, abbreviate most months and publishers' names (Dec. rather than December; Oxford UP instead of Oxford University Press), and include the name of the city in which the publisher is located but not the state (unless the city is obscure or ambiguous): Ithaca: Cornell UP. Use *n.p.* in place of publisher or location information if none is available. If the date of publication is not given, provide the approximate date, enclosed in brackets: [c. 1975]. If you cannot approximate the date, write *n.d.* for "no date."

- Do not use *p., pp.,* or *page(s)* (not italicized). Use *n. pag.* (not italicized) if the source lacks page or paragraph numbers or other divisions. When page spans over one hundred have the same first digit, do not repeat it for the second number: 243-47.

- Abbreviate all months except May, June, and July.

- For articles and other print sources that skip pages, provide the page number for the beginning of the article followed by a plus (+) sign.

- Use a hanging indent: Start the first line of each entry at the left margin, and indent all subsequent lines of the entry five spaces (or one-half inch in a word-processing program).

- Double-space within entries and between them.

8. Article or entry in a reference work Cite the author's name, title of the entry (in quotation marks), title of the reference work (italicized), editor, publication information, and medium. Omit page numbers if entries appear in alphabetical order. If the article is unsigned, start the entry with the title. For well-known reference works, omit the place and publisher.

> Hirsch, E. D. "Idioms." *Dictionary of Cultural Literacy.*
>
> 2nd ed. Boston: Houghton, 1993. 59. Print.

9. Preface, foreword, introduction, or afterword When the writer of some part of a book is different from the author of the book, use the word *By* after the book's title, and cite the author's full name. If the book's sole author wrote the part and the book has an editor, use only the author's last name after *By*. If there is no editor and the author wrote the part, cite the complete book.

> name of part of book
> Schlesinger, Arthur M. Jr. Introduction. *Pioneer*
>
> *Women: Voices from the Kansas Frontier.* By
>
> Joanna L. Stratton. New York: Simon, 1981.
>
> 11-15. Print.

10. Translation The translator's name goes after the title, with the abbreviation *Trans.*

> Freire, Paulo. *Pedagogy of the Oppressed.* Trans. Mara
>
> Bergman Ramos. New York: Continuum, 2005.
>
> Print.

11. Edition other than the first Include the number of the edition: *2nd ed., 3rd ed.* (not italicized) and so on. Place the number after the title, or if there is an editor, after that person's name.

Jenkins, Henry. *Convergence Culture: Where Old and New Media Collide.* 2nd ed. New York: New York UP, 2008. Print.

12. Religious text Give the version, italicized; the editor's or translator's name (if any); and the publication information including medium.

New American Standard Bible. La Habra: Lockman Foundation, 1995. Print.

The Upanishads. Trans. Eknath Easwaran. Tomales: Nilgiri, 1987. Print.

13. Multivolume work The first example indicates that the researcher used more than one volume of the work; the second shows that only the second volume was used *(to cite an individual article or chapter in a multivolume work or set of reference books, refer to no. 8).*

Manning, Martin J., and Clarence R. Wyatt. *Encyclopedia of Media and Propaganda in Wartime America.* 2 vols. Santa Barbara: ABC-CLIO, 2010. Print.

Manning, Martin J., and Clarence R. Wyatt. *Encyclopedia of Media and Propaganda in Wartime America.* Vol. 2. Santa Barbara: ABC-CLIO, 2010. Print.

14. Book in a series After the medium, put the name of the series and, if available on the title page, the number of the work.

Wimmer, Roger D., and Joseph R. Dominick. *Mass Media Research: An Introduction (with InfoTrac).*

Boston: Wadsworth, 2005. Print. Contributions

name of series not italicized

in Wadsworth Ser. in Mass Comm. and

Journalism.

15. Republished book Put the original date of publication, followed by a period, before the current publication data.

original publication date

Freire, Paulo. *Pedagogy of the Oppressed.* 1970. New

York: Continuum, 2005. Print.

16. Unknown author The citation begins with the title. In the list of works cited, alphabetize the citation by the first important word, excluding the articles *A, An,* and *The.*

Webster's College Dictionary. New York: Random;

New York: McGraw, 1991. Print.

Note that this entry includes both of the publishers listed on the dictionary's title page; they are separated by a semicolon.

17. Graphic novel or comic book Cite graphic narratives created by one person as you would any other book or multivolume work. For collaborations, begin with the person whose work you refer to most, and list others in the order in which they appear on the title page. Indicate each person's contribution. *(For part of a series, see no. 14.)*

Moore, Alan, writer. *Watchmen.* Illus. David

Gibbons. Color by John Higgins. New York: DC

Comics, 1995. Print.

Satrapi, Marjane. *Persepolis.* 2 vols. New York:

Pantheon-Random, 2004-05. Print.

Periodicals

Periodicals are published at set intervals, usually four times a year for scholarly journals, monthly or weekly for magazines, and daily or weekly for newspapers. Between the author and the publication data are two titles: the title of the article, in quotation marks, and the title of the periodical, italicized. Figure 15.2 on page 128 shows where the elements of a works-cited entry for a journal article can be found. *(For online versions of print periodicals and periodicals published only online, see pp. 136 and 143–44.)*

MLA

18. Article in a journal Most journals have a volume number corresponding to the year and an issue number for each publication that year. The issue may be indicated by a month or season. Put the volume number after the title. Follow it with a period and the issue number. Give the year of publication in parentheses, followed by a colon, a space, and the page numbers of the article. End with the medium. (If the journal does not use volume numbers, provide only the issue number, following the title.)

> Lacy, Stephen, et al. "Citizen Journalism Web Sites
>
> Complement Newspapers." *Newspaper Research*
>
> *Journal* 31.2 (2010): 34-46. Print.

19. Article in a magazine For a monthly magazine, provide the month and year, abbreviating all months except May, June, and July. For a weekly publication, include the complete date: day, month, and year.

> Robbins, Sarah. "One Mother's Fierce Love."
>
> *Glamour* Feb. 2008: 34. Print.

> Tresniowski, Alex, Jeff Truesdell, Siobhan
>
> Morrissey, and Howard Breuer. "A Cyberbully
>
> Convicted." *People* 15 Dec. 2008: 73-74. Print.

MLA

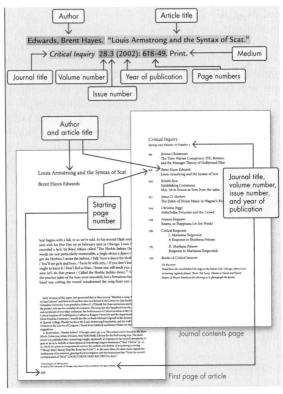

FIGURE 15.2 The elements of an MLA works-cited entry: journal articles. Some academic journals, like this one, provide most of the information needed for a citation on the first page of an article as well as, like others, on the cover or contents page. You will need to look at the article's final page for the last page number.

20. Article in a newspaper Provide the day, month, and year. If an edition is named on the top of the first page, specify the edition—*natl. ed.* or *late ed.* (without italics), for example—after the date. If the section letter is part of the page number, see the first example. Give the title of an unnumbered section with *sec.* (not italicized). If the article appears on nonconsecutive pages, put a plus (+) sign after the first page number.

> Gillis, Justin. "A Scientist, His Work and a Climate
> Reckoning." *New York Times* 22 Dec. 2010, natl.
> ed.: A1+. Print.

> Just, Julie. "Children's Bookshelf." *New York Times*
> 15 Mar. 2009, natl. ed., Book Review sec.: 13.
> Print.

21. Review Begin with the name of the reviewer and, if there is one, the title of the review. Add *Rev. of* (without italics, meaning "review of") and the title plus the author or performer of the work being reviewed.

> Want, Chun-Chi. Rev. of *Convergence Culture: Where*
> *Old and New Media Collide,* by Henry Jenkins.
> *Spectator* Fall 2007: 101-03. Print.

22. Editorial Treat editorials as articles, but add the word *Editorial* (not italicized) after the title. If the editorial is unsigned, begin with the title.

> Shaw, Theodore M. "The Debate over Race Needs
> Minority Students' Voices." Editorial. *Chronicle*
> *of Higher Education* 25 Feb. 2000: A72. Print.

23. Letter to the editor

> Tyler, Steve. Letter. *National Geographic Adventure*
> Apr. 2004: 11. Print.

Other print sources

24. Government document   Either the name of the government and agency or the name of the document's author comes first. If the government and agency name come first, follow the title of the document with the word *By* for a writer, *Ed.* for an editor, or *Comp.* for a compiler (if any), and give the name. Publication information and medium come last.

> United States. Bureau of Natl. Affairs. *The Civil Rights Act of 1964: Text, Analysis, Legislative History; What It Means to Employers, Businessmen, Unions, Employees, Minority Groups.* Washington: BNA, 1964. Print.

(For the format to use when citing the Congressional Record, *see no. 49.)*

25. Pamphlet or brochure   Treat a pamphlet or brochure as a book. If it has an author, list his or her name first; otherwise, begin with the title.

> *The Digital Derry Strategy.* Donegal: PIKE, 2009.

26. Conference proceedings   Cite as you would a book, but include information about the conference if it is not in the title.

> Mendel, Arthur, Gustave Reese, and Gilbert Chase, eds. *Papers Read at the International Congress of Musicology Held at New York September 11th to 16th, 1939.* New York: Music Educators' Natl. Conf. for the American Musicological Soc., 1944. Print.

27. Dissertation   Cite as you would a book. After the title, add *Diss.* (not italicized) for "dissertation,"

the name of the institution, the year the dissertation was written, and the medium. If a dissertation
is unpublished, begin by citing the author's name,
followed by the title in quotation marks, the abbreviation *Diss.* (not italicized), the institution, the
year it was written, and the medium.

> Ashman, Kathleen. *Online Composition Classes Call*
>
> > *for a Pedagogical Paradigm Shift: Students as*
> >
> > *Cartographers of Their Own Knowledge Maps.*
> >
> > Diss. Florida State U, 2006. Tallahassee:
> >
> > Florida State. 2006. Print.

28. Abstract of a dissertation Use the format
for an unpublished dissertation. After the dissertation date, give the abbreviation *DA* or *DAI* (for
Dissertation Abstracts or *Dissertation Abstracts
International*), then the volume number, the issue
number, the date of publication, the page number,
and the medium.

> Quinn, Richard Allen. "Playing Together:
>
> > Improvisation in Postwar American Literature
> >
> > and Culture." Diss. U of Iowa, 2000. *DAI* 61.6
> >
> > (2001): 2305A. Print.

29. Published interview Name the person interviewed, and give the title of the interview or the
descriptive term *Interview* (not italicized), the name
of the interviewer (if known and relevant), the publication information, and the medium.

> Pelosi, Nancy. "Minority Report." Interview
>
> > by Deborah Solomon. *The New York Times*
> >
> > *Magazine* 18 Nov. 2010: 18. Print.

30. Map or chart Cite as you would a book with
an unknown author. Italicize the title of the map

or chart, and add the word *Map* or *Chart* (not italicized) following the title.

> *Let's Go Map Guide to New Orleans.* Map. New York:
>
> St. Martin's, 1997. Print.

31. Cartoon or photograph in a print work

Include the artist's name, the title of the image (in quotation marks for cartoons, italicized for photographs), the publication information, and the medium. Include the word *Cartoon* or *Photograph* (not italicized) after the title.

> Dator, Joe. "14 Street." Cartoon. *New Yorker.* 10
>
> Jan. 2011: 72. Print.

> Wallace, Daniel. *Calvin Johnson Tries to Get by Bucs*
>
> *Cornerback Ronde Barber.* Photograph. *St.*
>
> *Petersburg Times.* 20 Dec. 2010: 1C. Print.

32. Advertisement
Name the item or organization being advertised, include the word *Advertisement* (not italicized), and indicate where the ad appeared.

> Hartwick College Summer Music Festival and
>
> Institute. Advertisement. *New York Times*
>
> *Magazine* 3 Jan. 1999: 54. Print.

33. Published letter
Treat like a work in an anthology, but include the date. Include the number, if one was assigned by the editor.

> Hughes, Langston. "To Arna Bontemps." 17 Jan.
>
> 1938. *Arna Bontemps-Langston Hughes Letters*
>
> *1925-1967.* Ed. Charles H. Nichols. New York:
>
> Dodd, 1980. 27-28. Print.

34. Personal letter To cite a letter you received, start with the writer's name, followed by the descriptive phrase *Letter to the author* (not italicized), the date, and *MS* (manuscript).

> Cogswell, Michael. Letter to the author. 15 Mar.
>
> 2008. MS.

MLA

To cite someone else's unpublished personal letter, give the author, the word *Letter,* the form (*MS* if handwritten, *TS* if typed), any identifying number, and the name and location of the institution housing the material. (Do not italicize any part of the citation.)

35. Legal source (print or online) To cite a specific act, give its name, Public Law number, its Statutes at Large number, page range, the date it was enacted, and the medium.

> Energy Policy Act of 2005. Pub. L. 109-58. 119 Stat.
>
> 594-1143. 8 Aug. 2005. Print.

To cite a law case, provide the names of the plaintiff and defendant, the case number, the court that decided the case, the date of the decision, and the medium.

PRINT

> Ashcroft v. the Free Speech Coalition. 535 US 234-73.
>
> Supreme Court of the US. 2002. Print.

WEB

> Ashcroft v. the Free Speech Coalition. 535 US 234-
>
> 73. Supreme Court of the US. 2002. *Supreme*
>
> *Court Collection.* Legal Information Inst.,
>
> Cornell U Law School, n.d. Web. 20 May 2008.

For more information about citing legal documents or case law, MLA recommends consulting *The Bluebook: A Uniform System of Citation,* published by the Harvard Law Review Association.

Online sources

The examples that follow are based on guidelines for the citation of electronic sources in the seventh edition of the *MLA Handbook for Writers of Research Papers* (2009).

For scholarly journals published online, see no. 59. For periodical articles from an online database, see no. 61. Cite most other Web sources according to nos. 36 and 37. For works that also exist in another medium (for example, print), the MLA recommends including information about the other version in your citation. See nos. 50–58. *(See Figure 15.3, which shows where the elements of a works-cited entry for a short work on a Web site can be found.)*

Basic Web sources

36. Web site or independent online work   Begin with the author, editor *(ed.)*, compiler *(comp.)*, director *(dir.)*, performer *(perf.)*, or translator *(trans.)*, if any, of the site. Give the title (italicized), the version or edition (if any), the publisher or sponsor (or *n.p.*), publication date (or last update, or *n.d.*), medium, and your access date. (Use italics for the title only.) Citations 36 through 49 follow this format. The following examples are of a government-sponsored Web site, a professional site, and a personal site.

> *Cyber Crimes Center.* U.S. Immigration and Customs
>
> Enforcement, 2010. Web. 18 Dec. 2010.

> Garrett, Chris. *The Business of Blogging and New*
> *Media.* Headway, n.d. Web. 20 Dec. 2010.
> <small>no date</small>

> <small>no publisher</small>
> Johnson, Steven. *StevenBerlinJohnson.com.* N.p.,
>
> 2002. Web. 19 Dec. 2010.

37. Page, selection, or part of a Web site or larger online work   Give the title of the part in quotation marks. If no title is available, use a descriptive term such as "Home page."

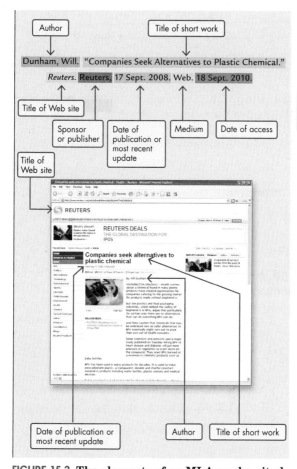

FIGURE 15.3 The elements of an MLA works-cited entry: Short work on a Web site. If you cannot find the source's author or sponsor, look for a link that says "About us" or "Contact us." If the source has an edition or version number, place it after the source title. See page 143 for online scholarly journals and page 140 for works existing online and in another medium (such as print or film).

> Oliver, Rachel. "All About: Forests and Carbon
>
> Trading." *CNN.com.* Cable News Network, 11
>
> Feb. 2008. Web. 14 Mar. 2008.

MLA

38. Blog The first example cites an entire blog; the second refers to a specific entry from one.

> McLennan, Doug. *Diacritical.* ArtsJournal, 2008.
>
> Web. 11 May 2008.

> McLennan, Doug. "The Rise of Arts Culture."
>
> *Diacritical.* ArtsJournal, 21 Nov. 2007. Web. 11
>
> May 2008.

39. Article in an online magazine or newspaper

> Castillo, Michelle. "FCC Passes Ruling to Protect
>
> Net Neutrality." *Time.com.* Time, 21 Dec. 2010.
>
> Web. 22 Dec. 2010.

> Kang, Cecilia. "FCC's Rules to Protect Internet
>
> Access Spark Claims of Violations." *Washington*
>
> sponsor
> *Post.* Washington Post, 24 Jan. 2011. Web. 4
>
> Mar. 2011.

40. Online editorial Include the word *Editorial* (not italicized) after the published title of the editorial.

> sponsor
> "Saner Gun Laws." Editorial. *New York Times.* New
>
> York Times, 22 Jan. 2011. Web. 23 Jan. 2011.

41. Online letter to the editor Include the word *Letter* (not italicized) after the name of the letter writer.

CITING ELECTRONIC SOURCES in MLA STYLE

- Begin with the name of the writer, editor, compiler, translator, director, or performer.
- Put the title of a short work in quotation marks.
- If there is no title, identify the genre of your source, such as *editorial* or *comment* (not italicized).
- Italicize the name of the publication or Web site. The online versions of some print magazines and newspapers have different titles than the print versions.
- Cite the date of publication or last update.
- For an online magazine or newspaper article or a Web original source, give the source (in quotation marks), the site title (italicized), version (if any), publisher or sponsor, date of publication, medium (Web), and access date. *(See pp. 134, 136.)*
- You may cite online sources that also appear in another medium with information about the other version *(see pp. 140–42)*. (Do not cite online versions of print newspapers and magazines in this way.)
- For a journal article, include the article title (in quotation marks), periodical title (italicized), volume and issue numbers, and inclusive page numbers or *n. pag.* (not italicized). Conclude with the medium (Web) and access date. *(See p. 143.)*
- To cite a periodical article from an online database, provide the print publication information, the database title (italicized), the medium, and your access date.
- If the source is not divided into sections or pages, include *n. pag.* (not italicized) for "no pagination." Give the medium (Web).
- Include your most recent date of access to the specific source (not the general site).
- Conclude the citation with a URL only if readers may have difficulty finding the source without it.

MLA

Dow, Roger. Letter. *SFGate.* San Francisco _{sponsor}

Chronicle, 10 Jan. 2008. Web. 12 May 2008.

42. Article in an online encyclopedia or other reference work   Begin with the author's name if any is given.

Hosch, William L. "Media Convergence and

Podcasting." *Encyclopaedia Britannica Online.*

Britannica, 2007. Web. 20 Dec. 2010.

43. Entry in a wiki   A wiki is a collaborative creation, so no author should be listed. Begin with the title of the entry or file, the wiki name, the sponsor, the date of latest update, the medium, and your access date. Check with your instructor before using a wiki as a source.

"Symphony." *Citizendium.* Citizendium Foundation,

1 Nov. 2007. Web. 12 May 2008.

44. Online visual (map, chart, or photograph—Web only)   Include the genre—*Map, Chart,* or similar term—unless the image is a photograph (do not italicize). Begin with the artist's name, if one is given.

"Denver, Colorado." Map. *Google Maps.* Google, 12

May 2008. Web. 12 May 2008.

Jelonek, Matt. "U2 perform in Perth, Australia."

Rolling Stone. Rolling Stone, 21 Dec. 2010.

Web. 22 Dec. 2010.

45. Audio or video podcast

Powell, Padgett. "Padgett Powell: The Interrogative

Mood." Interview by St. John Flynn. *Cover to*

> *Cover.* Natl. Public Radio. GPB, Atlanta, 29
> Mar. 2010. Web. 4 Mar. 2011.

46. Online video (Web original)

> Wesch, Michael. "The Machine Is Us/ing Us."
> *Digital Ethnography.* Kansas State U, 31 Jan.
> 2007. Web. 12 May 2008.

For material posted online from a film, TV series, or other non-Web source, see nos. 50–58.

47. Posting to a news group, electronic forum, or e-mail discussion list   Treat an archived posting as a Web source. Include the author and use the subject line as the title of the posting. If there is no subject, substitute *Online posting* (not italicized).

> Harbin, David. "Furtwangler's Beethoven 9
> Bayreuth." *Opera-L Archives.* City U of New
> York, 3 Jan. 2008. Web. 12 May 2008.

> Pomeroy, Leslie K., Jr. "Racing with the Moon."
> *Rec.music.bluenote.* N.p., 4 May 2008. Web.
> 12 May 2008.

48. Online government publication other than the *Congressional Record*   Begin with the name of the country, followed by the name of the sponsoring department, the title of the document, and the names (if listed) of the authors.

> United States. National Commission on Terrorist
> Attacks upon the United States. *The 9/11
> Commission Report.* By Thomas H. Kean, et al. 5
> Aug. 2004. Web. 12 May 2008.

49. *Congressional Record* (online or print)
The *Congressional Record* has its own citation format, which is the same for print and online (apart from the medium). Abbreviate the title, and include the date and page numbers. Give the medium (print or Web).

> *Cong. Rec.* 28 Apr. 2005: D419-D428. Web. 12 May
>
> 2008.

Web sources also available in another medium

If an online work also appears in another medium (for example, print), the MLA recommends (but does not require) that your citation include information about the other version of the work. (Information about the editor or sponsor of the Web site or database is optional in this model.) If the facts about the other version of the source are not available, cite it as a basic Web source. (Articles on the Web sites of newspapers and magazines are never cited with print publication information.)

50. Online or electronic book (e-book)   Cite a book you download from a database such as *Bartleby .com* as a print book *(no. 1)*. Instead of ending with *Print* (not italicized), give the Web site or database, the medium (Web), and your access date.

> Arter, Jared Maurice. *Echoes from a Pioneer Life.*
>
> Atlanta: Caldwell, 1922. *Documenting the*
>   name and location (optional) of Web publisher
> *American South.* U of North Carolina, Chapel
>
> Hill. Web. 21 May 2008.

For an e-book that you download from an online bookseller or library, use the same format as a print book *(no. 1)*, but change the medium from *Print* to the kind of e-book (for example, *Kindle e-book file*).

> Schiff, Stacy. *Cleopatra: A Life.* New York: Little,
>
> Brown, 2010. Kindle e-book file.

51. Selection from an online book   Add the title of the selection after the author. If the online version of the work lacks page numbers, use *n. pag.* instead (capitalize the *n* in *n. pag.* when it follows a period).

> Sandburg, Carl. "Chicago." *Chicago Poems*. New
>
>> York: Holt, 1916. N. pag. *Bartleby.com*. Web. 12
>>
>> May 2008.

52. Online dissertation   Give the Web site or database, the medium (Web), and your access date. Or cite as a basic Web source *(see nos. 36 and 37)*.

> Kosiba, Sara A. "A Successful Revolt? The
>
>> Redefinition of Midwestern Literary Culture
>>
>> in the 1920s and 1930s." Diss. Kent State U,
>>
>> 2007. *OhioLINK*. Web. 12 May 2008.

53. Online pamphlet or brochure (also in print)   Cite as a book. Give the title of the Web site or database, the medium (Web), and your access date. Or cite as a basic Web source *(see no. 36)*.

> United States. Securities and Exchange
>
>> Commission. Division of Corporate
>>
>> Finance. *International Investing: Get the Facts*.
>>
>> Washington: GPO, 1999. *US Securities and*
>>
>> *Exchange Commission*. Web. 12 May 2008.

54. Online map or chart (also in print)   See no. 30 for a print map. Remove the medium; add the title of the database or Web site, the medium (Web), and your access date. *(See no. 44 for a Web-only map.)* Or cite as a basic Web source *(see nos. 36 and 37)*.

> *MTA New York City Subway*. New York: Metropolitan
>
>> Transit Authority, 2008. *MTA New York City*
>>
>> *Transit*. Web. 12 May 2008.

55. Online rendering of visual artwork Cite as you would the original *(no. 76)*. Remove the medium; add the database or Web site, the medium (Web), and your access date. Or cite as a basic Web source *(see nos. 36 and 37)*.

> Seurat, Georges-Pierre. *Evening, Honfleur.* 1886.
>
> Museum of Mod. Art, New York. *MoMA.org.*
>
> Web. 8 May 2008.

56. Online video or film (also on film or DVD) See nos. 70 and 71 for a film, DVD, or Blu-ray. Remove the medium; add the database or site, the medium (Web), and your access date. Or cite as a basic Web source *(see nos. 36 and 37)*.

> *Night of the Living Dead.* Dir. George A. Romero.
>
> Image Ten, 1968. *Internet Archive.* Web.
>
> 12 May 2008.

57. Online radio or television program See no. 72 for a radio or television program. Remove the medium; add the database or site, the medium (Web), and your access date. Or cite as a basic Web source *(see nos. 36 and 37)*.

> "Bill Evans: 'Piano Impressionism.' " *Jazz Profiles.*
>
> Narr. Nancy Wilson. Natl. Public Radio.
>
> WGBH, Boston, 27 Feb. 2008. *NPR.org.* Web.
>
> 16 Mar. 2008.
>
>   episode   director
> (not series)   of episode   series
> "Local Ad." Dir. Jason Reitman. *The Office.* Perf.
> performer in series
>   Steve Carrell. NBC. WNBC, New York, 12 Dec.
>
> 2007. *NBC.com.* Web. 12 May 2008.

58. Online archival material Provide the information for the original. Add the Web site or database, the medium (Web), and your access date. Otherwise, cite as a basic Web source *(see nos. 36 and 37).*

Whitman, Walt. "After the Argument." [c. 1890].
date uncertain

The Charles E. Feinberg Collection of the

Papers of Walt Whitman, Lib. of Cong. *The*

Walt Whitman Archive. Web. 13 May 2008.

Works in online scholarly journals

Use the same format for all online journals, including those with print editions.

59. Article in an online journal Give the author, the article title (in quotation marks) or a term such as *Editorial* (not italicized), the journal title (italicized), the volume number, issue number, date, and the inclusive page range (or *n. pag.*—not italicized—if the source lacks page numbers). Conclude with the medium (Web) and your access date.

Ridolfo, Jim, and Danielle Nicole DeVoss.

"Composing for Recomposition: Rhetorical

Velocity and Delivery." *Kairos* 13.2 (2009):

n. pag. Web. 25 April 2011.

60. Editorial or letter to the editor in an online journal

Heitmeyer, Wilhelm, et al. "Letter from the

Editors." Editorial. *International Journal of*

Conflict and Violence 1.1 (2007): n. pag. Web. 14

May 2008.

Destaillats, Frédéric, Julie Moulin, and Jean-

Baptiste Bezelgues. Letter. *Nutrition &*

Metabolism 4.10 (2007): n. pag. Web. 14 May

2008.

Works from online databases

In addition to information about the print version of the source, provide the title of the database (in italics), the medium (Web), and your access date. Figure 15.4 on page 145 shows where the elements of a works-cited entry for a journal article from an online database can be found.

61. Newspaper or magazine article from an online database

> Blumenfeld, Larry. "House of Blues." *New York Times* 11 Nov. 2007: A33. *Academic Universe.* Web. 31 Dec. 2007.

> Farley, Christopher John. "Music Goes Global." *Time* 15 Sept. 2001: 4+. *General OneFile.* Web. 31 Dec. 2007.

62. Journal article or abstract from an online database

> Nielson, Aldon Lynn. "A Hard Rain." *Callaloo* 25.1 (2002): 135-45. *Academic Search Premier.* Web. 17 Mar. 2008.

> Dempsey, Nicholas P. "Hook-Ups and Train Wrecks: Contextual Parameters and the Coordination of Jazz Interactions." *Symbolic Interaction* 31.1 (2008): 57-75. Abstract. *Academic Search Premier.* Web. 17 Mar. 2008.

Other electronic (non-Web) sources

63. E-mail Include the author, the subject line (if any) in quotation marks, the descriptive term *Message to* (not italicized), and the name of the recipient, the date of the message, and the medium.

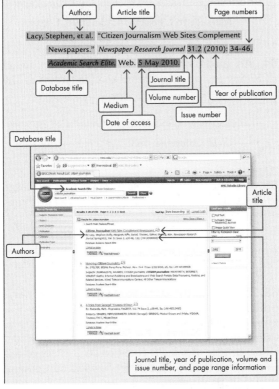

FIGURE 15.4 The elements of an MLA works-cited entry: Journal article from an online database A citation for an article obtained from an online database includes information about the database, the medium, and the date of access in addition to the information about the print version of the article. Information about the date of access comes from the researcher's notes.

> Hoffman, Esther. "Re: My Louis Armstrong Paper."
>
> Message to J. Peritz. 14 Apr. 2008. E-mail.

64. An audio file Use the format for a sound recording *(see no. 74)*. Record the file format as the medium.

> Holiday, Billie. "God Bless the Child." *God Bless the*
>
> *Child.* Columbia, 1936. MP3 file.

65. A visual file Cite local image files as works of visual art. Record the file format as the medium.

> Gursky, Andreas. *Times Square, New York.* 1997.
>
> Museum of Mod. Art, New York. JPEG file.

66. CD-ROM or DVD-ROM published periodically If a CD-ROM or DVD-ROM is revised on a regular basis, include in its citation the author, title of the work, any print publication information, medium, title of the CD-ROM or DVD-ROM (if different from the original title), vendor, and date of electronic publication.

> Ross, Alex. "Separate Worlds, Linked
>
> Electronically." *New York Times* 29 Apr. 1996,
>
> late ed.: A22. CD-ROM. *New York Times Ondisc.*
>
> UMI-ProQuest. Dec. 1996.

67. CD-ROM or DVD-ROM not published periodically Works on CD-ROM or DVD-ROM are usually cited like books or parts of books if they are not revised periodically. The medium and the name of the vendor (if different from the publisher) appear after the publication data. For a work that also exists in print, give the print publication information followed by the medium, electronic publisher, and date of electronic publication.

Jones, Owen. *The Grammar of Ornament.* London,
    print publisher omitted for pre-1900 work
    1856. CD-ROM. Octavo, 1998.

If there are multiple discs, list the total number of discs at the end of the entry, or give the number of the disc you reviewed if you used only one.

68. Computer software Include the title, version, publisher, and date in your text or in an explanatory note. Do not include an entry in your works-cited list.

69. Video game In your entry, include the title, version, publisher, date of publication, and medium.

Europa 1400: The Guild. Vienna: JoWood

    Entertainment AG, 2002. DVD.

Audiovisual and other nonprint sources

70. Film Begin with the title (italicized) unless you want to highlight a particular contributor. For a film, cite the director and the featured performer(s) or narrator (*Perf.* or *Narr.,* neither italicized), followed by the distributor and year. Conclude with the medium.

Artists and Models. Dir. Raoul Walsh. Perf. Jack

    Benny, Ida Lupino, and Alan Townsend.

    Paramount, 1937. Film.

71. DVD or Blu-ray See no. 70. Include the original film's release date if relevant. Conclude with the medium (for example, DVD, Blu-ray).

Casablanca. Dir. Michael Curtiz. Perf. Humphrey

    Bogart and Ingrid Bergman. 1942. Warner,

    2000. DVD.

72. Radio or television program Give the episode title (in quotation marks), the program title (italicized), the name of the series (if any), the network (call letters), the city, the broadcast date, and the medium (*Radio* or *Television,* neither italicized). Name individuals if relevant.

> "Who's Carl This Time?" *Wait, Wait . . . Don't Tell*
>
> *Me.* NPR, Washington, 18 Dec. 2010. Radio.

> episode   director
> (not series)   of episode   series
> "Local Ad." Dir. Jason Reitman. *The Office.* Perf.
>   performer in series
>   Steve Carrell. NBC. WNBC, New York, 12 Dec.
>
>   2007. Television.

73. Broadcast interview Give the name of the person interviewed, followed by the word *Interview* (not italicized) and the name of the interviewer if you know it. End with information about the broadcast and the medium.

> Meacham, Jon. Interview by Jon Stewart. *The Daily*
>
> *Show with Jon Stewart.* Comedy Central, 5 May
>
> 2010. Television.

74. Sound recording Start with the composer, conductor, or performer, depending on your focus. Include the following information: the work's title (italicized); the artist(s), if not already mentioned; the manufacturer; the date of release; and the medium. In the first example, an individual song on a recording is noted (in quotation marks) before the album title.

> Arcade Fire. "We Used to Wait." *The Suburbs.*
>
> Merge/Mercury, 2010. MP3 file.

> Yanni. *Truth of Touch.* Virgin Records/EMI, 2011. LP.

75. Musical composition Include only the composer and title, unless you are referring to a published score (see the third example). Published scores are treated like books except that the date of composition appears after the title. Titles of instrumental pieces are not italicized when known only by form and number, unless the reference is to a published score.

> Ellington, Duke. *Satin Doll.*

> Haydn, Franz Josef. Symphony No. 94 in G Major.

> reference to a published score
> Haydn, Franz Josef. *Symphony No. 94 in G Major.*
>
> 1791. Ed. H. C. Robbins Landon. Salzburg:
>
> Haydn-Mozart, 1965. Print.

76. Artwork Provide the artist's name, the title of the artwork (italicized), the date (if unknown, write *n.d.*), the medium, and the institution or private collection and city (or *n.p.*) in which the artwork can be found. For anonymous collectors, write *Private collection,* and omit city (do not write *n.p.*).

> Warhol, Andy. *Campbell's Soup Can.* 1962. Oil on
>
> Canvas. Saatchi Collection, London.

77. Personal, telephone, or e-mail interview Begin with the person interviewed, followed by *Personal interview, Telephone interview,* or *E-mail interview* (not italicized) and the date of the interview. *(See no. 29 for a published interview.)*

> Jacobs, Phoebe. Personal interview. 5 May 2008.

78. Lecture or speech Give the speaker, the title (in quotation marks), the name of the forum or sponsor, the location, and the date. Conclude with a description such as *Speech, Lecture,* or *Presentation* (not italicized). If you access the speech online, include that information and replace the medium *Speech* with *Web.*

> Beaufort, Anne. "All Talk, No Action? Or, Does
>
> Transfer Really Happen after Reflective
>
> Practice?" Conference on College Composition
>
> and Communication. San Francisco, CA, 13
>
> March 2009. Presentation.

79. Live performance To cite a play, opera, dance performance, or concert, begin with the title; followed by the authors *(By);* information such as the director *(Dir.)* and major performers; the site; the city; the performance date; and the word *Performance* (not italicized).

> *Ragtime.* By Terrence McNally, Lynn Athrens, and
>
> Stephen Flaherty. Dir. Frank Galati. Ford
>
> Performing Arts Center, New York. 11 Nov.
>
> 1998. Performance.

16 MLA style: Explanatory notes and acknowledgments

Explanatory notes are used to cite multiple sources for borrowed material or to give readers supplemental information. You can also use explanatory notes to acknowledge people who helped you with research and writing. Acknowledgments are a courteous gesture. If you acknowledge someone's assistance in your explanatory notes, be sure to send that person a copy of your research project.

The example that follows is a note that provides additional information—one blogger's opinion about the nature of his audience.

TEXT

Mainstream media companies, such as the *New York Times, Newsweek,* BBC, and CNN, have started their own blogs and have adopted other forms of new media, such as *Twitter,* in an effort to expand their audience base.[1]

NOTE

1. Former librarian and public administrator Will Manley notes that, in contrast to face-to-face audiences or print media audiences, his blogging audience is "solid and real" because of the sheer volume of daily traffic on his blog.

MLA

17 MLA style: Format

The following guidelines will help you prepare your research project in the format recommended by the seventh edition of the *MLA Handbook for Writers of Research Papers.* For sample pages from a research project that has been prepared using MLA style, see pages 154–58.

Materials

Back up your final draft on a flash drive, CD, or DVD. Use a high-quality printer and high-quality, white 8½-by-11-inch paper. Put the printed pages together with a paper clip.

Heading and title

Include a separate title page if your instructor requires one. In the upper left-hand corner of the first page of the paper, one inch from the top and side, enter on separate, double-spaced lines your name, your instructor's name, the course number, and the date. (Check with your instructor about the course information you should provide.) Double-space between the date and the title and between the title and the first line of text, as well as throughout your paper. The title should be centered and properly capitalized *(see p. 154)*. Do not italicize the title or put it in quotation marks or bold type.

If your instructor requires a title page, prepare it according to his or her instructions. If your instructor requires a final outline, place it between the title page and the first page of the paper.

Margins and spacing

Use one-inch margins all around, except for the top right-hand corner, where the page number goes. Your right margin should be ragged (not "justified," or even).

Double-space lines throughout, including in quotations, notes, and the works-cited list. Indent the first word of each paragraph one-half inch (or five spaces) from the left margin. For block quotations, indent one inch (or ten spaces) from the left.

Page numbers

Put your last name and the page number in the upper right-hand corner of the page, one-half inch from the top and flush with the right margin.

Visuals

Place visuals (tables, charts, graphs, and images) close to the place in your text where you refer to them. Label and number tables consecutively *(Table 1, Table 2)*, and give each one an explanatory caption; put this information above the table. The term *Figure* (abbreviated *Fig.*) is used to label all other kinds of visuals, except for musical illustrations, which are labeled *Example* (abbreviated *Ex.*). Place a figure or an example caption below each visual. Below all visuals, cite the source of the material, and provide explanatory notes as needed. *(For more on using visuals effectively, see Chapter 6: Designing Documents for Page and Screen.)*

18 Pages from a research project in MLA style

As a first-year college student, Rebecca Hollingsworth wrote a research project about the impact of blogging on traditional news for her composition course. The following sample pages are from Hollingsworth's research project.

Place your name, your professor's name, your course title, and the date at the left margin, double-spaced.

Rebecca Hollingsworth

Professor Spaulding

English 120

7 May 2011

Title centered, not italicized.

Breaking News:

Blogging's Impact on Traditional and

New Media

In previous decades, when people wanted to know what was happening in the world, they turned to the daily newspaper and their television sets. Today, many of us are more likely to go online, where a simple *Google* search on any subject can produce

Double-spaced throughout.

thousands of hits and open doors to seemingly limitless sources of information. Much of this information comes from the online journals known as blogs, which have redefined the concept of news and multiplied our ways of obtaining it. To survive, journalism must blend traditional forms of reporting with new methods that get news and opinion to the people instantaneously and universally.

Blogging has become an extremely popular activity; many people are doing it for a wide variety of reasons. Arts and crafts, politics, sustainable living, pets, pop music, and astrophysics are just a few of the countless topics currently discussed in the millions of blogs on the

Internet. *Encyclopaedia Britannica* defines a *blog,* short for *Web log,* as an "online journal where an individual, group, or corporation presents a record of activities, thoughts, or beliefs" ("Blog"). This definition points out an important aspect of blogs: some are maintained by companies and organizations, but many are maintained by people not necessarily affiliated with traditional news outlets. New York University professor and media consultant Clay Shirky explains that this aspect of blogging is a fundamental transformation, "in the definition of news: from news as an institutional prerogative to news as part of a communications ecosystem, occupied by a mix of formal organizations, informal collectives, and individuals" (*Here Comes Everybody* 65-66). Like *Britannica*'s definition of *blog,* Shirky's definition of *news* emphasizes the range of people producing the news today, from multinational corporations to college students. By noting the interdependence of all news producers, Shirky reveals an important insight about the evolution of journalism: new forms of media, especially blogs and other social media, have allowed average citizens to influence and even create the very news we consume.

MLA in-text citation: title of the encyclopedia entry is given in parentheses.

MLA in-text citation: author (Shirky) named in signal phrase; short title included before page numbers to identify which one of two works by same author in Works Cited list is cited.

155

Notes

1. Former librarian and public administrator Will Manley notes that, in contrast to face-to-face audiences or print media audiences, his blogging audience is "solid and real" because of the sheer volume of daily traffic on his blog.

2. The editors of the *New Atlantis* point out in "Blogs Gone Bad" that because online content has an immediate and widespread impact, bloggers and other Web writers need to be especially careful in what they post online (106).

3. Jon Meacham argues that media outlets need to shift their attention to digital over print content and delivery in order to thrive.

Works Cited

"Blog." *Encyclopaedia Britannica Online*.
Encyclopaedia Britannica, 2010. Web. 25
Apr. 2011.

"Blogs Gone Bad." Editorial. *New Atlantis* 8
(2005): 106-09. Print.

Cass, Stephen. "Mainstream News Taps into
Citizen Journalism." *Technology Review*
Jan.-Feb. 2010: 62-63. Print.

Gillmor, Dan. Interview by Eric Olsen. *State of
the Blogosphere 2009*. Technorati, 2009.
Web. 21 Apr. 2011.

Goldhammer, Gary. *The Last Newspaper:
Reflections on the Future of News*. N.p.:
Lulu, 2009. Print.

Ingram, Mathew. Interview by Eric Berlin. *State
of the Blogosphere 2009*. Technorati, 2009.
Web. 21 Apr. 2011.

Lacy, Stephen, et al. "Citizen Journalism
Web Sites Complement Newspapers."
Newspaper Research Journal 31.2 (2010):
34-46. *Academic Search Elite*. Web. 21 Apr.
2011.

Manley, Will. "My Favorite Medium." *American
Libraries* Apr. 2010: 64. *Academic Search
Elite*. Web. 21 Apr. 2011.

Meacham, Jon. Interview by Jon Stewart.
The Daily Show with Jon Stewart. Comedy
Central. 5 May 2010. Television.

Title centered; entries in alphabetical order.

Source: online encyclopedia.

Source: journal editorial.

Source: magazine article.

Source: online interview.

Source: whole book (no place of publication).

Source: online interview.

Source: journal article by more than three authors in online database.

Source: one-page magazine article in online database.

Source: broadcast interview.

157

Perlmutter, David D., and Misti McDaniel.

    "The Ascent of Blogging." *Nieman Reports*

    Fall 2005: 60-64. Print.

Pew Research Center. Project for Excellence in

    Journalism. *The State of the News Media*

    2010: An Annual Report on American

    Journalism. Journalism.org. Project for

    Excellence in Journalism, 2010. Web. 22

    Apr. 2011.

Rosen, Jay. "The New News." *Technology Review*

    Jan.-Feb. 2010: 15. Print.

Shirky, Clay. *Here Comes Everybody: The Power*

    of Organizing without Organizations. New

    York: Penguin, 2008. Print.

---. "Newspapers and Thinking the

    Unthinkable." *Risk Management* May

    2009: 24-29. *Academic Search Elite.* Web.

    21 Apr. 2011.

Source:
magazine
article by
two authors.

Source:
online report
by corpo-
rate author.

Source:
one-page
magazine
article.

Source:
entire book.

Source:
magazine
article in
online data-
base. Three
hyphens are
used instead
of repeat-
ing author's
name

Take the whole range of imaginative literature, and we are all wholesale borrowers. In every matter that relates to invention, to use, or beauty or form, we are borrowers.

—WENDELL PHILLIPS

PART 4

APA Documentation Style

The charts on pages 160–62 can help you locate the right example of a reference-list entry for a particular kind of source. Answering the questions provided will usually lead you to the sample entry you need. You can also use the directory on pages 174–76 in Chapter 20.

Entries in a List of References:
BOOKS (172–73, 177)

❓ *Is your source a complete book or part of a book?*

No Yes
↓   ↓

	Go to this entry on page	
Is it a complete book with one named author?		
Is it the only book by this author that you are citing?	**1**	170
Are you citing more than one book by this author?	**4**	172
Is it a complete book with more than one named author?	**2**	170
Is it a complete book without a named author or editor?		
Is the author an organization?	**3**	172
Is the author unknown?	**9**	173
Is it a complete book with an editor or a translator?		
Is there an editor instead of an author?	**5**	172
Is it a translation?	**7**	173
Is it a complete book with an edition or a volume number?		
Does it have an edition number (for example, Second Edition)?	**10**	177
Is it part of a multivolume work (such as Volume 3)?	**11**	177
Is your source a work from an anthology or a chapter in an edited book?	**6**	172
Is it an article in a reference work (such as an encyclopedia)?	**8**	173
Is it a published presentation from a conference?	**23**	181

Check the next page or the directory on pages 174–75, or consult your instructor.

Entries in a List of References:
PRINT PERIODICALS OR OTHER PRINT SOURCES (177–82)

❓ *Is your source from a journal, a magazine, or a newspaper?*

No Yes
  ↓

	Go to this entry on page	
Is it from an academic journal?	**12**	177
Does it have three to seven authors, or more than seven?	**13**	177
Is it an abstract (a brief summary) of a journal article?	**14**	178
Is it a review (for example, a review of a book)?	**19**	180
Is it a published presentation from a conference?	**23**	181
Is it from a monthly or weekly magazine?		
Is it an article?	**16**	179
Is it an editorial or a letter to the editor?	**18**	180
Is it a review (such as a review of a book)?	**19**	180
Is it an interview?	**20**	180
Is it from a newspaper?		
Is it an article?	**17**	180
Is it an editorial or a letter to the editor?	**18**	180
Is it a review (such as a review of a book)?	**19**	180
Is it an interview?	**20**	180
Is the author unknown?	**9**	173
Are you citing two or more articles published in the same year by the same author?	**15**	178

APA

❓ *Is it a print source but not a book or a periodical article?*

No Yes
  ↓

	Go to this entry (or these entries) on page(s)	
Is it published by the government or a nongovernment organization?		
Is it a government document?	**21, 43**	181, 188
Is it a report, a working paper, or a conference presentation?	**22, 23**	181
Is it an unpublished work?		
Is it an unpublished conference presentation?	**23**	181
Is it an unpublished dissertation or a dissertation abstract?	**24**	182

Check the next page or the directory on pages 174–75, or consult your instructor.

Entries in a List of References:
ELECTRONIC OR OTHER NONPRINT SOURCES (182–93)

❓ *Did you find your nonprint source online?*

No Yes
↓

Go to this entry (or these entries) on page

Is it an article or abstract?		
Is it an article with a Digital Object Identifier (DOI)?	**31**	183
Is it an article without a DOI?	**32**	184
Is it an abstract (a brief summary of an article) from a collection of abstracts?	**33**	184
Is it an article from a database?	**34**	184
Is it a newspaper or magazine article from a database?	**35**	185
Is it from an online newspaper or magazine?	**36, 37**	186
Is it online exclusive material from a magazine with a print edition?	**38**	187
Is it a review from an online publication or database?	**39**	187
Is it a document or report on a Web site?	**40**	188
Is it from an online reference work?	**46**	189
Is it an electronic book?		
Is it an electronic version of a print book?	**41**	188
Is it an electronic book with no print edition?	**42**	188
Is it a government publication?		
Is it from the *Congressional Record*?	**44**	189
Is it another government document available online?	**43**	188
Is it an online policy brief or white paper?	**45**	189
Is it a posting to an online forum?	**49**	191
Is it a personal e-mail or instant message?	**50**	192
Is it an entry from a blog?	**48**	191
Is it part of a wiki?	**47**	190
Is it an MP3 or audio podcast?	**51, 52**	192
Is it a video podcast?	**53**	192
Is it an online video?	**54**	194

❓ *Is your source a nonprint source that is **not** published online?*

No Yes
↓

Go to this entry (or these entries) on page

Is it a film, DVD, or Blu-ray?	**25**	182
Is it a CD or an audio recording?	**26**	182
Is it a musical composition?	**29**	183
Is it a television series or an episode?	**27, 28**	182
Is it computer software?	**55**	194
Is it a personal interview?	**30**	182

Check the directory on pages 174–75, or consult your instructor.

Instructors of courses in psychology, sociology, political science, communications, education, and business usually prefer a documentation style that emphasizes the author and the year of publication.

The information in Chapters 19 through 22 is based on the sixth edition of the American Psychological Association's *Publication Manual* (Washington: APA, 2010). For updates, check the APA-sponsored Web site at <www.apastyle.org>.

APA documentation style has two mandatory parts:

- In-text citations
- List of references

19 APA style: In-text citations

In-text citations let readers know that they can find full information about the source of an idea you have paraphrased or summarized, or the source of a quotation, in the list of references at the end of your project.

1. Author named in sentence   Follow the author's name with the year of publication (in parentheses).

signal phrase
In her book, *Generation Me,* Jean M. Twenge (2006) explains that Americans of current college age are preoccupied with amassing wealth and achieving material goals but claims these aims and giving back to others aren't mutually exclusive.

2. Author named in parentheses   If you do not name the source's author in your sentence, then you must include the name in the parentheses, followed by the date and, if you are giving a quotation or a specific piece of information, the page number. Separate the name, date, and page number with commas.

> This trend, which counters the stereotype of the self-centered college student, is expected to continue (Jaschik, 2006).

APA

3. Books with two or more authors If a source has five or fewer authors, name all of them the first time you cite the source.

> Policy professors Bruce L. R. Smith and A. Lee Fritschler (2009) argue that service learning requires context: volunteering itself does not guarantee students learn the lessons intended about citizenship or social policies.

If you put the names of the authors in parentheses, use an ampersand *(&)* instead of *and*.

> Similarly, a study conducted for the Higher Education Research Institute found that "students develop a heightened sense of civic responsibility and personal effectiveness through participation in service-learning courses" because they connect the academic discussions of the classroom to the practical application of providing service in the community (Astin, Vogelgesang, Ikeda, & Yee, 2000, p. 2).

ampersand used within parentheses

After the first time you cite a work by three or more authors, use the first author's name plus *et al.* (as an abbreviation, the *al.* has a period following it): (Astin et al., 2000). Always use both names when citing a work by two authors.

For in-text citations of a work by six or more authors, always give the first author's name plus *et al.*: As Barbre et al. have argued . . . In the reference

APA IN-TEXT CITATIONS: DIRECTORY to SAMPLE TYPES

(See pp. 170–93 for examples of references entries.)

APA

list, however, list up to seven author names. For more than seven, list the first six authors' names, followed by an ellipsis mark (three spaced periods) and the last author's name.

4. Organization as author   Treat the organization as the author, and spell out its name the first time the source is cited. If the organization is well known, you may use an abbreviation thereafter.

> According to the Pew Research Center for the
>
> People and the Press (2007), the roles food bank
>
> workers, role models for children in single-parent

households, and youth drug counselors—to name a few—occupy today provide critical support, yet they were not as necessary to society years ago.

Public service announcements were used to inform parents of these findings (National Institute of Mental Health [NIMH], 1991).

APA In subsequent citations, only the abbreviation and the date need to be given: (NIMH, 1991).

APA IN-TEXT CITATIONS

- Identify the author(s) of the source, either in the sentence or in a parenthetical citation.
- Indicate the year of publication of the source following the author's name, either in parentheses if the author's name is part of the sentence or, if the author is not named in the sentence, after the author's name and a comma in the parenthetical citation.
- Include a page reference for a quotation or specific piece of information. Put "p." before the page number. If the author is named in the text, the page number appears in the parenthetical citation following the borrowed material. Page numbers are not necessary when you are summarizing the source as a whole or paraphrasing an idea found throughout a work. *(For more on summary, paraphrase, and quotation, see Chapter 12: Working with Sources and Avoiding Plagiarism, pp. 84–90.)*
- If the source does not have page numbers (as with many online sources), do your best to direct readers. If the source has no page or paragraph numbering or easily identifiable headings, just use the name and date. *(See no. 12 and note on p. 169.)*

5. Unknown author   Give the first one or two important words of the title. Use quotation marks for titles of articles, chapters, or Web pages and italics for titles of books, periodicals, or reports.

> The transformation of women's lives has been
> hailed as "the single most important change of the
> past 1,000 years" ("Reflections," 1999, p. 77).

APA

6. Two or more authors with the same last name   If the authors of two or more sources have the same last name, always include their first initial, even if the year of publication differs.

> M. Smith (1988) showed how globalization has
> restructured both cities and states.

7. Two or more works by the same author in the same year   Alphabetize the works by their titles in your reference list, and assign a letter in alphabetical order (for example, *2006a, 2006b*). Use that same year-letter designation in your in-text citation.

> J. P. Agarwal (1996b) described the relationship
> between trade and foreign direct investment (FDI).

8. Two or more sources cited at one time   Cite the authors in the order in which they appear in the list of references, separated by a semicolon.

> They contribute to the continual efforts to improve
> society without expecting that significant change
> will occur; they expect to make a difference in
> society locally, one citizen at a time, and they hope
> to gain personally while doing so (Astin & Sax,
> 1998; Friedman, 2007).

APA

9. E-mails, letters, and conversations To cite information received from unpublished forms of personal communication—such as conversations, letters, notes, and e-mail messages—give the source's first initial or initials and last name, and provide as precise a date as possible. Because readers do not have access to them, do not include personal communications in your reference list.

> According to scholar T. Williams (personal communication, June 10, 2010), many students volunteer because they believe in giving back to the community they grew up in.

10. Specific part of a source Include the chapter *(Chapter)*, page *(p.)*, figure, or table number.

> Despite the new law, the state saw no drop in car fatalities involving drivers ages 16–21 (Johnson, 2006, Chapter 4).

11. Indirect (secondary) source When referring to a source that you know only from reading another source, use the phrase *as cited in,* followed by the author of the source you actually read and its year of publication.

> Peter Levine, director of the Center for Information and Research on Civic Learning and Engagement at the University of Maryland, credits students with utilizing the Internet to effect change, "relying less on street protests and more on lobbying and volunteering" (as cited in Koch, 2008, p. 3a).

The work by Koch would be included in the references list, but the work by Peter Levine would not.

12. Electronic source Cite the author's last name or the name of the site's sponsor (if an author's name is not available) and the publication date. If the document is a PDF (portable document format) file with stable page numbers, cite the page number. If the source has paragraph numbers instead of page numbers, use *para.* instead of *p.*

> CNCS (2010) defines *service learning* as a practice
> that "engages students in the educational process,
> using what they learn in the classroom to solve
> real-life problems."

> **Note:** If the specific part lacks page or paragraph numbering, cite the heading and the number of the paragraph under that heading where the information can be found. If the heading is long, use a short version in quotation marks. If you cannot determine the date, use the abbreviation *n.d.* in its place: (CNCS, n.d.).

13. Two or more sources in one sentence   Include a parenthetical reference after each fact, idea, or quotation you have borrowed.

> As *New York Times* columnist Thomas L. Friedman
> (2007) has observed, while this generation might
> be less politically motivated than generations past,
> it does work quietly toward its own idealistic goals,
> which according to Bringle and Hatcher (1996)
> aligns with the motivation that students volunteer
> so that they can be a part of a community.

14. Sacred or classical text   Cite these within your text only, and include the version you consulted as well as any standard book, part, or section numbers.

> The famous song sets forth a series of opposites,
> culminating in "a time to love, and a time to hate; a
> time of war, and a time of peace" (Eccles. 3:8, King
> James Bible).

APA documentation style requires a list of references where readers can find complete bibliographical information about the sources referred to in your project. The list should appear at the end of your research project, beginning on a new page titled "References."

To format entries in a list of references correctly, it is important to know what kind of source you are citing. The directory that follows will help you find the appropriate sample to use as your model. As an alternative, you can use the charts on pages 160–62 to help you locate the right example. If you cannot find what you are looking for after consulting the appropriate directory or chart, ask your instructor for help.

To help locate the information you need in an actual source, consult the facsimiles on pages 171, 179, 186, and 190.

Books

1. Book with one author

> Twenge, J. M. (2006). *Generation me: Why today's young Americans are more confident, assertive, entitled—and more miserable—than ever before.* New York, NY: Free Press.

2. Book with two or more authors   Precede the final name with an ampersand *(&)*.

> Astin, A. W., Vogelgesang, L. J., Ikeda, E. K., & Yee, J. A. (2000). *How service learning affects students.* Los Angeles, CA: Higher Education Research Institute.

For more than seven authors, list the first six, three ellipses, and the final author *(see no. 13).*

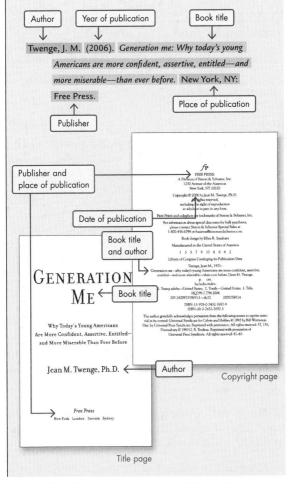

FIGURE 20.1 The Elements of an APA Reference-List Entry: Books. Information for a book citation can be found on the book's title and copyright pages.

3. Organization as author   When the publisher is the author, use *Author* instead of repeating the organization's name as the publisher.

> Corporation for National and Community Service.
>
> > (2010). *What is service learning?* Washington,
> >
> > DC: Author.

4. Two or more works by the same author List the works in publication order, with the earliest one first. If a university publisher's name includes the state (note the second example), do not repeat it.

> Eller, C. (2003). *Am I a woman? A skeptic's guide to*
>
> > *gender.* Boston, MA: Beacon Press.
>
> Eller, C. (2011). *Gentlemen and amazons: The myth*
>
> > *of matriarchal prehistory, 1861–1900.* Berkeley:
> >
> > University of California Press.

If the works were published in the same year, put them in alphabetical order by title and add a letter *(a, b, c)* to the year to distinguish each entry in your in-text citations.

5. Book with editor(s)   Add *(Ed.)* or *(Eds.)* after the name. If a book lists an author and an editor, treat the editor like a translator *(see no. 7)*.

> Ferrari, J., & Chapman, J. G. (Eds.). (1999).
>
> > *Educating students to make a difference:*
> >
> > *Community-based service learning.* New York, NY:
> >
> > Haworth Press.

6. Selection in an edited book or anthology The selection's author, year of publication, and title come first, followed by the word *In* and information about the edited book. The page numbers of the selection go in parentheses after the book's title.

> Primavera, J. (1999). The unintended consequences
> of volunteerism: positive outcomes for those
> who serve. In Ferrari, J., & Chapman, J. G.
> (Eds.), *Educating students to make a difference:*
> *community-based service learning* (pp. 125–140).
> New York, NY: Haworth Press.

7. Translation After the title of the translation, put the name(s) of the translator(s) in parentheses, followed by the abbreviation *Trans.*

> Jarausch, K. H., & Gransow, V. (1994). *Uniting*
> *Germany: Documents and debates, 1944–1993*
> (A. Brown & B. Cooper, Trans.). Providence,
> RI: Berg.

8. Article in an encyclopedia or other reference work Begin with the author of the selection, if given. If no author is given, begin with the selection's title.

title of the selection
> Arawak. (2000). In *The Columbia encyclopedia*
> (6th ed., p. 2533). New York, NY: Columbia
> University Press.

9. Unknown author or editor Start with the title. When alphabetizing, use the first important word of the title (excluding articles such as *The, A,* or *An*).

> *Give me liberty.* (1969). New York, NY: World.

APA Reference Entries: Directory to Sample Types

(See pp. 163–69 for examples of in-text citations.)

APA

APA

APA LIST of REFERENCES

- Begin on a new page with the centered title "References."
- Include a reference for every in-text citation except personal communications and sacred or classical texts *(see in-text citations no. 9 on p. 167 and no. 14 on p. 169).*
- Put references in alphabetical order by author's last name.
- Give the last name and first or both initials for each author. If the work has more than one author, see no. 2 *(pp. 163–64)* or no. 13 *(p. 169).*
- Put the publication year in parentheses following the author or authors' names.
- Capitalize only the first word and proper nouns in titles. Also capitalize the first word following the colon in a subtitle.
- Use italics for titles of books but not articles. Do not enclose titles of articles in quotation marks.
- Include the city and publisher for books. Give the state or country. If a university publisher's name includes the state, do not repeat it.
- Include the periodical name and volume number (both in italics) as well as the page numbers for a periodical article.
- End with the DOI, if any *(see nos. 12 and 31 and the box on p. 185).*
- Separate the author's or authors' name(s), date (in parentheses), title, and publication information with periods.
- Use a hanging indent: Begin the first line of each entry at the left margin, and indent all subsequent lines of an entry (five spaces).
- Double-space within and between entries.

10. Edition other than the first

Smyser, W. R. (1993). *The German economy: Colossus at crossroads* (2nd ed.). New York, NY: St. Martin's Press.

11. One volume of a multivolume work   If the volume has its own title, put it before the title of the whole work.

Google. (2003). The ultimate online learning resource. In *E.enyclopedia* (Vol. 1). New York, NY: D. K. Publishing.

Periodicals

12. Article in a journal (paginated by volume or issue)   Provide the issue number—*not* italicized—in parentheses after the italicized volume number, with no space between them. A DOI ends the entry if available *(also see no. 31)*.

Inzlicht, M., & Kang, S. K. (2010). Stereotype threat spillover: How coping with threats to social identity affects aggression, eating, decision making, and attention. *Journal of Personality and Social Psychology, 99*(3), 467–481. doi:10.1037/a0018951

13. Article with three to seven authors or with more than seven authors   If a work has up to seven authors, list them all (see first example); if it has more than seven authors, list the first six followed by a comma, three ellipses, and the final author's name (see the second example).

Hilgers, T., Hussey, E., & Stitt-Bergh, M. (1999). As you're writing, you have these epiphanies. *Written Communication, 16*(3), 317–353.

Plummer, C. A., Ai, A. L., Lemieux, C., Richardson, R., Dey, S., Taylor, P., . . . Hyun-Jun, K. (2008). Volunteerism among social work students during Hurricanes Katrina and Rita. *Journal of Social Service Research, 34*(3), 55–71. doi:10.1080/01488370802086328

APA

14. Abstract For an abstract that appears in the original source, add the word *Abstract* in brackets after the title. If the abstract appears in a printed source that is different from the original publication, first give the original publication information for the article, followed by the publication information for the source of the abstract. If the dates of the publications differ, cite them both, with a slash between them, in the in-text citation: Murphy (2003/2004).

Burnby, J. G. L. (1985, June). Pharmaceutical connections: The Maw's family [Abstract]. *Pharmaceutical Historian, 15*(2), 9–11.

Murphy, M. (2003). Getting carbon out of thin air. *Chemistry & Industry, 6,* 14–16. Abstract retrieved from *Fuel and Energy Abstracts, 45*(6), 389.

15. Two or more works in one year by the same author Alphabetize by title, and attach a letter to each entry's year of publication, beginning with *a*. In-text citations must use the letter as well as the year.

Agarwal, J. P. (1996a). *Does foreign direct investment contribute to unemployment in home countries? An empirical survey* (Discussion Paper No. 765). Kiel, Germany: Institute of World Economics.

Agarwal, J. P. (1996b). Impact of Europe agreements on FDI in developing countries. *International Journal of Social Economics, 23*(10/11), 150–163.

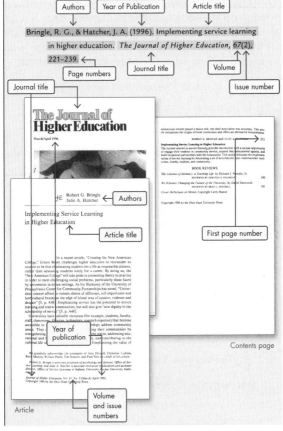

FIGURE 20.2 The Elements of an APA Reference-List Entry: Journal Articles. In this journal, the information needed for a citation appears on the first page of an article. Some journals list their contents and publication information on the cover.

16. Article in a magazine After the year, add the month for magazines published monthly or the month and day for magazines published weekly. Note that the volume and issue numbers are also included.

> Gross, P. (2001, February). Exorcising sociobiology.
>
> *New Criterion, 19*(6), 24.

17. Article in a newspaper   Use *p.* or *pp.* (not italicized) with the section and page number. List all page numbers, separated by commas, if the article appears on discontinuous pages: pp. C1, C4, C6. If there is no identified author, begin with the title of the article.

> Smith, T. (2003, October 8). Grass is green for
>
> Amazon farmers. *The New York Times,* p. W1.

18. Editorial or letter to the editor   Note the use of brackets to identify the genre.

> Krugman, P. (2011, January 28). Their own private
>
> Europe [Editorial]. *The New York Times,* p. A31.

19. Review   If the review is untitled, use the bracketed description in place of a title.

> Dargis, M. (2011, March 4). Creepy people with a
>
> plan, and a couple on the run [Review of the
>
> motion picture *The adjustment bureau,* 2011].
>
> *The New York Times,* pp. C1, C10.

> MacFarquhar, Roderick (2011, February 10). The
>
> worst man-made catastrophe, ever [Review
>
> of the book *Mao's great famine: The history*
>
> *of China's most devastating catastrophe* by F.
>
> Dikotter]. *The New York Review of Books, 58*(2),
>
> 26–28.

20. Interview   Cite an interview as you would an article in a journal, newspaper, or magazine. List the interviewer as author.

> Solomon, D. (2010, November 18). Minority
>
> Report. *The New York Times Magazine,* 18.

Other Print and Audiovisual Sources

21. Government document When no author is listed, use the government agency as the author.

> U.S. Bureau of the Census. (1976). *Historical statistics of the United States: Colonial times to 1970*. Washington, DC: Government Printing Office.

For an enacted resolution or piece of legislation, see no. 43.

22. Report or working paper If the issuing agency numbered the report, include that number in parentheses after the title.

> Agarwal, J. P. (1996a). *Does foreign direct investment contribute to unemployment in home countries? An empirical survey* (Discussion Paper No. 765). Kiel, Germany: Institute of World Economics.

23. Conference presentation Treat published conference presentations as a selection in a book *(no. 6),* as a periodical article *(nos. 16 and 17),* or as a report *(no. 22),* whichever applies. For unpublished conference presentations, provide the author, the year and month of the conference, the italicized title of the presentation, and the presentation's form, forum, and place.

> Desantis, R. (1998, June). *Optimal export taxes, welfare, industry concentration and firm size: A general equilibrium analysis*. Poster session presented at the First Annual Conference in Global Economic Analysis, West Lafayette, IN.

Markusen, J. (1998, June). *The role of multinationals in global economic analysis.* Paper presented at the First Annual Conference in Global Economic Analysis, West Lafayette, IN.

APA

24. Dissertation or dissertation abstract Use this format for an unpublished dissertation.

Luster, L. (1992). *Schooling, survival and struggle: Black women and the GED* (Unpublished doctoral dissertation). Stanford University, Palo Alto, CA.

If you use an abstract from *Dissertation Abstracts International,* treat the entry like a periodical article.

Weinbaum, A. E. (1998). Genealogies of "race" and reproduction in transatlantic modern thought. *Dissertation Abstracts International, 58,* 229.

25. Film, DVD, or Blu-ray Begin with the cited person's name and, if appropriate, a parenthetical notation of his or her role. After the title, identify the medium, followed by the country and name of the distributor. *(For online video, see no. 54.)*

Rowling, J. K., Kloves, S. (Writers), Yates, D. (Director), & Barron, D. (Producer). (2009). *Harry Potter and the half-blood prince* [Motion picture]. United States: Warner Brothers Pictures.

26. CD or audio recording See no. 51 for an MP3 or no. 52 for an audio podcast.

title of piece
Corigliano, J. (2007). Red violin concerto
title of album
    [Recorded by J. Bell]. On *Red violin concerto*

    [CD]. New York, NY: Sony Classics.

27. TV series   For an entire TV series or specific news broadcast, treat the producer as author.

    Simon, D., & Noble, N. K. (Producers). (2002). *The*

        wire [Television series]. New York, NY: HBO.

28. Episode from a TV series   Treat the writer as the author and the producer as the editor of the series. See no. 53 for a podcast TV series episode.

    Burns, E., Simon, D. (Writers), & Johnson, C.

        (Director). (2002). The target [Television

        series episode]. In D. Simon & N. K. Noble

        (Producers), *The wire*. New York, NY: HBO.

29. Musical composition

    Rachmaninoff, S. (1900). *Piano concerto no. 2, opus*

        18 [Musical composition].

30. Personal interview   Like other unpublished personal communications, personal interviews are not included in the reference list. See in-text citation entry no. 9 *(p. 168)*.

Electronic Sources

31. Online journal article with a Digital Object Identifier (DOI)   If your source has a DOI, include it at the end of the entry; URL and access date are not needed.

Ray, R., Wilhelm, F., & Gross, J. (2008). All in the
mind's eye? Anger rumination and reappraisal.
Journal of Personality and Social Psychology, 94,
133–145. doi:10.1037/0022-3514.94.1.133

32. Online journal article without a DOI Include the URL of the journal's home page.

Chan, L. (2004). Supporting and enhancing
scholarship in the digital age: The role of open
access institutional repository. *Canadian Journal
of Communication, 29,* 277–300. Retrieved from
http://www.cjc-online.ca

33. Abstract from an online journal article
Treat much like a journal article, but include the word *Abstract* before retrieval information.

Plummer, C. A., Ai, A. L., Lemieux, C., Richardson,
R., Dey, S., Taylor, P., . . . Hyun-Jun, K. (2008).
Volunteerism among social work students
during Hurricanes Katrina and Rita. *Journal of
Social Service Research, 34*(3), 55–71. Abstract
retrieved from Refdoc.fr

34. Journal article from an online, subscription, or library database Include database information only if the article is rare or found in just a few databases. *(Otherwise, see nos. 31 and 32.)* Give the URL of the database's home page.

Gore, W. C. (1916). Memory, concept, judgment,
logic (theory). *Psychological Bulletin, 13,* 355–
358. Retrieved from PsycARTICLES database:
http://psycnet.apa.org

APA ELECTRONIC REFERENCES

- Many print and online books and articles have a Digital Object Identifier (DOI), a unique alphanumeric string. Citations of online documents with DOIs do not require the URL.
- Include a retrieval date only for items that probably will change (such as a wiki).
- Do not include information about a database or library subscription service in the citation unless the work is difficult to find elsewhere (for example, archival material).
- Include the URL of the home page for journal, magazine, and newspaper articles lacking a DOI.
- Include the full URL for all other items lacking a DOI.
- For nonperiodicals, name the site sponsor in the retrieval statement unless the author is the sponsor *(see no. 37)*. This format derives from the APA model for an online report.

author
Butler, R. A. (2008, July 31). *Future threats to*

the Amazon rain forest. Retrieved from
Web site sponsor
Mongabay.com website: http://news

.mongabay.com/2009/0601-brazil

_politics.html

author as Web site sponsor
Sisters in Islam. (2007). *Mission.* Retrieved

from http://sistersinislam.org.my/mission

.htm

35. Newspaper or magazine article from a database Include database information for archival material not easily found elsewhere. Give the URL of the database's home page. *(Otherwise, see no. 36 for an online newspaper article or no. 37 for an online magazine article.)*

APA

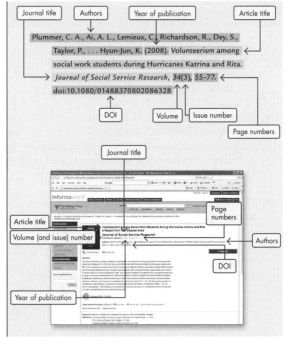

FIGURE 20.3 The Elements of an APA Reference-List Entry: Journal Article with DOI Assigned
This article lists the DOI beneath the journal and citation information. For journals paginated by issue, include the issue number in parentheses after the volume number. For an article with more than seven authors, list the first six, followed by an ellipsis mark (three spaced periods) and the last author's name.

Culnan, J. (1927, November 20). Madison to celebrate arrival of first air mail plane. *Wisconsin State Journal,* p. A1. Retrieved from Wisconsin Historical Society database: http://www.wisconsinhistory.org/WLHBA

36. Article in an online newspaper

Rohter, L. (2004, December 12). South America
seeks to fill the world's table. *The New York
Times.* Retrieved from http://www.nytimes.com

37. Article in an online magazine   Include the volume and issue numbers after the magazine title.

Biello, D. (2007, December 5). Thunder, hail, fire:
What does climate change mean for the U.S.?
Scientific American, 297(6). Retrieved from
http://www.sciam.com

38. Online exclusive magazine content   *Online exclusive* in brackets indicates that the material is distributed only in online venues.

Perry, A. (2004, January 26). The future lies in
democracy [Online exclusive]. *Time.* Retrieved
from http://www.time.com

39. Review from an online publication

Goodsell, C. T. (1993, January/February). Reinvent
government or rediscover it? [Review of
the book *Reinventing government: How the
entrepreneurial spirit is transforming the public
sector,* by T. Gaebler & D. Osborne]. *Public
Administration Review, 53*(1), 85–87. Retrieved
from JSTOR database.

40. Document or report on a Web site Include the Web site sponsor in the retrieval statement unless the author of the work is also the sponsor. Here, the author is the World Health Organization, and the sponsor is BPD Sanctuary.

> World Health Organization. (1992). *ICD-10 criteria
>   for borderline personality disorder.* Retrieved
>   from BPD Sanctuary website: http://www
>   .mhsanctuary.com/borderline/icd10.htm

41. Electronic version of a print book Provide a DOI, if it is available, instead of the URL.

> Mill, J. S. (1869). *On liberty* (4th ed.). Retrieved from
>   http://books.google.com/books

> Schiraldi, G. R. (2001). *The post-traumatic stress
>   disorder sourcebook: A guide to healing, recovery
>   and growth* [Adobe Digital Editions version].
>   doi:10.1036/0071393722

42. Electronic book, no print edition

> Stevens, K. (n.d.). *The dreamer and the beast.*
>   Retrieved from http://www.onlineoriginals
>   .com/showitem.asp?itemID=321

43. Online government document other than the *Congressional Record*

> National Commission on Terrorist Attacks upon
>   the United States. (2004). *The 9/11 Commission
>   report.* Retrieved from Government Printing

Office website: http://www.gpoaccess
.gov/911/index.html

44. *Congressional Record* (online or in print)
For enacted resolutions or legislation, give the number of the Congress after the number of the resolution or legislation, the *Congressional Record* volume number, the page number(s), and year, followed by *(enacted)*.

H. Res. 2408, 108th Cong., 150 Cong. Rec. 1331–
1332 (2004) (enacted).

Give the full name of the resolution or legislation when citing it within your sentence, but abbreviate the name when it appears in a parenthetical in-text citation: *(H. Res. 2408, 2004)*.

45. Online policy brief or white paper
Cramer, K., Shelton, L., Dietz, N., Dote, L.,
Fletcher, C., Jennings, S., . . . Silsby, J. (2010).
*Volunteering in America 2010: National, state, and
city information.* Retrieved from Corporation
for National and Community Service website:
http://www.volunteeringinamerica.gov/assets
/resources/IssueBriefFINALJune15.pdf

46. Article in an online reference work
Begin with the author's name, if given, followed by the publication date. If no author is given, place the title before the date. Include the full URL.

Attribution theory. (2009). In *Encarta.*
Retrieved from http://encarta.msn.com
/encyclopedia_761586848/Attribution
_Theory.html

APA

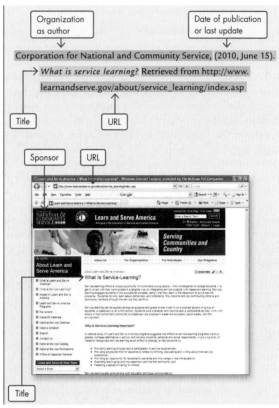

FIGURE 20.4 The Elements of an APA Reference-List Entry: Short Work on a Web Site. List an individual author's last name first. Supplemental information about format may follow the title. Here, the author is also the Web site sponsor. When the author is not the sponsor, name the sponsor after "Retrieved from" *(see no. 40 on p. 188).* You may need to search on a site to find author, date, and other information. Include the home page URL for magazine, newspaper, and journal articles (lacking a DOI). Give the full URL for other sources.

47. Wiki article Wikis are collaboratively written Web sites. Most are updated regularly, so include the access date in your citation. Check with your instructor before using a wiki article as a source.

Demographic transition. (2007, October 8).

> Retrieved from Citizendium website:
>
> http://en.citizendium.org/wiki
>
> /Demographic_transition

48. Blog posting This model is for a blog post. For an example of a video blog post, see the second example; use the description "video file." For a comment, use the same format but substitute "Web log comment" for "Web log post."

APA

Eggers, A. (2009, May 20). Debates on government

> transparency websites [Web log post].
>
> Retrieved from Social Science Statistics Blog
>
> website: http://www.iq.harvard.edu/blog/sss

Underwood, Elizabeth. (2010, May 17). Audubon

> oil spill response volunteer. [Video file].
>
> Retrieved from BirdLife International website:
>
> http://www.birdlife.org/community/2010/05
>
> /audubon-oil-spill-response-volunteer-liz-video/

49. Post to an electronic mailing list, newsgroup, or discussion forum Provide the message's author, its date, and its subject line as the title. For a post to a mailing list, provide the description *Electronic mailing list message* in brackets. For a post to a newsgroup or discussion forum, give the identifying information *Online forum comment* in brackets. Conclude either entry with the words *Retrieved from,* followed by the URL of the archived message.

Glick, D. (2007, February 10). Bio-char

> sequestration in terrestrial ecosystems—
>
> A review [Electronic mailing list message].
>
> Retrieved from http://bioenergylists.org
>
> /newsgroup-archive/terrapreta_bioenergylists
>
> .org/2007-February/000023.html

APA

Jones, D. (2001, February 3). California solar power

[Online forum comment]. Retrieved from

http://yarchive.net/space/politics/california

_power.html

50. E-mail or instant message (IM) E-mail, instant messages, or other nonarchived personal communication should be cited in the body of your text but not given in the references list *(see in-text citation entry no. 9, on p. 168).*

51. MP3 or other digital audio file Use brackets to identify the file type.

Hansard, G., & Irglova, M. (2006). Falling slowly.

On *The swell season* [MP3]. Chicago, IL:

Overcoat Recordings.

52. Audio podcast

Glass, I. (Host). (2008, June 30). Social engineering.

This American life [Audio podcast]. Retrieved

from http://www.thisamericanlife.org

53. Video podcast

Reitman, J. (Director), & Novak, B. J. (Writer).

(2007). Local ad [Television series episode].

In S. Carrell, M. Kaling, L. Eisenberg, & G.

Stupnitsky (Producers), *The office* [Video

podcast]. Retrieved from http://www.nbc

.com/the_office/video/episodes.shtml

54. Online video

Wesch, M. (2007, March 8). The machine is

us/ing us [Video file]. Retrieved from http://

mediatedcultures.net/ksudigg/?p=84

55. Computer software or video game Cite only specialized software. Familiar software such as Microsoft Word doesn't need to be cited.

L.A. noire. (2011). [Video game]. New York:

Rockstar Games.

21   APA style: Format

The following guidelines are recommended by the *Publication Manual of the American Psychological Association,* sixth edition. For sample pages from a research paper that has been prepared using APA style, see pages 196–99.

Materials   Back up your final draft. Use a high-quality printer and high-quality white 8½-by-11-inch paper. Do not justify your text or hyphenate words at the right margin; it should be ragged right.

Title page   The first page of your research report should be a title page. Center the title between the left and right margins in the upper half of the page, and put your name and your school's name a few lines below the title. *(See p. 196 for an example.)*

Margins and spacing Use one-inch margins all around, except for the upper right-hand corner, where the page number goes, and the upper left-hand corner, where the running head goes.

Double-space lines throughout, including in the abstract, within any notes or captions, and in the list of references. Indent the first word of each paragraph one-half inch (or five spaces).

For quotations of more than forty words, use block format, and indent five spaces from the left margin. Double-space the quoted lines.

Page numbers and abbreviated titles All pages, including the title page, should have a short version of your title in uppercase letters. On the title page, preface this with the words "Running head" and a colon. Put this information in the upper left-hand corner of each page, about one-half inch from the top. Put the page number in the upper right-hand corner.

Abstract Instructors sometimes require an abstract—a summary of your paper's thesis, major points or lines of development, and conclusions. The abstract appears on its own numbered page, entitled "Abstract," right after the title page. It should not exceed 150 to 250 words.

Headings Primary headings should be boldfaced and centered. All key words in the heading should be capitalized.

Secondary headings should be boldfaced and appear flush against the left-hand margin. Do not use a heading for your introduction, however. *(For more on headings, see Chapter 6: Designing Academic Texts, pp. 36–37.)*

Visuals   Place each visual (table, chart, graph, or image) on its own page following the reference list and any content notes. Tables precede figures. Label each visual as a table or a figure, and number each kind consecutively (Table 1, Table 2). Provide an informative caption for each visual. Cite the source of the material, and provide explanatory notes as needed. *(For more on using visuals effectively, see Chapter 6: Designing Academic Texts, pp. 38–41.)*

APA

22 Pages from a research project in APA style

Tina Schwab researched the topic of student volunteerism and wrote a report about it for her introductory sociology course. Her sources included books, journal articles, and Web documents. The following sample pages are from Schwab's research project.

All pages: short title and page number; on title page only: "Running head"

The New Volunteer:

College Students' Involvement in Community

Giving Grows

Tina Schwab

Sociology 101

Professor Morgan

May 15, 2010

Title appears in full and centered on separate page with student's name, course information, and date.

Abstract

College students today are volunteering in record numbers. Research indicates that today's youth are just as committed to community service as the young Americans of the 1960s, who are often perceived as the most civic-minded of American generations. However, current college students have reasons for volunteering beyond the desire to do good. Today, volunteerism is built into the academic curriculum, aids career development, and provides a sense of community. While the motivations for and methods of volunteering may vary from one generation to another, the fact remains that today's students are committed to serving their communities and making their world a better place for all.

Abstract appears on a new page after the title page. The first line is not indented.

Essay is concisely and objectively summarized—key points included but not details or statistics.

Paragraph should not exceed 150 to 250 words.

196

½"

↕ 1"

The New Volunteer:

College Students' Involvement in Community

Giving Grows

Are college students today concerned with helping others? It may not seem so to older generations, to whom today's students may appear obsessed with social networking, text messaging, and materialistic values. In her book, *Generation Me,* Jean M. Twenge (2006) explains that Americans of current college age are preoccupied with amassing wealth and achieving material goals but claims these aims and giving back to others aren't mutually exclusive. "As long as time spent volunteering does not conflict with other goals, GenMe finds fulfillment in helping others" (Twenge, 2006, p. 5). Attitudes and perceptions aside, today's college students actively help others in their communities, in ways that make a collective impact on the world. Their approach, however, differs from that of the previous generation. Today's college students tend to volunteer for at least one of three reasons: to satisfy a curricular requirement, to prepare for the financial success they hope to achieve professionally, and to be active members of their communities.

Full title is repeated on first page only.

Paraphrase from a source; the author is named in the text, so date follows her name in parentheses.

Direct quote from a source; page number is included in parenthetical citation.

References

Astin, A. W. (1998). The changing American
    college student: Thirty-year trends,
    1966–1996. *The Review of Higher
    Education, 21*(2), 115–135. Retrieved from
    http://www.press.jhu.edu/journals
    /review_of_higher_education

Astin, A. W., & Sax, L. J. (1998). How
    undergraduates are affected by service
    participation. *Journal of College Student
    Development, 39*(3), 251–263.

Astin, A. W., Vogelgesang, L. J., Ikeda, E. K.,
    & Yee, J. A. (2000). *How service learning
    affects students*. Los Angeles, CA: Higher
    Education Research Institute.

Bringle, R. G., & Hatcher, J. A. (1996).
    Implementing service learning in higher
    education. *Journal of Higher Education,
    67*(2), 221–239.

Corporation for National and Community
    Service. (2009, July). *Volunteering in
    America research highlights*. Retrieved from
    http://www.volunteeringinamerica
    .gov/assets/resources/Volunteering
    InAmericaResearchHighlights.pdf

Annotations (left margin):

New page, title centered. Entries are in alphabetical order by author's last name or, if no author, by first important word in the title.

Source: journal article with volume and issue number, retrieved online.

Source: entire book by four authors.

Source: report by a corporate author, retrieved online.

Twenge, J. M. (2006). *Generation me: Why today's young Americans are more confident, assertive, entitled—and more miserable—than ever before.* New York, NY: Free Press.

PART
5

Chicago
Documentation
Style

23 Chicago documentation style: Elements

The note and bibliography style presented in the sixteenth edition of *The Chicago Manual of Style* (Chicago: University of Chicago Press, 2010) is used in many disciplines, including history, art, philosophy, business, and communications. This style has three parts:

- Numbered in-text citations
- Numbered footnotes or endnotes
- A bibliography of works consulted

The first two parts are necessary; the third is optional, unless your instructor requires it. (Chicago also has an alternative author-date system that is similar to APA style.) For more information on this style, consult *The Chicago Manual of Style.* For updates and answers to frequently asked questions about this style, go to the University of Chicago Press's Web site at <http://www.press.uchicago.edu>, and click on "*Chicago Manual of Style* Web site."

23a Using numbered in-text citations and notes

Whenever you use information or ideas from a source, you need to indicate what you have borrowed by putting a superscript number in the text ([1]) at the end of the borrowed material. These superscript numbers are placed after all punctuation marks except for the dash.

> New York University professor and media
> consultant Clay Shirky explains that this change
> "isn't a shift from one kind of news institution to
> another, but rather in the definition of news."[2]

If a quotation is fairly long, you can set it off as a block quotation. Indent it five spaces or one-half inch from the left margin, and double-space the quotation, leaving an extra space above and below it. Place the superscript number after the period that ends the quotation.

Each in-text superscript number must have a corresponding note either at the foot of the page or at the end of the text. Indent the first line of each footnote like a paragraph. Footnotes begin with the number and are single-spaced, with a double space between notes.

If you are using endnotes instead of footnotes, they should begin after the last page of your text on a new numbered page titled "Notes." The list of endnotes can be double-spaced, unless your instructor prefers that you make them single-spaced.

The first time you cite a source in either a footnote or an endnote, you should include a full citation. Subsequent citations require less information.

23a Chicago

FIRST REFERENCE TO SOURCE

2. Clay Shirky, *Here Comes Everybody: The Power of Organizing without Organizations* (New York: Penguin, 2008), 65–66.

ENTRY FOR SOURCE ALREADY CITED

6. Shirky, 80.

If several pages pass between references to the same title, include a brief version of the title to clarify the reference.

ENTRY FOR SOURCE ALREADY CITED IN LONGER PAPER

7. Shirky, *Here Comes Everybody,* 99–100.

If you quote from the same work immediately after providing a full footnote, use the abbreviation *Ibid.* (Latin for "in the same place"), followed by the page number.

8. Ibid., 135.

23b Preparing a separate bibliography or list of works cited if your instructor requires one

Some instructors require a separate list of works cited or of works consulted. If you are asked to provide a works-cited list, do so on a separate, numbered page titled "Works Cited." If the list should include all works you consulted, title it "Bibliography." Here is a sample entry.

> Shirky, Clay. *Here Comes Everybody: The Power of Organizing without Organizations.* New York: Penguin, 2008.

23c Using the correct Chicago style for notes and bibliography entries

Books

1. Book with one author

NOTE

1. Michael Lewis, *Next: The Future Just Happened* (New York: Norton, 2001), 29.

BIBLIOGRAPHY ENTRY

Lewis, Michael. *Next: The Future Just Happened.* New York: Norton, 2001.

If the publisher's name is not available, include the place of publication with the date *(see p. 228)*.

2. Multiple works by the same author After providing complete information in the first footnote, include only a shortened version of the title with the author's last name and the page number

CHICAGO STYLE: DIRECTORY to SAMPLE TYPES

23c Chicago

**23c
Chicago**

in any subsequent footnotes. In the bibliography, list entries either in alphabetical order by title or from earliest to most recent. After the first listing, replace the author's name with a "three-em" dash (type three hyphens in a row).

NOTES

2. Shirky, *Cognitive Surplus,* 15.

3. Shirky, *Here Comes Everybody,* 65–66.

BIBLIOGRAPHY ENTRIES

Shirky, Clay. *Cognitive Surplus: Creativity and Generosity in a Connected Age.* New York: Penguin, 2010.

———. *Here Comes Everybody: The Power of Organizing without Organizations.* New York: Penguin, 2008.

3. Book with two or more authors In notes, you can name up to three authors. When there are three authors, put a comma after the first name and a comma plus *and* after the second.

BIBLIOGRAPHY or WORKS-CITED LIST in CHICAGO STYLE

- Begin on a new page.
- Begin with the centered title "Works Cited" if you are including only works referred to in your research project. Use the title "Bibliography" if you are including every work you consulted.
- List sources alphabetically by author's (or editor's) last name.
- Capitalize the first and last words in titles as well as all important words and words that follow colons.
- Indent all lines except the first of each entry five spaces, using your word processor's hanging indent feature.
- Use periods between author and title as well as between title and publication data.
- Double-space both within each entry and between entries, unless your instructor prefers that you make the entries single-spaced.

NOTE

4. Joelle Reeder and Katherine Scoleri, *The IT Girl's Guide to Blogging with Moxie* (Hoboken, NJ: Wiley, 2007), 45.

BIBLIOGRAPHY ENTRY

Reeder, Joelle, and Katherine Scoleri. *The IT Girl's Guide to Blogging with Moxie.* Hoboken, NJ: Wiley. 2007.

When more than three authors are listed on the title page, use *and others* or *et al.* after the first author's name in the note.

NOTE

5. Julian Henriques and others, *Changing the Subject: Psychology, Social Regulation and Subjectivity* (New York: Methuen, 1984), 275.

BIBLIOGRAPHY ENTRY

Henriques, Julian, Wendy Holloway, Cathy Urwin, Couze Venn, and Valerie Walkerdine. *Changing the Subject: Psychology, Social Regulation and Subjectivity.* New York: Methuen, 1984.

Give all author names in bibliography entries.

4. Book with an author and an editor or a translator (or both)   Put the author's name first, and add the editor's *(ed.)* or translator's *(trans.)* name after the title. Spell out *Edited* or *Translated* in the bibliography entry.

**23c
Chicago**

NOTE

6. Anton Chekhov, *The Essential Tales of Chekhov,* ed. Richard Ford, trans. Constance Garnett (Boston: Ecco, 1998).

BIBLIOGRAPHY ENTRY

Chekhov, Anton. *The Essential Tales of Chekhov.* Edited by Richard Ford. Translated by Constance Garnett. Boston: Ecco, 1998.

5. Anthology or other book with an editor in place of an author   Put the editor's name first, followed by the abbreviation *ed.* Otherwise, use the same format as for an author-based note.

NOTE

7. Victor Villanueva, ed., *Cross-Talk in Comp Theory* (Urbana, IL: NCTE Press, 2003).

BIBLIOGRAPHY ENTRY

Villanueva, Victor, ed. *Cross-Talk in Comp Theory.* Urbana, IL: NCTE Press, 2003.

6. Organization as author   Treat the organization as the author, and use the same format as for an author-based note.

NOTE

8. Centre for Contemporary Cultural Studies, *Making Histories: Studies in History Writing and Politics* (London: Hutchinson, 1982), 10.

BIBLIOGRAPHY ENTRY

Centre for Contemporary Cultural Studies. *Making Histories: Studies in History Writing and Politics.* London: Hutchinson, 1982.

23c
Chicago

7. Work in an anthology or part of an edited book Begin with the author and title of the specific work or part.

NOTES

9. Walter R. Fisher, "Narration, Knowledge, and the Possibility of Wisdom," in *Rethinking Knowledge: Reflections across the Disciplines,* ed. Robert F. Goodman and Walter R. Fisher (Albany: SUNY Press, 1995), 169.

10. Arthur M. Schlesinger, introduction to *Pioneer Women: Voices from the Kansas Frontier,* by Joanna L. Stratton (New York: Simon & Schuster, 1981).

BIBLIOGRAPHY ENTRIES

Fisher, Walter R. "Narration, Knowledge, and the Possibility of Wisdom." In *Rethinking Knowledge: Reflections across the Disciplines,* edited by Robert F. Goodman and Walter R. Fisher, 169–192. Albany: SUNY Press, 1995.

Schlesinger, Arthur M. Introduction to *Pioneer Women: Voices from the Kansas Frontier,* by Joanna L. Stratton, 11–15. New York: Simon & Schuster, 1981.

In notes, descriptive terms such as *introduction* are not capitalized. In bibliography entries, these descriptive terms are capitalized.

8. Article in an encyclopedia or a dictionary

For well-known reference works, publication data can be omitted from a note, but the edition or copyright date should be included. There is no need to include page numbers for entries in reference works that are arranged alphabetically; the abbreviation *s.v.* (meaning "under the word") plus the entry's title can be used instead.

NOTES

11. Joseph F. Kett, "American History since 1865," in *The Dictionary of Cultural Literacy: What Every American Needs to Know,* by E. D. Hirsch Jr., Joseph F. Kett, and James Trefil (Boston: Houghton Mifflin, 1993), 269–70.

12. *Webster's New College Dictionary,* 3rd ed., s.v. "Blog."

Reference works are not listed in the bibliography unless they are unusual or crucial to your project.

BIBLIOGRAPHY ENTRY

Kett, Joseph F. "American History since 1865." In *The Dictionary of Cultural Literacy: What Every American Needs to Know.* 2nd ed. By E. D. Hirsch Jr., Joseph F. Kett, and James Trefil. Boston: Houghton Mifflin, 1993.

9. The Bible
Abbreviate the name of the book, and use Arabic numerals for chapter and verse, separated by a colon. Name the version of the Bible cited, and do not include the Bible in your bibliography.

NOTE

13. Eccles. 8:5 (Jerusalem Bible).

10. Edition other than the first
Include the number of the edition after the title or, if there is an editor, after that person's name.

NOTE

14. Henry Jenkins, *Convergence Culture: Where Old and New Media Collide,* 2nd ed. (New York: New York University Press, 2008), 54.

BIBLIOGRAPHY ENTRY

Jenkins, Henry. *Convergence Culture: Where Old and New Media Collide.* 2nd ed. New York: New York University Press, 2008.

11. Reprint of an older book   Include the original publication date and other publication details if they are relevant. If referencing page numbers, be sure to note the date of the cited edition.

NOTE

15. Ernest Hemingway, *The Sun Also Rises* (1926; repr., New York: Scribner, 2006), 94.

BIBLIOGRAPHY ENTRY

Hemingway, Ernest. *The Sun Also Rises.* New York: Scribner, 1926. Reprint, New York: Scribner, 2006. Page references are to the 2006 edition.

12. Multivolume work   Put the volume number in Arabic numerals followed by a colon, before the page number.

NOTE

16. Martin J. Manning and Clarence R. Wyatt, *Encyclopedia of Media and Propaganda in Wartime America* (Santa Barbara, CA: ABC-CLIO, 2010), 2:40–42.

BIBLIOGRAPHY ENTRY

Manning, Martin J., and Clarence R. Wyatt. *Encyclopedia of Media and Propaganda in Wartime America.* Vol. 2. Santa Barbara, CA: ABC-CLIO, 2010.

13. Work in a series   Include the name of the series as well as the book's series number, if available. The series name should not be italicized or underlined.

NOTE

17. Roger D. Wimmer and Joseph R. Dominick, *Mass Media Research: An Introduction,* Contributions in Wadsworth Series in Mass Communication and Journalism (Boston: Wadsworth, 2005), 5.

BIBLIOGRAPHY ENTRY

Wimmer, Roger D., and Joseph R. Dominick. *Mass Media Research: An Introduction.* Contributions in Wadsworth Series in Mass Communication and Journalism. Boston: Wadsworth, 2005.

23c Chicago

14. Unknown author   Cite anonymous works by title, and alphabetize them by the first word, ignoring *A, An,* or *The.*

NOTE

18. *The British Album* (London: John Bell, 1790), 2:43–47.

BIBLIOGRAPHY ENTRY

The British Album. Vol. 2. London: John Bell, 1790.

15. Source quoted in another source   Quote a source within a source only if you are unable to find the original source. List both sources in the entry.

NOTE

19. Peter Gay, *Modernism: The Lure of Heresy* (New York: Norton, 2007), 262, quoted in Terry Teachout, "The Cult of the Difficult," *Commentary* 124, no. 5 (2007): 66–69.

BIBLIOGRAPHY ENTRY

Gay, Peter. *Modernism: The Lure of Heresy.* New York: Norton, 2007. Quoted in Terry Teachout. "The

Cult of the Difficult." *Commentary* 124, no. 5
(2007): 66–69.

Periodicals

16. Article in a journal paginated by volume
When journals are paginated by yearly volume, your
citation should include the following: author, title of
article in quotation marks, title of journal, volume
number and year, and page number(s).

**23c
Chicago**

NOTE

20. Frank Tirro, "Constructive Elements in Jazz
Improvisation," *Journal of the American Musicological
Society* 27 (1974): 300.

BIBLIOGRAPHY ENTRY

Tirro, Frank. "Constructive Elements in Jazz
Improvisation." *Journal of the American
Musicological Society* 27 (1974): 285–305.

17. Article in a journal paginated by issue   If
the periodical is paginated by issue rather than by
volume, add the issue number, preceded by the abbreviation *no.*

NOTE

21. Sarah Appleton Aguiar, " 'Everywhere
and Nowhere': Beloved's 'Wild' Legacy in Toni
Morrison's *Jazz*," *Notes on Contemporary Literature*
25, no. 4 (1995): 11.

BIBLIOGRAPHY ENTRY

Aguiar, Sarah Appleton. " 'Everywhere and
Nowhere': Beloved's 'Wild' Legacy in Toni
Morrison's *Jazz*." *Notes on Contemporary
Literature* 25, no. 4 (1995): 11–12.

18. Article in a magazine   Identify magazines
by week (if available) and month of publication. If

the article cited does not appear on consecutive pages, do not put any page numbers in the bibliography entry. You can, however, give specific pages in the note. In Chicago style, the month precedes the date, and months are not abbreviated.

NOTE

22. Alex Tresniowski, Jeff Truesdell, Siobhan Morrissey, and Howard Breuer, "A cyberbully convicted," *People,* December 15, 2008, 73.

BIBLIOGRAPHY ENTRY

Tresniowski, Alex, Jeff Truesdell, Siobhan Morrissey, and Howard Breuer. "A cyberbully convicted." *People,* December 15, 2008.

23c
Chicago

19. Article in a newspaper Provide the author's name (if known), the title of the article, the name of the newspaper, and the date of publication. Do not give a page number. Instead, give the section number or title if it is indicated. If applicable, indicate the edition (for example, *national edition*) before the section number.

NOTE

23. Justin Gillis, "A Scientist, His Work, and a Climate Reckoning," *New York Times,* December 22, 2010, national edition, sec A.

Newspaper articles cited in the text of your paper do not need to be included in a bibliography or works-cited list. If you are asked to include articles in the list, however, or if you did not provide full citation information in the essay or the note, format the entry as follows.

BIBLIOGRAPHY ENTRY

Gillis, Justin. "A Scientist, His Work and a Climate Reckoning." *New York Times,* December 22, 2010, national edition, sec. A.

20. Unsigned article or editorial in a newspaper
Begin the note with the name of the article; if you provide a bibliography or works-cited list entry, begin it with the name of the newspaper.

NOTE

24. "A Promising Cloning Proposal," *New York Times,* October 15, 2004.

Other Sources

21. Review
If the review is untitled, start with the author's name (if any) and *review of* for a note or *Review of* for a bibliography entry.

NOTE

25. Chun-Chi Wang, review of *Convergence Culture: Where Old and New Media Collide,* by Henry Jenkins, *Spectator,* Spring 2007, 102.

BIBLIOGRAPHY ENTRY

Wang, Chun-Chi. Review of *Convergence Culture: Where Old and New Media Collide,* by Henry Jenkins. *Spectator,* Spring 2007, 101–103.

22. Interview
Treat published print interviews like articles *(see no. 16)*. However, unless an interview has a given title (such as "Talking with the Dead: An Interview with Yiyun Li"), start with the name of the person interviewed. If a record of an unpublished interview exists, note the medium and where it may be found; the first example here is for a broadcast interview. Only interviews accessible to your readers are listed in the bibliography; the second example shown here, for a personal interview, would require only a note.

NOTES

26. Jon Meacham, Interview by Jon Stewart, *The Daily Show with Jon Stewart,* Comedy Central, May 5, 2010.

27. James Warren, personal interview by author, May 31, 2010, tape recording, Tallahassee, FL.

BIBLIOGRAPHY ENTRY

Meacham, Jon. Interview by Jon Stewart. *The Daily Show with Jon Stewart.* Comedy Central. May 5, 2010.

23. Published letter   For a letter published in a collection, begin the entry with the letter writer's name, followed by *to* and the name (or in this case, the relationship) of the addressee. An approximate date for when the letter was written can be prefaced with the abbreviation *ca.* for *circa.* Follow information about the letter with publication information about the source it appears in.

23c
Chicago

NOTE

28. C. S. Lewis to his brother, ca. November 1905, in *The Collected Letters of C. S. Lewis, Vol. 1: Family Letters, 1905–1931,* ed. Walter Hooper (New York: Harper Collins, 2004), 2–3.

BIBLIOGRAPHY ENTRY

Lewis, C. S. C. S. Lewis to his brother, ca. November 1905. In *The Collected Letters of C. S. Lewis, Vol. 1: Family Letters, 1905–1931,* edited by Walter Hooper. New York: HarperCollins, 2004.

24. Personal letter or e-mail   Do not list a letter that readers could not access in your bibliography.

NOTES

29. Jorge Ramados, letter to author, November 30, 2007.

30. George Hermanson, e-mail message to author, November 15, 2007.

25. Government document If it is not already obvious in your text, name the country first.

NOTE

31. Bureau of National Affairs, *The Civil Rights Act of 1964: Text, Analysis, Legislative History; What It Means to Employers, Businessmen, Unions, Employees, Minority Groups* (Washington, DC: BNA, 1964), 22–23.

BIBLIOGRAPHY ENTRY

U.S. Bureau of National Affairs. *The Civil Rights Act of 1964: Text, Analysis, Legislative History; What It Means to Employers, Businessmen, Unions, Employees, Minority Groups.* Washington, DC: BNA, 1964.

26. Unpublished document or dissertation Include a description of the document as well as information about where it is available. If more than one item from an archive is cited, include only one entry for the archive in your bibliography.

NOTES

32. Joe Glaser to Lucille Armstrong, September 28, 1960, Louis Armstrong Archives, Rosenthal Library, Queens College CUNY, Flushing, NY.

33. Deidre Dowling Price, "Confessional Poetry and Blog Culture in the Age of Autobiography." (PhD diss., Florida State University, 2010), 20–22.

BIBLIOGRAPHY ENTRIES

Glaser, Joe. Letter to Lucille Armstrong. Louis Armstrong Archives. Rosenthal Library, Queens College CUNY, Flushing, NY.

Price, Deidre Dowling. "Confessional Poetry and Blog Culture in the Age of Autobiography." PhD diss., Florida State University, 2010.

27. DVD or other form of recorded video Include the original release date before the publication information if it differs from the release date for the DVD.

NOTE

35. *Wit,* directed by Mike Nichols (2000; New York: HBO Home Video, 2001), DVD.

BIBLIOGRAPHY

Wit. Directed by Mike Nichols. 2000. New York: HBO Home Video, 2001. DVD.

23c
Chicago

28. Sound recording Begin with the composer or other person responsible for the content.

NOTE

36. Yanni, *Truth of Touch.* Virgin Records/EMI, 2011, compact disc.

BIBLIOGRAPHY ENTRY

Yanni. *Truth of Touch.* Virgin Records/EMI, 2011. compact disc.

29. Artwork Begin with the artist's name, and include both the name and the location of the institution holding the work. Italicize the name of any photograph or work of fine art. Works of art are usually not included in the bibliography.

NOTE

37. Andy Warhol, *Campbell's Soup Can* (oil on canvas, 1962, Saatchi Collection, London).

30. CD-ROM or other electronic non-Internet source Indicate the format after the publication information.

NOTE

38. Owen Jones, *The Grammar of Ornament* (London, 1856; repr., Oakland: Octavo, 1998), CD-ROM.

BIBLIOGRAPHY ENTRY

Jones, Owen. *The Grammar of Ornament*. London, 1856. Reprint, Oakland: Octavo, 1998. CD-ROM.

23c Chicago

Online Sources

The sixteenth edition of *The Chicago Manual of Style* specifically addresses the documentation of electronic and online sources. In general, citations for electronic sources include all of the information required for print sources, in addition to a URL (universal resource locator) or DOI (direct object identifier) and, in some cases, the date of access. There are three key differences between Chicago- and MLA-style online citations:

- Chicago recommends URLs or DOIs (preferring the latter when available) for all online sources. They should not be enclosed in angle brackets.

- Months are not abbreviated, and the date is usually given in the following order: month, day, year (September 13, 2011).

- Chicago recommends including dates of access only for sources that do not disclose a date of publication or revision. However, many instructors require students to include access dates for all online sources. Ask your instructor for his or her policy. If access dates are required, include them *before* the URL or DOI.

Use a period after any URL or DOI. If the URL or DOI has to be broken across lines, the break should occur *before* a single slash (/), a period, a hyphen, an underscore, or a tilde (~). However, a break should occur *after* a double slash (//) or a colon.

31. Electronic book Online versions of books are available either free of charge on the Web (often older titles that are in the public domain and out of print) or in versions that can be downloaded from a library or bookseller and also exist in a print version. For an older book you have accessed on the Web, include the date of access before the URL—or DOI if it is available—if your instructor requires it, as in the following example.

NOTE

39. Carl Sandburg, *Chicago Poems* (New York: Henry Holt, 1916), accessed March 18, 2008, http://www.bartleby.com/165/index.html.

BIBLIOGRAPHY ENTRY

Sandburg, Carl. *Chicago Poems.* New York: Henry Holt, 1916. Accessed March 18, 2008. http://www.bartleby.com/165/index.html.

For an electronic book you have purchased or obtained from a library, follow the guidelines for citing a print book *(see nos. 1–6),* but indicate the format at the end of the citation (for example, *Kindle edition, PDF e-book*). Because page numbers can vary, use the chapter number, section number, or another means of referring your reader to a specific part of the text.

NOTE

40. Stacy Schiff, *Cleopatra: A Life.* New York: Little, Brown, 2010. Kindle edition, chap. 3.

BIBLIOGRAPHY

Schiff, Stacy. *Cleopatra: A Life.* New York: Little, Brown, 2010. Kindle edition.

32. Partial or entire Web site Identify as many of the following as you can: author (if any), title of short work or page (if applicable), title or sponsor of site, and URL.

23c
Chicago

NOTES

41. Chris Garrett, "How I Use My Blog as a Fulcrum and You Can Too," *The Business of Blogging and New Media,* accessed January 28, 2011, http://www.chrisg.com/fulcrum/.

42. Chris Garrett, *The Business of Blogging and New Media,* last modified January 16, 2011, http://www.chrisg.com/.

43. Will Allison's Facebook page, last modified January 29, 2011, http://www.facebook.com/profile.php?id=591079933#!/profile.php?id=519407651.

BIBLIOGRAPHY ENTRIES

Garrett, Chris. "How I Use My Blog as a Fulcrum and You Can Too." *The Business of Blogging and New Media.* Accessed January 28, 2011. http://www.chrisg.com/fulcrum/.

Garrett, Chris. *The Business of Blogging and New Media.* Last modified on January 16, 2011. http://www.chrisg.com/.

33. Article in an online reference work (dictionary or encyclopedia) Widely used reference works are usually cited in notes, not bibliographies, and most publication information can be omitted. Signed entries, however, should include the entry author's name.

NOTE

44. *Encyclopedia of World Biography,* s.v. "Warren Zevon," accessed December 18, 2010, http://www.notablebiographies.com/newsmakers2/2004-Q-Z/Zevon-Warren.html.

34. Article from an online periodical (with a DOI) Whenever a DOI is available for an article, use it instead of the URL. Include the date of access before the DOI if required.

NOTE

45. Carol Ann Plummer, et al., "Volunteerism among Social Work Students during Hurricanes Katrina and Rita," *Journal of Social Service Research* 34, no. 3 (2008): 55–71, doi: 10.1080 /01488370802086328.

BIBLIOGRAPHY ENTRIES

Plummer, Carol Ann, Amy L. Ai, Catherine M. Lemieux, Roslyn Richardson, Sharbari Dey, Patricia Taylor, Susie Spence, and Hyun-Jun Kim. "Volunteerism among Social Work Students during Hurricanes Katrina and Rita." *Journal of Social Service Research* 34, no. 3 (2008): 55–71. doi: 10.1080/01488370802086328.

**23c
Chicago**

35. Article from an online journal, magazine, or newspaper (with no DOI)   When no DOI is available, provide the source's direct URL.

NOTES

46. Jay Rosen, "The New News," *Technology Review,* January/February 2010, http://www.technologyreview.com /communications/24175/?a=f.

47. Michelle Castillo, "FCC Passes Ruling to Protect Net Neutrality." *Time.com,* December 21, 2010, http://techland.time.com/2010/12/21 /fcc-passes-ruling-to-protect-net-neutrality/.

48. Larry Magid, "FCC Network Neutrality Rules Neither Socialism nor Sell-out," *The Huffington Post,* December 21, 2010, http://www .huffingtonpost.com/larry-magid/fcc-network -neutrality-ru_b_799999.html.

BIBLIOGRAPHY ENTRIES

Rosen, Jay. "The New News," *Technology Review,* January/February 2010. http://www .technologyreview.com/communications /24175/?a=f.

Castillo, Michelle. "FCC Passes Ruling to Protect Net Neutrality." *Time.com*. December 21, 2010. http://techland.time.com/2010/12/21 /fcc-passes-ruling-to-protect-net-neutrality/.

Magid, Larry. "FCC Network Neutrality Rules Neither Socialism nor Sell-out." *The Huffington Post*. December 21, 2010. http://www .huffingtonpost.com/larry-magid/fcc-network -neutrality-ru_b_799999.html.

23c Chicago

36. Journal, magazine, or newspaper article from a library subscription database

Give the name of the database after information about the article. An access date is required only if items do not include a publication or revision date. If a stable/permanent URL is provided for the source, include it, but otherwise provide the name of the database. If an identifying reference number is provided for the source, include it in parentheses (between the database name and the closing period).

NOTE

49. T. J. Anderson, "Body and Soul: Bob Kaufman's *Golden Sardine*," *African American Review* 34, no. 2 (Summer 2000): 329–46, EBSCOhost.

BIBLIOGRAPHY ENTRY

Anderson, T. J. "Body and Soul: Bob Kaufman's *Golden Sardine*." *African American Review* 34, no. 2 (Summer 2000): 329–46. EBSCOhost.

37. Blog posting

Individual blog posts are cited in the notes, along with the description *blog* in parentheses after the larger blog's title. A frequently cited blog can also be cited in the works-cited list or bibliography, as in this example.

NOTE

50. Rich Copley, "Major Universities Can Have a Major Impact on Local Arts," *Flyover* (blog),

March 15, 2008, http://www.artsjournal.com
/flyover/2008/03/major_ universities_can_have_a
.html.

BIBLIOGRAPHY ENTRY

Copley, Rich. *Flyover* (blog). http://www.artsjournal
.com/flyover/.

38. Posting to an electronic mailing list   Give
the URL if the posting is archived. If included, the
name or number of a posting should be noted after
the date. Do not create a bibliography entry.

NOTE

51. Roland Kayser to Opera-L mailing list,
January 3, 2008, http://listserv.bccls.org/cgi-bin
/wa?A2=ind0801A&L=OPERA-L&D=0&P=57634.

39. Podcast   The note should include any important name(s); the title; the source; the description,
such as *podcast audio;* and the date. Bibliographic
items follow the same sequence.

NOTE

52. Margaret Atwood, "Readings from Her
Recent Work," *Southeast Review Online,* podcast
audio, February 2010, http://southeastreview
.org/2010/02/margaret-atwood.html.

BIBLIOGRAPHY ENTRY

Atwood, Margaret. "Readings from Her Recent
Work." *Southeast Review Online.* Podcast
audio. February 2010. http://southeastreview
.org/2010/02/margaret-atwood.html.

40. Online video   Notes for online videos include
the relationship of the video to another source.

NOTE

53. Steven Johnson, "Where Good Ideas Come From," YouTube video, 4:07, as a trailer for Johnson's book *Where Good Ideas Come From,* posted by "RiverheadBooks," September 17, 2010, http://www.youtube.com/watch?v=NugRZGDbPFU.

BIBLIOGRAPHY ENTRY

Johnson, Steven. "Where Good Ideas Come From." YouTube video, 4:07. Posted September 17, 2010. http://www.youtube.com /watch?v=NugRZGDbPFU.

41. Online broadcast interview

NOTE

54. Jon Meacham, interview by Jon Stewart, *The Daily Show with Jon Stewart,* Comedy Central video posted May 5, 2010, http://www .thedailyshow.com/watch/wed-may-5-2010 /jon-meacham/jon-meacham.

BIBLIOGRAPHY ENTRY

Meacham, Jon. "Interview with Jon Meacham." By Jon Stewart. *The Daily Show with Jon Stewart,* Comedy Central video. Posted May 5, 2010. http://www.thedailyshow.com/watch /wed-may-5-2010/jon-meacham.

The following excerpt from Rebecca Hollingsworth's
project on blogging's impact on new media has been
adapted and put into Chicago style so that you can see
how citation numbers and endnotes work together.

The Chicago Manual of Style is primarily a
guide for publishers or those who wish to submit
work to be published. To prepare a research project using Chicago documentation style, you can use
the guidelines provided in Chapter 6 *(pp. 32–38)* or
check with your instructor. The formatting of the
following sample pages is consistent with the guidelines found in *A Manual for Writers of Research Papers, Theses, and Dissertations,* Seventh Edition, by
Kate Turabian, which is based on Chicago style.

Chicago style allows you the option of including
a title page. If you do provide a title page, count it as
page 1, but do not include the number on the page.
Put page numbers in the upper right-hand corner of
the remaining pages.

Blogging has become an extremely popular activity; many people are doing it for a wide variety of reasons. *Encyclopaedia Britannica* defines a *blog,* short for *Web log,* as an "online journal where an individual, group, or corporation presents a record of activities, thoughts, or beliefs."[1] This definition points out an important aspect of blogs: some are maintained by companies and organizations, but many are maintained by people not necessarily affiliated with traditional news outlets. New York University professor and media consultant Clay Shirky explains how this aspect of blogging is affecting news: "The change isn't a shift from one kind of news institution to another, but rather in the definition of news: from news as an institutional prerogative to news as part of a communications ecosystem, occupied by a mix of formal organizations, informal collectives, and individuals."[2] Like *Britannica*'s definition of *blog,* Shirky's definition of *news* emphasizes the range of people producing the news today, from multinational corporations to college students. To survive, journalism must blend traditional forms of reporting with new methods that get news and opinion to the people instantaneously and universally.

Blogs have turned citizens into novice reporters, but what do they mean for mainstream news outlets? Traditional forms of reporting, such as newspapers and televised news broadcasts, have always depended on the objectivity and credibility of their journalists, the reliability of their sources, and the extensive research and fact-checking that inform every news story. Blogs are a fast and easy way to publicize current issues and events, but many wonder if they can offer information that is as reliable as that provided by traditional news organizations and their carefully researched news. . . . During a recent interview about the struggling news industry alongside the burgeoning blogosphere, Jon Stewart asks Jon Meacham, the editor of *Newsweek,* a central question: "Who exactly is going to be doing the reporting?"[3] Formerly a newspaper reporter and currently a blogger, media consultant, and senior vice president for Edelman Digital, Gary Goldhammer tackles this question in his book *The Last Newspaper:* "every citizen can be a reporter, but not every citizen should or will. Every person will get news, but not in the same way, not at the same time, and not with the same perspective."[4] . . .

12

Notes

1. *Encyclopaedia Britannica Online,* s.v. "Blog," accessed April 25, 2010, http://www.britannica.com/EBchecked/topic/869092/blog.

2. Clay Shirky, *Here Comes Everybody: The Power of Organizing without Organizations* (New York: Penguin, 2008), 65–66.

3. Jon Meacham, interview by Jon Stewart, *The Daily Show with Jon Stewart,* Comedy Central video posted May 5, 2010, http://www.thedailyshow.com/watch/wed-may-5-2010/jon-meacham.

4. Gary Goldhammer, *The Last Newspaper: Reflections on the Future of News* (Lulu, 2009), 13.

13

Bibliography

Goldhammer, Gary. *The Last Newspaper: Reflections on the Future of News.* Lulu, 2009.

Meacham, Jon. "Interview with Jon Meacham." By Jon Stewart. *The Daily Show with Jon Stewart,* Comedy Central video. Posted May 5, 2010. http://www.thedailyshow.com/watch/wed-may-5-2010/jon-meacham.

Perlmutter, David D., and Misti McDaniel. "The Ascent of Blogging." *Nieman Reports* 59, no. 43 (2005): 60–64.

Shirky, Clay. *Here Comes Everybody: The Power of Organizing without Organizations.* New York: Penguin, 2008.

PART 6

Editing for Clarity

A sentence does not have to be short and simple to be concise, but every word in it must count.

25a Eliminating redundancies and unnecessary modifiers

Be on the lookout for redundancies such as *first and foremost, full and complete, final result, past histories, round in shape,* and *refer back.*

25b
w

► Students living ~~in close proximity~~ in the

dorms need to cooperate ~~together if they~~

~~want~~ to live in harmony.

Usually, modifiers such as *very, rather,* and *really* and intensifiers such as *absolutely, definitely,* and *incredibly* can be deleted.

► The ending ~~definitely~~ shocked us ~~very much~~.

25b Replacing wordy phrases

Make your sentences more concise by replacing wordy phrases with appropriate alternatives.

► ~~It is necessary at this point in time that~~
  Tests must now
  tests be run ~~for the purposes of measuring~~
  to measure
  the switch's strength.
  ^

	Concise
Wordy Phrases	**Alternatives**
at that point in time	then
at this point in time	now
due to the fact that	because
for the reason that	because

Wordy Phrases	Concise Alternatives
in close proximity to	near
in order to	to
in spite of the fact that	although
in the event that	if
in the final analysis	finally
in the not-too-distant future	soon
is able to	can
is necessary that	must

25c Editing roundabout sentences

Eliminate expletive constructions like *there is, there are,* and *it is;* replace the static verbs *be* and *have* with active verbs; and beware of overusing nouns derived from verbs.

► ~~There are~~ ^The^ stylistic similarities between "This Lime-Tree Bower" and "Tintern Abbey,"^indicate^ ~~which are indications of the influence~~ that Coleridge ~~had on~~ ^influenced^ Wordsworth.

For conciseness and clarity, simplify your sentence structure by turning modifying clauses into phrases.

► The film *The Social Network*, ~~which was~~ directed by David Fincher, portrays the turbulent founding of Facebook.

Often, you can reduce phrases to single words.

► David Fincher's film *The Social Network* portrays the turbulent founding of Facebook.

IDENTIFY AND EDIT
Wordy Sentences

Ask yourself these questions as you edit:

[w]

❷ 1. *Do any sentences contain wordy or empty phrases such as at this point in time? Do any contain redundancies or other unnecessary repetitions?*

> - ~~The fact is that at this point in time~~ ^{More} women
>   than men attend college. ^{now}
>
> - College enrollments have increased steadily
>   ~~upward~~ since the 1940s, but since the 1970s
>   women have enrolled in greater numbers than
>   men ~~have~~.

❷ 2. *Can any clauses be reduced to phrases, or phrases to single words? Can any sentences be combined to reduce repetitive information?*

> - ~~Reports that come from college~~ ^{College} officials ~~indicate~~ ^{report}
>   that more women are applying than men/ ~~This~~
>   ~~pattern indicates~~ ^{and} that women will outnumber
>   men in college for some time to come.

❷ 3. *Do any sentences include there is, or there are, or it is expressions; weak verbs; or nouns derived from verbs?*

> - In 1970, ~~there were~~ ^{men outnumbered women in college by} more than 1.5 million. ~~more~~
>   ~~men in college than women.~~
> - This trend ~~is a reflection of~~ ^{reflects} broad changes in
>   gender roles throughout U.S. society.

You can combine short, repetitive sentences.

► Hurricane Ike ~~had a devastating effect on~~ *'s torrential rains devastated*

our town., ~~The destruction resulted from~~

~~torrential rains. Flooding~~ submerg*ing*ed Main

Street under eight feet of water. ~~The rain~~ *and*

~~also~~ trigger*ing*ed mudslides that destroyed two

nearby towns.

26 Add missing words.

Do not omit words the reader needs to understand your sentence.

26a Adding needed words to compound structures

For conciseness, words can sometimes be omitted from compound structures: *His anger is extreme and his behavior [is] violent.* But do not leave out part of a compound structure unless both parts of the compound are the same.

► The gang members neither cooperated *with* nor

listened to the authorities.

26b Adding the word *that* when needed

Add the word *that* if doing so makes the sentence clearer.

▶ The attorney argued ⌃*that* men and women
should receive equal pay for equal work.

26c Making comparisons clear

To be clear, comparisons must be complete. Check comparisons to make sure your meaning is clear. In the following example, does the writer mean that she loved her grandmother more than her sister did—or more than she loved her sister? To clarify, add the missing words.

▶ I loved my grandmother more than my sister. ⌃*did*

▶ I loved my grandmother more than my sister. ⌃*I loved*

When you use *as* to compare people or things, be sure to use it twice.

▶ Napoleon's temper was ⌃*as* volatile as a volcano.

Include *other* or *else* to indicate that people or things belong to the group with which the subject is being compared.

▶ High schools and colleges stage *The Laramie Project* more than any *other* play.

▶ Professor Koonig wrote more books than anyone *else* in the department.

Use a possessive form when comparing attributes or possessions.

▶ Plato's philosophy is easier to read than
⌃ ~~that of Aristotle.~~ *Aristotle's*

Complex comparisons may require more than one addition to be clear.

► Smith's book is longer, *than Jones's book* but his account of
^
the war is more interesting than ~~Jones's.~~ *Jones's account*
^

26d Adding the articles *a, an,* or *the* as appropriate

Omitting an article usually sounds odd, unless the omission occurs in a series of nouns.

► He gave me *the* books he liked best.
^

► He gave me books, CDs, and games.

If the articles in a series are not all the same, each one must be included.

► I have a fish tank, birdcage, and rabbit hutch.

► I have *an* aquarium, *a* birdcage, and *a* rabbit
^   ^
hutch.

(For more information about the use of articles, multilingual writers should consult Chapter 43, pp. 326–29.)

27 Unscramble mixed constructions.

Sentences that do not fit together grammatically or logically can confuse readers and must be revised.

27a Untangling mixed-up grammar

A sentence should not start one way and then midway through change grammatical direction.

► *Family*
~~For family~~ members who enjoy one
 ^
another's company often choose a vacation

spot together.

A prepositional phrase cannot be the subject of a
sentence. Eliminating the preposition *for* makes it
clear that *family members* is the subject.

► *can be*
In Mexico, ~~when~~ a curandero ~~is~~ consulted
 for ^
~~can address~~ spiritual or physical illness.
 ^

The dependent clause *when a curandero is consulted*
cannot serve as the subject of the sentence. Transforming the dependent clause into an independent
clause with a subject and predicate fixes the problem.

27b Repairing illogical predicates

A sentence's subject and verb must match both logically and grammatically. When they do not, the result is faulty predication.

► ~~The best kind of education for me would be~~
 A
~~a~~ university with both a school of music and
 ^
 would be best for me
a school of government.
 ^

A university is an institution, not a type of
education.

The phrases *is when, is where,* and *the reason is . . .
because* may sound logical, but they usually result
in faulty predication.

► *the production of carbohydrates from the interaction of*
Photosynthesis is ~~where~~ carbon dioxide,
 ^
water, and chlorophyll ~~interact~~ in the

presence of sunlight. ~~to form carbohydrates.~~
 ^

Photosynthesis is a process, not a place, so *is where*
is illogical.

▶ The reason the joint did not hold is ~~because~~ *that*
the coupling bolt broke.

or

▶ The ~~reason the~~ joint did not hold ~~is~~ because
the coupling bolt broke.

28 Fix confusing shifts.

Revise confusing shifts in point of view, tense, mood,
or voice.

28a Fixing shifts in point of view

A writer has three points of view to choose from:
first person *(I or we),* second person *(you),* and third
person *(he, she, it, one,* or *they).* Once you choose a
point of view, use it consistently.

▶ Students will have no trouble getting a
they
good seat if ~~you~~ arrive at the theater before
7 o'clock.

Note: When making a general statement about what
people should or should not do, use the third person, not
the second person.

Do not switch from singular to plural or plural to
singular for no reason. When correcting such shifts,
choose the plural to avoid using *his or her* or introducing gender bias. *(See Chapter 34, pp. 261–62.)*

► *People are*
~~A person is~~ often surprised when they are
^
complimented.

28b Fixing shifts in tense

Verb tenses show the time of an action in relation to other actions. Choose a time frame—present, past, or future—and use it consistently, changing tense only when the meaning of your text requires you to do so.

► The wind was blowing a hundred miles an
was
hour when suddenly there ~~is~~ a big crash,
^
fell
and a tree ~~falls~~ into the living room.
^

► She has admired many strange buildings
thinks
at the university but ~~thought~~ that the new
^
looks
Science Center ~~looked~~ completely out of
^
place.

NAVIGATING THROUGH COLLEGE AND BEYOND

Present Tense and Literary Works

By convention—because as long as a book is read, it is "alive"—we use the present tense to write about the content of literary works.

► **David Copperfield describes villains**
such as Mr. Murdstone and heroes such
as Mr. Micawber in unforgettable detail.
is
But Copperfield ~~was~~ not himself an
^
especially interesting person.

IDENTIFY AND EDIT
Confusing Shifts

To avoid confusing shifts, ask yourself these questions as you edit your writing:

shift

? 1. *Does the sentence shift from one point of view to another, for example, from third person to second?*

> • Over the centuries, millions of laborers helped build and maintain the Great Wall of China, and ~~if you were one, you probably~~ suffered great hardship as a result.
>
> *most of them*

? 2. *Are the verbs in your sentence consistent in the following ways:*

In tense (past, present, or future)?

> • Historians call the period before the unification of China the Warring States period. It ~~ends~~ when the ruler of the Ch'in state conquered the last of his independent neighbors.
>
> *ended*

In mood (statements versus commands or hypothetical conditions)?

> • If a similar wall ~~is~~ built today, it would cost untold amounts of time and money.
>
> *were*

In voice (active or passive)?

> • The purpose of the wall was to protect against invasion, but commerce. ~~was promoted by it also.~~
>
> *it also promoted*

? 3. *Are quotations and questions clearly phrased in either direct or indirect form?*

> • The visitor asked the guide ~~when~~ did construction of the Great Wall begin?"
>
> *, "When*
>
> • The visitor asked the guide when ~~did~~ construction of the Great Wall ~~begin?~~
>
> *began.*

28c Avoiding unnecessary shifts in mood and voice

Verbs have a mood and a voice. There are three basic moods: the **indicative,** used to state or question facts, acts, and opinions; the **imperative,** used to give commands or advice; and the **subjunctive,** used to express wishes, conjectures, and hypothetical conditions. Unnecessary shifts in mood can confuse and distract your readers.

>   *could go*
> If he ~~goes~~ to night school, he would take a
>   ^
> course in accounting.

> The sign says that in case of emergency
>
> passengers should follow the instructions
>   *should not*
> of the train crew and ~~don't~~ leave the train
>   ^
> unless instructed to do so.

Most verbs have two voices. In the **active voice,** the subject does the acting; in the **passive voice,** the subject is acted on. Do not shift abruptly from one voice to the other.

> The Impressionist painters hated black.
> *They favored violet,*
> ~~Violet,~~ green, blue, pink, and red. ~~were~~
> ^   ^
> ~~favored by them.~~

The revision uses *they* to make "the Impressionist painters" the subject of the second sentence as well as the first.

28d Avoiding shifts between direct and indirect quotations and questions

Indirect quotations report what others wrote or said without repeating their words exactly. **Direct quotations** report the words of others exactly and should be enclosed in quotation marks. *(For more on* *punctuating quotations, see Chapter 48, pp. 361–62.)* Do not shift from one form of quotation to the other within a sentence.

► **In his inaugural speech, President Kennedy**

called on Americans not to ask what their

to
country could do for them but instead ⸌ask
they could   *their*
what ~~you can~~ do for ~~your~~ country.⸢"
   ^   ^

The writer could have included the quotation in its entirety: *In his inaugural speech, President Kennedy said, "My fellow Americans, ask not what your country can do for you; ask what you can do for your country."*

Similarly, do not shift from an indirect to a direct question.

29
//

► **The performance was so bad the audience**
       whether   *had*
wondered ~~had~~ the performers ever
       ^   ^

rehearsed.

As an alternative, the writer could ask the question directly: *Had the performers ever rehearsed? The performance was so bad the audience wasn't sure.*

29 Use parallel constructions.

Parallel constructions present equally important ideas in the same grammatical form.

► **At Gettysburg in 1863, Lincoln said that the Civil War was being fought to make sure that government *of the people, by the people,* and *for the people* might not perish from the earth.**

Correct items in a series or paired ideas that do not have the same grammatical form by making them parallel. Put items at the same level in an outline or items in a list in parallel form.

29a Making items in a series parallel

A list or series of equally important items should be parallel in grammatical structure.

▶ **The Census Bureau classifies people as**

employed if they receive payment for any

kind of labor, are temporarily absent from

     work

their jobs, or ~~working~~ at least fifteen hours

    ^

as unpaid laborers in a family business.

Parallel construction can make a sentence more forceful and memorable.

▶ **My sister obviously thought that I was too**

  too   *too troublesome*

young, ignorant, and ~~a troublemaker~~.

  ^   ^

29b Making paired ideas parallel

Paired ideas connected with a coordinating conjunction *(and, but, or, nor, for, so, yet),* a correlative conjunction *(not only . . . but also, both . . . and, either . . . or, neither . . . nor),* or a comparative expression *(as much as, more than, less than)* must have parallel grammatical form.

       both

▶ **Successful teachers must inspire ~~students~~**

  challenge their students ^

and ~~challenging them is also important~~.

 ^

▶ **I dreamed not only of getting the girl but**

  winning

also of the gold medal.

 ^

IDENTIFY AND EDIT
Faulty Parallelism

To avoid faulty parallelism, ask yourself these
questions as you edit your writing:

❓ 1. *Are the items in a series in parallel form?*

> * The senator stepped to the podium, ~~an angry~~
>   *glanced angrily at*
>   ^
>   ~~glance shooting toward~~ her challenger, and
>
>   began to refute his charges.

❓ 2. *Are paired items in parallel form?*

> * Her challenger, she claimed, ~~had~~ not only
>   *had*
>   accused her falsely of accepting illegal campaign
>   ^   *had accepted illegal contributions himself.*
>   contributions, but ~~his contributions were from~~
>   ^
>   ~~illegal sources also.~~

❓ 3. *Are the items in outlines and lists in parallel form?*

FAULTY PARALLELISM	She listed four reasons for voters to send her back to Washington:
	1. Ability to protect the state's interests
	2. Her seniority on important committees
	3. Works with members of both parties to get things done
	4. Has a close working relationship with the President
REVISED	She listed four reasons for voters to send her back to Washington:
	1. *Her ability* to protect the state's interests
	2. *Her seniority* on important committees
	3. *Her ability* to work with members of both parties to get things done
	4. *Her* close working *relationship* with the President

29b
//

► **Many people find that having meaningful**
earning
work is more important than high pay.
^

29c Repeating function words as needed

Function words such as prepositions *(to, for, by)* and subordinating conjunctions *(although, that)* give information about a word or indicate the relationships among words in a sentence. Although they can sometimes be omitted, include them whenever they signal a parallel structure that might be missed by readers.

30a
mm

► **The project has three goals: to survey the**
to
valley for Inca-period sites, excavate a test
^
to
trench at each site, and excavate one of
^

those sites completely.

The writer added *to* to make it clear where one goal ends and the next begins.

30 Fix misplaced and dangling modifiers.

For a sentence to make sense, its parts must be arranged appropriately. When a modifying word, phrase, or clause is misplaced or dangling, readers get confused.

30a Fixing misplaced modifiers

Modifiers should usually come immediately before or after the words they modify. In the following sentence, the clause *after the police arrested them* modifies *protesters,* not *property.*

► *After the police had arrested them, the*
~~The~~ protesters were charged with

destroying college property. ~~after the police~~
~~had arrested them.~~

Prepositional phrases used as adverbs are easy to
misplace.

► *From the cabin's porch, the*
~~The~~ hikers watched the storm gathering

force. ~~from the cabin's porch.~~

30b Clarifying ambiguous modifiers

30b
mm

Adverbs can modify words that precede or follow
them. When they are ambiguously placed, they are
called **squinting modifiers.** The following revision shows that the objection is vehement, not the
argument.

► *vehemently*
Historians who object to this account

~~vehemently~~ argue that the presidency was

never endangered.

Problems occur with limiting modifiers such as
only, even, almost, nearly, and *just.* Check every sentence that includes one of these modifiers.

AMBIGUOUS	That restaurant *only offers* seafood for dinner.
REVISED	That restaurant *offers* *only* seafood for dinner.
	or
	That restaurant *offers* seafood *only* for dinner.

IDENTIFY AND EDIT
Misplaced Modifiers

mm

To avoid misplaced modifiers, ask yourself these questions:

? 1. *Are all the modifiers close to the expressions they modify?*

> *At the beginning of the Great Depression, people*
> - ~~People~~ panicked and all tried to get their money
>   ^
>   out of the banks at the same time, forcing many
>
>   banks to close. ~~at the beginning of the Great~~
>   ^
>   ~~Depression.~~

? 2. *Are any modifiers placed in such a way that they modify more than one expression? Pay particular attention to limiting modifiers such as only, even, and just.*

> *quickly*
> - President Roosevelt declared a bank holiday,
>   ^   ^
>   ~~quickly~~ helping to restore confidence in the
>
>   nation's financial system.
>
> - Congress enacted many programs to combat the
>   *only*
>   Depression ~~only~~ within the first one hundred
>   ^
>   days of Roosevelt's presidency.

? 3. *Do any modifiers disrupt the relationships among the grammatical elements of the sentence?*

> *Given how entrenched segregation was at the time, the*
> - ~~The~~ president's wife, Eleanor, was a surprisingly
>   ^
>   strong, ~~given how entrenched segregation was at~~
>
>   ~~the time,~~ advocate for racial justice in Roosevelt's
>
>   administration.

30c Moving disruptive modifiers

Separating grammatical elements that belong together, such as a subject and verb, with a lengthy modifying phrase or clause disrupts the connection between the two sentence elements.

▶ *Despite their similar conceptions of the self,*
  Descartes and Hume, despite their similar
  ^
  conceptions of the self, deal with the issue

  of personal identity in different ways.

30d Avoiding split infinitives

30e
dm

An **infinitive** couples the word *to* with the base form of a verb. In a **split infinitive,** one or more words intervene between *to* and the verb form. Avoid splitting infinitives with a modifier unless keeping them together results in an awkward or ambiguous construction.

In the example that follows, the modifier *successfully* should be moved. The modifier *carefully* should probably stay where it is, however, even though it splits the infinitive *to assess.*

▶   *successfully,*
  To successfully complete this assignment,
  ^
  students have to carefully assess projected

  economic benefits.

30e Fixing dangling modifiers

A **dangling modifier** is a descriptive phrase that implies an actor different from the sentence's subject. When readers try to connect the modifying phrase with the subject, the result may be humorous as well as confusing.

DANGLING   *Swimming toward the boat on*
MODIFIER   *the horizon,* the crowded beach
                felt as if it were miles away.

**30e
dm**

IDENTIFY AND EDIT
Dangling Modifiers

dm

To avoid dangling modifiers, ask yourself these questions when you see a descriptive phrase at the beginning of a sentence:

? 1. *What is the subject of the sentence?*

- Snorkeling in Hawaii, ancient sea turtles were an amazing sight.

   The subject of the sentence is *sea turtles.*

? 2. *Could the phrase at the beginning of the sentence possibly describe this subject?*

- Snorkeling in Hawaii, ancient sea turtles were an amazing sight.

   No, sea turtles do not snorkel in Hawaii or anywhere else.

? 3. *Who or what is the phrase really describing? Either make that person or thing the subject of the main clause, or add a subject to the modifier.*

   we saw
- Snorkeling in Hawaii, ancient sea turtles, ~~were~~ an amazing sight.

   While we were snorkeling   amazed us.
- ~~Snorkeling~~ in Hawaii, ancient sea turtles ~~were an amazing sight.~~

To fix a dangling modifier, name its implied actor explicitly, either as the subject of the sentence or in the modifier itself.

REVISED   Swimming toward the boat on the horizon, *I* felt as if the crowded beach were miles away.

or

As *I swam* toward the boat on the horizon, the crowded beach seemed miles away.

Simply moving a dangling modifier won't fix the problem. To make the meaning clear, you must make the implied actor in the modifying phrase explicit.

DANGLING MODIFIER   *After struggling for weeks in the wilderness,* the town pleased them mightily.

REVISED   After struggling for weeks in the wilderness, *they* were pleased to come upon the town.

or

After *they had struggled* for weeks in the wilderness, the town appeared in the distance.

**31
coord/sub**

31 Use coordination and subordination effectively.

Coordination and subordination allow you to combine and develop ideas in ways that readers can follow and understand.

Coordination gives two or more ideas equal weight. To coordinate parts within a sentence, join them with a coordinating conjunction *(and, but, or, for, nor, yet,* or *so).* To coordinate two or more sentences, use a comma plus a coordinating conjunction, or insert a semicolon.

► The auditorium was huge, *and* the acoustics were terrible.

► The tenor bellowed the aria, *but* no one in the back could hear him.

► The student was *both* late for class *and* unprepared.

▶ **Jones did not agree with her position on health care; *nevertheless,* he supported her campaign for office.**

Note: When a semicolon is used to coordinate two sentences, it is often followed by a conjunctive adverb such as *moreover, nevertheless, however, therefore,* or *subsequently.*

Subordination makes one idea depend on another. Less important ideas belong in subordinate clauses. Subordinate clauses start with a relative pronoun *(who, whom, that, which, whoever, whomever, whose)* or a subordinating conjunction such as *after, although, because, if, since, when,* or *where.*

**31a
coord/sub**

▶ **The blue liquid, *which will be added to the beaker later,* must be kept at room temperature.**

▶ **Christopher Columbus discovered the New World in 1492, *although he never understood just what he had found.***

▶ ***After writing the opening four sections,* Wordsworth put the work aside for two years.**

Note: Commas often set off subordinate ideas, especially when the subordinate clause or phrase opens the sentence. *(For more on using commas, see Chapter 44, pp. 340–52.)*

If you do not fix the following problems with coordination and subordination, your readers will have difficulty following your train of thought.

31a Using subordination, not coordination, for ideas of unequal importance

Coordination should be used only when two or more ideas deserve equal emphasis: *Smith supports bilingual education, but Johnson does not.* Subordination, not coordination, should be used to indicate information of secondary importance and to show its logical relation to the main idea.

▶ When the
  ~~The~~ police arrived, ~~and~~ the burglars ran
  ^
  away.

31b Keeping major ideas in main clauses

Major ideas belong in main clauses, not in subordinate clauses or phrases. The writer revised the following sentence because the subject of the paper was definitions of literacy, not those who value literacy.

► *Highly valued by businesspeople as well as academics, literacy*
   ~~Literacy, which~~ has been defined as the

   ability to talk intelligently about many

   topics/. ~~is highly valued by businesspeople~~

   ~~as well as academics.~~

**31c
coord/sub**

31c Combining short, choppy sentences

Short sentences are easy to read, but several of them in a row can become so monotonous that meaning gets lost. Use subordination to put the idea you want to emphasize in the main clause, and use subordinate clauses and phrases for the other ideas.

CHOPPY	My cousin Jim is not an accountant. But he does my taxes every year. He suggests various deductions. These deductions reduce my tax bill considerably.
REVISED	Even though he is not an accountant, *my cousin Jim does my taxes every year,* suggesting various deductions that reduce my tax bill considerably.

If a series of short sentences includes two major ideas of equal importance, use coordination for the two major ideas and subordinate the secondary information.

CHOPPY	Bilingual education is designed for children. The native language of these children is not English. Smith supports expanding bilingual education. Johnson does

not support expanding bilingual
education.

REVISED Smith supports bilingual education for children whose native
language is not English; Johnson,
however, does not.

31d Avoiding excessive subordination

When a sentence seems overloaded, separate it into
two or more sentences.

▶ Big-city majors, ~~who are supported by~~
~~public funds,~~ should be cautious about
spending taxpayers' money for personal
needs, ~~such as furnishing official residences,~~
especially when municipal budget shortfalls

They risk
have caused extensive job layoffs/. angering
by using public funds for furnishing official residences.
city workers and the general public/
                                    ^

32 Vary sentence patterns.

Enliven your prose by using a variety of sentence
patterns.

32a Varying sentence openings

When all the sentences in a passage begin with
the subject, you risk losing your readers' attention.
Vary your sentences by moving a modifier to the
beginning. The modifier may be a single word, a
phrase, or a clause.

► Eventually,
Louis Armstrong's innovations on the
^

trumpet ~~eventually~~ **became the standard.**

► In at least two instances, this
~~**Armstrong's**~~ **money-making strategy**
^

backfired. ~~in at least two instances.~~
^

► After Glaser became his manager,
Armstrong no longer had to worry about
^

business. ~~after Glaser became his manager.~~
^

A **participial phrase** begins with an *-ing* verb *(driving)* or a past participle *(moved, driven)* and is used as a modifier. You can often move it to the beginning of a sentence for variety, but make sure that the phrase describes the explicit subject of the sentence, or you will end up with a dangling modifier *(see pp. 247–49).*

32b
var

► Pushing the other children aside,
Joseph, ~~pushing the other children aside,~~
^

demanded that the teacher give him a

cookie first.

► Stunned by the stock market crash in 1929, many
~~**Many**~~ **brokers,** ~~stunned by the stock market~~
^

~~crash in 1929,~~ **committed suicide.**

32b Varying sentence length and structure

Short, simple sentences (under ten words) will keep your readers alert if they occur in a context that also includes longer, complex sentences.

As you edit your work, check to see if you have overused one kind of sentence structure. Are most of your sentences short and simple? If so, use subordination to combine some of them *(see pp. 251–52).* However, if most of your sentences are long and complex, put at least one of your ideas into a short, simple sentence. Your goal is to achieve a satisfying mix.

DRAFT I dived quickly into the sea. I peered through my mask at the watery world. It turned darker. A school of fish went by. The distant light glittered on their bodies, and I stopped swimming. I waited to see if the fish might be chased by a shark. I was satisfied that there was no shark and continued down.

REVISED I dived quickly into the sea, peering through my mask at a watery world that turned darker as I descended. A school of fish went by, the distant light glittering on their bodies. I stopped swimming and waited. Perhaps the fish were being chased by a shark? Satisfied that there was no shark, I continued down.

(For more on coordination and subordination, see pp. 249–52.)

32c

32c | Including a few cumulative and periodic sentences

Cumulative sentences, which add a series of descriptive participial or absolute phrases to the basic subject-plus-verb pattern, make writing more forceful. They can also be used to add details. They work best in personal essays and the humanities.

► **The motorcycle spun out of control,** *plunging down the ravine, crashing through the fence,* **and** *coming to rest on its side.*

You can also make your writing more forceful by using periodic sentences. In a **periodic sentence,** the key word, phrase, or idea appears at the end.

► **In 1946 and 1947, young people turned away from the horrors of World War II and fell in love—with the jukebox.**

32d Trying an occasional inversion, a rhetorical question, or an exclamation

Most sentences are declarative and follow the normal sentence pattern of subject plus verb plus object. Occasionally, though, you might try using an inverted sentence pattern or another sentence type, such as a rhetorical question or an exclamation.

You can create an **inversion** by putting the verb before the subject.

► **Characteristic of Issey Miyake's work are bold design and original thinking.**

Because many inversions sound odd, they should be used infrequently and carefully.

Asking a question invites your readers to participate more actively in your work. Because you do not expect your audience to answer, this kind of question is called a **rhetorical question.**

► **Athletes injured at an early age too often find themselves without a job, a college degree, or their health. Is it any wonder that a few turn to drugs and alcohol?**

Rhetorical questions work best in the middle or at the end of a long, complicated passage. Sometimes they can help make a transition from one topic to another. Use them selectively, however, and avoid using them to begin an essay.

In academic writing, **exclamations** are rare. If you decide to use one, be sure that strong emotion is appropriate and worth risking a loss of credibility.

► **Wordsworth completed the thirteen-book *Prelude* in 1805, after seven years of hard work. Instead of publishing his masterpiece, however, he devoted himself to revising it—for forty-five years! The poem, in a fourteen-book version, was finally published in 1850, after he had died.**

32d
var

33 Choose active verbs.

Active verbs such as *run, shout, write,* and *think* are more direct and forceful than forms of the verb *be (am, are, is, was, were, been, being)* or passive-voice constructions. The more active your verbs, the stronger and clearer your writing will be.

33a Considering alternatives to *be* verbs

Be does a lot of work in English.

> **BE AS A LINKING VERB**

> ▶ **Germany *is* relatively poor in natural resources.**

33b

> **BE AS HELPING VERB**

> ▶ **Macbeth *was* returning from battle when he met the three witches.**

Be verbs are so useful that they get overworked. Watch for weak, roundabout sentences with *be* verbs, and consider replacing those verbs with active verbs.

> ▶ **The mayor's refusal to meet with our group**
> ~~**is a demonstration of**~~ *demonstrates* **his lack of respect for**
> **us, as well as for the environment.**

33b Preferring the active voice when writing for a general audience

Verbs can be in the active or passive voice. In the **active voice,** the subject of the sentence acts; in the **passive voice,** the subject is acted on.

ACTIVE	The Senate finally passed the bill.
PASSIVE	The bill was finally passed by the Senate.

The passive voice downplays the actors as well as the action, so much so that the actors are often left out of the sentence.

> PASSIVE   The bill was finally passed.

The active voice is more forceful, and readers usually want to know who or what does the acting.

> PASSIVE   Polluting chemicals were dumped into the river.
>
> ACTIVE   Industrial Products Corporation dumped polluting chemicals into the river.

However, when the recipient of the action is more important than the doer of the action, the passive voice is appropriate.

33b

► **After her heart attack, my mother was taken to the hospital.**

Mother and the fact that she was taken to the hospital are more important than who took her to the hospital.

NAVIGATING THROUGH COLLEGE AND BEYOND

Passive Voice

The passive voice is often used in scientific reports to keep the focus on the experiment and its results rather than on the experimenters.

> **The bacteria were treated carefully with nicotine and stopped reproducing.**

34 Use appropriate language.

Language is appropriate when it fits your writing situation: your topic, purpose, and audience. You can develop a sense of audience through reading how other writers in the field handle your topic.

34a Avoiding slang, regional expressions, and nonstandard English

In college writing, slang terms and the tone that goes with them should be avoided.

34b
d

> **SLANG** In *Heart of Darkness,* we hear a lot about a *dude* named Kurtz, but we don't see the *guy* much.
>
> **REVISED** In *Heart of Darkness,* Marlow, the narrator, talks continually about Kurtz, but we meet Kurtz himself only at the end.

Like slang, regional and nonstandard expressions such as *y'all, hisself,* and *don't be doing that* work fine in conversation but not in college writing.

34b Using an appropriate level of formality

College writing assignments usually call for a style that avoids the extremes of the stuffy and the casual, the pretentious and the chatty. Revise passages that veer toward one extreme or the other.

> **PRETENTIOUS** Romantic lovers are characterized by a preoccupation with a deliberately restricted set of qualities in the love object that are viewed as means to some ideal end.
>
> **REVISED** People in love see what they want to see, usually by idealizing the beloved.

34c Avoiding jargon

When specialists communicate with each other, they often use technical language. **Jargon** is the inappropriate use of specialized or technical language. You should not use language that is appropriate for specialists when you are writing for a general audience.

JARGON	Pegasus Technologies developed a Web-based PSP system to support standard off-line brands in meeting their loyalty-driven marketing objectives via the social networking space.
REVISED	Pegasus Technologies developed a system that helps businesses create networking sites to run promotions for their customers.

34d d

If you must use technical terms when writing for nonspecialists, be sure to provide definitions.

▶ **Armstrong's innovative singing style featured "scat," a technique that combines "nonsense syllables [with] improvised melodies" (Robinson 515).**

34d Avoiding euphemisms and doublespeak

Euphemisms substitute nice-sounding words like *correctional facility* and *passing away* for such harsh realities as *prison* and *death*. Doublespeak is used to obscure facts and evade responsibility.

DOUBLESPEAK	Pursuant to the environmental protection regulations enforcement policy of the Bureau of Natural Resources, special management area land use permit issuance procedures have been instituted.

REVISED   The Bureau of Natural Resources has established procedures for issuing land use
permits.

Avoid using words that evade or deceive.

34e Avoiding biased or sexist language

Biased or sexist language can undermine your
credibility with readers.

1. Biased language

Always review your writing to see if it is unintentionally biased. Be on the lookout for stereotypes,
rigid, unexamined generalizations that demean,
ignore, or patronize people on the basis of gender,
race, religion, national origin, ethnicity, physical
ability, sexual orientation, occupation, or any other
human condition. Revise for inclusiveness.

For example, do not assume that Irish Catho-
lics have large families.

> *The* *an* *Catholic family with*
> **Although the Browns are Irish ~~Catholics,~~**
> ^ ^ ^
> **~~there are only~~ two children. ~~in the family.~~**
> ^

In addition, remember that a positive stereotype is
still an overgeneralization, which listeners hear as

NAVIGATING THROUGH COLLEGE AND BEYOND

Biased Language

The American Psychological Association recommends this test: Substitute your own group
for the group you are discussing. If you are of-
fended by the resulting statement, revise your
phrasing to eliminate bias.

34e
sexist

patronizing, that is, as coming from someone who believes she or he is superior.

► ~~Because Asian students are whizzes at~~
We   *math whizzes*
~~math, we~~ all wanted ~~them~~ in our study
    ^   ^
group.

2. The generic use of *he* or *man*

Traditionally, the pronoun *he* and the noun *man* have been used to represent either gender. Today, however, the use of *he* or *man* or any other masculine noun to represent people in general is considered offensive.

BIASED	Everybody had his way.
REVISED	We all had our way.
BIASED	It's every man for himself.
REVISED	All of us have to save ourselves.

34e
sexist

Follow these simple principles to avoid gender bias in your writing:

- Replace terms that indicate gender with their gender-free equivalents:

No	Yes
chairman	chair, chairperson
congressman	representative, member of Congress
forefathers	ancestors
man, mankind	people, humans, humankind
man-made	artificial
policeman	police officer
spokesman	spokesperson

- Refer to men and women in parallel ways: *ladies and gentlemen*, *men and women*, *husband and wife*.

BIASED	D. H. Lawrence and Mrs. Woolf met each other, but Lawrence did not like the Bloomsbury circle that revolved around Virginia.

REVISED D. H. Lawrence and Virginia Woolf met each other, but Lawrence did not like the Bloomsbury circle that revolved around Woolf.

■ Replace the masculine pronouns *he, him, his,* and *himself* when they are being used generically to refer to both women and men. One way to replace masculine pronouns is to use the plural.

>   *Senators*   *their districts*
> ▶ ~~Each senator~~ returned to ~~his district~~
> during the break.

>   *Lawyers need*   *their*
> ▶ ~~A lawyer needs~~ to be frank with ~~his~~
> clients.

34e
sexist

Some writers alternate *he* and *she,* and *him* and *her.* This strategy is effective but distracting. The constructions *his or her* and *he or she* are acceptable as long as they are not used more than once in a sentence.

> ▶ **Each student in the psychology class**
> **was to choose a book,** ~~according to~~
>   *it*
> ~~his or her interests, to~~ **read** ~~the book~~
> **overnight,** ~~to~~ **do without** ~~his or her~~
> **normal sleep,** ~~to~~ **write a short**
>   *the book the next morning,*
> **summary of** ~~what he or she had read,~~
> **and then** ~~to~~ **see whether he or she**
> **dreamed about the book the following**
> **night.**

The constructions *his/her* and *s/he* are not acceptable.

Note: Using the neuter impersonal pronoun *one* can sometimes help you avoid masculine pronouns, but it can make your writing sound stuffy.

(For more on editing to avoid the generic use of he, him, his, *or* himself, *see Chapter 41, p. 312.)*

3. Sexist language
Avoid language that demeans or stereotypes women and men. Women are usually the explicit targets. For example, many labels and clichés imply that women are not as able or mature as men. Consider the meaning of words and phrases like *the fair sex, acting like a girl, poetess,* and *coed.*

35 Use exact language.

To convey your meaning clearly, you need to choose the right words. Is your choice of words as precise as it should be?

35a Choosing words with suitable connotations

Words have denotations and connotations. **Denotations** are the primary meanings of the word. **Connotations** are the feelings and images associated with a word.

As you revise, replace any word whose connotation does not fit what you want to say.

> The players' union should ~~request~~ that the
>   demand
>   ^
> NFL amend its pension plan.

If you cannot think of a more suitable word, consult a print or online thesaurus for **synonyms**—words with similar meanings. Keep in mind, however, that most words have connotations that allow them to work in some contexts but not in others. To find out more about a synonym's connotations, look the word up in a dictionary.

35b Including specific and concrete words

Specific words name particular kinds of things or items, such as *pines* or *college sophomores.*

Concrete words name things we can sense by touch, taste, smell, hearing, and sight, such as *velvet* or *sweater.*

By creating images that appeal to the senses, specific and concrete words make writing more precise.

> VAGUE   The trees were affected by the bad weather.
>
> PRECISE   The tall pines shook in the gale.

As you edit, develop specific and concrete details. Also check for overused, vague terms—such as *factor, thing, good, nice,* and *interesting*—and replace them with more specific and concrete words.

▶   **The protesters were charged with ~~things~~** ^crimes^
they never ~~did.~~ ^committed.^

35c Using standard idioms

Idioms are customary forms of expression. They are not always logical and are hard to translate. Often they involve selecting the right preposition. If you are not sure which preposition to use, look up the main word in a dictionary.

Some verbs, called **phrasal verbs,** include a preposition to make their idiomatic meaning complete:

- Henry *made up* with Gloria.
- Henry *made off* with Gloria.
- Henry *made out* with Gloria.

35d Avoiding clichés

A **cliché** is an overworked expression that no longer creates a vivid picture in a reader's imagination. Rephrase clichés in plain language.

> *made some good observations.*
> ► The speaker at our conference ~~hit the nail on the head.~~
>   ^

The list that follows gives some clichés to avoid:

Examples of Clichés

agony of suspense
beat a hasty retreat
beyond the shadow of
  a doubt
blind as a bat
calm, cool, and
  collected
cold, hard facts
cool as a cucumber
dead as a doornail
deep, dark secret
depths of despair
few and far between
flat as a pancake
green with envy
heave a sigh of relief
hit the nail on the head
last but not least

the other side of the
  coin
pass the buck
pretty as a picture
quick as a flash
rise to the occasion
sadder but wiser
sink or swim
smart as a whip
sneaking suspicion
straight and narrow
tired but happy
tried and true
ugly as sin
untimely death
white as a sheet
worth its weight in
  gold

35e Using suitable figures of speech

Figures of speech make writing vivid by supplementing the literal meaning of words. A **simile** is a comparison that contains the word *like* or *as*.

> ► **Hakim's smile was like sunshine after a rainstorm.**

A **metaphor** is an implied comparison. It treats one thing or action as if it were something else.

▶ **The senator's speech rolled along a familiar highway, past the usual landmarks: taxes and foreign policy.**

Because it is compressed, a metaphor is often more forceful than a simile.

Only compatible comparisons make prose vivid. Be careful not to mix metaphors.

| MIXED | His presentation of the plan was such a *well-constructed tower of logic* that we immediately decided *to come aboard.* |
| REVISED | His clear presentation of the plan immediately convinced us to come aboard. |

35f Avoiding the misuse of words

Avoid mistakes in your use of new terms and unfamiliar words. Consult a dictionary whenever you include an unfamiliar word in your writing.

▶ **The aristocracy ~~exuded~~ *exhibited* numerous vices, including greed and ~~license.~~ *licentiousness.***

36 Glossary of usage

The following words and expressions are often confused, misused, or considered nonstandard. This list will help you use these words precisely.

a, an Use *a* with a word that begins with a consonant sound: *a cat, a dog, a one-sided argument, a house.* Use *an* with a word that begins with a vowel sound: *an apple, an X-ray, an honor* (*h* is silent).

accept, except   *Accept* is a verb meaning "to receive willingly": *Please accept my apologies. Except* is a preposition meaning "but": *Everyone except Julie saw the film.*

adapt, adopt   *Adapt* means "to adjust or become accustomed to": *They adapted to the customs of their new country. Adopt* means "to take as one's own": *We adopted a puppy.*

advice, advise   *Advice* is a noun; *advise* is a verb: *I took his advice and deeply regretted it. I advise you to disregard it, too.*

affect, effect   As a verb, *affect* means "to influence": *Inflation affects our sense of security.* As a noun, *affect* means "a feeling or an emotion": *To study affect, psychologists probe the unconscious.* As a noun, *effect* means "result": *Inflation is one of the many effects of war.* As a verb, *effect* means "to make or accomplish": *Inflation has effected many changes in the way we spend money.*

36
usage

agree to, agree with   *Agree to* means "consent to"; *agree with* means "be in accord with": *They will agree to a peace treaty, even though they do not agree with each other on all points.*

ain't   A slang contraction for *is not, am not,* or *are not, ain't* should not be used in formal writing or speech.

all ready, already   *All ready* means "fully prepared"; *already* means "previously": *We were all ready to go out when we discovered that Jack had already ordered a pizza.*

all right, alright   *Alright* is nonstandard. Use *all right. He told me it was all right to miss class tomorrow.*

all together, altogether   *All together* expresses unity or common location; *altogether* means "completely," often in a tone of ironic understatement: *At the casino, it was altogether startling to see so many kinds of gambling all together in one place.*

allude, elude, refer to   *Allude* means "to refer indirectly": *He alluded to his miserable adolescence. Elude* means "to avoid" or "to escape from": *She eluded the police for nearly two days.* Do not use *allude* to mean "to refer directly": *The teacher referred* [not *alluded*] *to page 468 in the text.*

almost, most   *Almost* means "nearly." *Most* means "the greater part of." Do not use *most* when you mean *almost: He wrote to me about almost* [not *most*] *everything he did. He told his mother about most things he did.*

a lot   *A lot* is always two words. Do not use *alot.*

A.M., AM, a.m. These abbreviations mean "before noon" when used with numbers: *6 A.M., 6 a.m.* Be consistent, and do not use the abbreviations as a synonym for *morning: In the morning* [not *a.m.*], *the train is full.*

among, between Generally, use *among* with three or more nouns and *between* with two: *The distance between Boston and Knoxville is a thousand miles. The desire to quit smoking is common among those who have smoked for a long time.*

amoral, immoral *Amoral* means "neither moral nor immoral" and "not caring about moral judgments"; *immoral* means "morally wrong": *Unlike such amoral natural disasters as earthquakes and hurricanes, war is intentionally violent and therefore immoral.*

amount, number Use *amount* for quantities you cannot count; use *number* for quantities you can count: *The amount of oil left underground in the United States is a matter of dispute, but the number of oil companies losing money is tiny.*

an *See* a, an.

anxious, eager *Anxious* means "fearful": *I am anxious before a test. Eager* signals strong interest or desire: *I am eager to be done with that exam.*

anymore, any more *Anymore* means "no longer." *Any more* means "no more." Both are used in negative contexts: *I do not enjoy dancing anymore. I do not want any more peanut butter.*

anyone/any one, anybody/any body, everyone/ every one, everybody/every body *Anyone, anybody, everyone,* and *everybody* are indefinite pronouns: *Anybody can make a mistake.* When the pronoun *one* or the noun *body* is modified by the adjective *any* or *every,* the words should be separated by a space: *A good mystery writer accounts for every body that turns up in the story.*

as Do not use *as* as a synonym for *since, when,* or *because: I told him he should visit Alcatraz since* [not *as*] *he was going to San Francisco. When* [not *as*] *I complained about the meal, the cook said he did not like to eat there himself. Because* [not *as*] *we asked her nicely, our teacher decided to cancel the exam.*

as, like In formal writing, avoid the use of *like* as a conjunction: *He sneezed as if* [not *like*] *he had a cold. Like* is perfectly acceptable as a preposition that introduces a comparison: *She handled the reins like an expert.*

36
usage

at   Avoid the use of *at* to complete the notion of *where:* not *Where is Michael at?* but *Where is Michael?*

awful, awfully   Use *awful* and *awfully* to convey the emotion of terror or wonder (awe-full): *The vampire flew out the window with an awful shriek.* In writing, do not use *awful* to mean "bad" or *awfully* to mean "very" or "extremely."

awhile, a while   *Awhile* is an adverb: *Stay awhile with me* [but not *for awhile with me*]. *A while* consists of an article and a noun and can be used with or without a preposition: *A while ago I found my red pencil. I was reading under the tree for a while.*

bad, badly   *Bad* is an adjective used after a linking verb such as feel; *badly* is an adverb: *She felt bad about playing the piano badly at the recital.*

being as, being that   Do not use *being as* or *being that* as synonyms for *since* or *because: Because* [not *being as*] *the mountain was there, we had to climb it.*

belief, believe   *Belief* is a noun meaning "conviction"; *believe* is a verb meaning "to have confidence in the truth of": *Her belief that lying was often justified made it hard for us to believe her story.*

beside, besides   *Beside* is a preposition meaning "next to" or "apart from": *The ski slope was beside the lodge. She was beside herself with joy. Besides* is both a preposition and an adverb meaning "in addition to" or "except for": *Besides a bicycle, he will need a tent and a pack.*

better   Avoid using *better* in expressions of quantity: *Crossing the continent by train took more than* [not *better than*] *four days.*

between   *See* among, between.

bring, take   Use *bring* when an object is being moved toward you and *take* when it is being moved away: *Please bring me a new disk, and take the old one home with you.*

but that, but what   In expressions of doubt, avoid writing *but that* or *but what* when you mean *that: I have no doubt that* [not *but that*] *you can learn to write well.*

can, may   *Can* refers to ability; *may* refers to possibility or permission: *I see that you can Rollerblade without crashing into people; nevertheless, you may not Rollerblade on the promenade.*

can't hardly   This double negative is ungrammatical and self-contradictory: *I can* [not *can't*] *hardly understand algebra. I can't understand algebra.*

36 usage

capital, capitol *Capital* can refer to wealth or resources or to a city; *capitol* refers to a building where lawmakers meet: *Protesters traveled to the state capital to converge on the capitol steps.*

censor, censure *Censor* means "to remove or suppress material"; *censure* means "to reprimand formally": *The Chinese government has been censured by the U.S. Congress for censoring Web access.*

cite, sight, site The verb *cite* means "to quote or mention": *Be sure to cite all your sources in your bibliography.* As a noun, the word *sight* means "view": *It was love at first sight. Site* is a noun meaning "a particular place" as well as "a location on the Internet."

compare to, compare with Use *compare to* to point out similarities between two unlike persons or things: *She compared his singing to the croaking of a wounded frog.* Use *compare with* for differences or likenesses between two things in the same general category: *Compare Shakespeare's* Antony and Cleopatra *with Dryden's* All for Love.

complement, compliment *Complement* means "to go well with": *I consider sauerkraut the perfect complement to sausages. Compliment* means "praise": *She received many compliments on her thesis.*

conscience, conscious The noun *conscience* means "a sense of right and wrong": *His conscience bothered him.* The adjective *conscious* means "awake" or "aware": *I was conscious of a presence in the room.*

continual, continuous *Continual* means "repeated regularly and frequently": *She continually checked her computer for new e-mail. Continuous* means "extended or prolonged without interruption": *The car alarm made a continuous wail in the night.*

could care less *Could care less* is nonstandard; use *does not care at all* instead: *She does not care at all about her physics homework.*

could of, should of, would of Avoid these ungrammatical forms of *could have, should have,* and *would have.*

criteria, criterion *Criteria* is the plural form of the Latin word *criterion,* meaning "standard of judgment": *The criteria are not very strict. The most important criterion is whether you can do the work.*

data *Data* is the plural form of the Latin word *datum,* meaning "fact." Although *data* is often used informally as a singular noun, in writing, treat *data* as a plural noun: *The data indicate that recycling has gained popularity.*

differ from, differ with   *Differ from* expresses a lack of similarity; *differ with* expresses disagreement: *The ancient Greeks differed less from the Persians than we often think. Aristotle differed with Plato on some important issues.*

different from, different than   Use *different from*: *The east coast of Florida is very different from the west coast.*

discreet, discrete   *Discreet* means "tactful" or "prudent"; *discrete* means "separate" or "distinct": *What's a discreet way of telling them that these are two discrete issues?*

disinterested, uninterested   *Disinterested* means "impartial": *We expect members of a jury to be disinterested. Uninterested* means "indifferent" or "unconcerned": *Most people today are uninterested in alchemy.*

don't, doesn't   *Don't* is the contraction for *do not* and is used with *I, you, we, they,* and plural nouns; *doesn't* is the contraction for *does not* and is used with *he, she, it, one,* and singular nouns: *You don't know what you're talking about. He doesn't know what you're talking about either.*

each and every   Use one of these words or the other but not both: *Every cow came in at feeding time. Each one had to be watered.*

each other, one another   Use *each other* in sentences involving two subjects and *one another* in sentences involving more than two: *Husbands and wives should help each other. Classmates should share ideas with one another.*

eager   *See* anxious, eager.

effect   *See* affect, effect.

either, neither   Both *either* and *neither* are singular: *Neither of the two girls has played the game. Either of the two boys is willing to show you the way home. Either* has an intensive use that *neither* does not, and when it is used as an intensive, *either* is always negative: *She told him she would not go either. (For* [either . . . or] *and* [neither . . . nor] *constructions, see p. 293.)*

elicit, illicit   The verb *elicit* means "to draw out"; the adjective *illicit* means "unlawful": *The detective was unable to elicit any information about other illicit activities.*

elude   *See* allude, elude, refer to.

emigrate, immigrate   *Emigrate* means "to move away from one's country": *My father emigrated from*

36 usage

Vietnam in 1980. Immigrate means "to move to another country and settle there": *Father immigrated to the United States.*

eminent, imminent, immanent   *Eminent* means "celebrated" or "well known": *Many eminent Victorians were melancholy. Imminent* means "about to happen" or "about to come": *In August 1939, many Europeans sensed that war was imminent. Immanent* refers to something invisible but dwelling throughout the world: *Medieval Christians believed that God's power was immanent through the universe.*

etc.   The abbreviation *etc.* stands for the Latin *et cetera,* meaning "and others" or "and other things." Because *and* is included in the abbreviation, do not write *and etc.* In a series, a comma comes before *etc.,* just as it would before the coordinating conjunction that closes a series: *He brought string, wax, paper, etc.* In most college writing, it is better to end a series of examples with a final example or the words *and so on.*

36
usage

everybody/every body, everyone/every one   *See* anyone/any one . . .

except   *See* accept, except.

expect, suppose   *Expect* means "to hope" or "to anticipate": *I expect a good grade on my final paper. Suppose* means "to presume": *I suppose you did not win the lottery on Saturday.*

explicit, implicit   *Explicit* means "stated outright"; *implicit* means "implied, unstated": *Her explicit instructions were to go to the party without her, but the implicit message she conveyed was disapproval.*

farther, further   *Farther* describes geographical distances: *Ten miles farther on is a hotel. Further* means "in addition" when geography is not involved: *He said further that he didn't like my attitude.*

fewer, less   *Fewer* refers to items that can be counted individually; *less* refers to general amounts: *Fewer people signed up for indoor soccer this year than last. Your argument has less substance than you think.*

firstly   *Firstly* is common in British English but not in the United States. *First, second, third,* and so on are the accepted forms.

flaunt, flout   *Flaunt* means "to wave" or "to show publicly" with a delight tinged with pride and even arrogance: *He flaunted his wealth by wearing many gold chains. Flout* means "to scorn" or "to defy," especially in public without concern for the consequences: *She flouted the traffic laws by running through red lights.*

former, latter   *Former* refers to the first and *latter* to the second of two things mentioned previously: *Mario and Alice are both good cooks; the former is fonder of Chinese cooking, the latter of Mexican.*

further   *See* farther, further.

get   In formal writing, avoid colloquial uses of *get,* as in *get with it, get it all together, get-up-and-go, get it,* and *that gets me.*

good, well   *Good* is an adjective and should not be used in place of the adverb *well: He felt good about doing well on the exam.*

half, a half, half a   Write *half, a half,* or *half a* but not *half of, a half a,* or *a half of: Half the clerical staff went out on strike. I want a half-dozen eggs to throw at the actors. Half a loaf is better than none, unless you are on a diet.*

**36
usage**

hanged, hung   People are *hanged* by the neck until dead. Pictures and all other things that can be suspended are *hung.*

hopefully   *Hopefully* means "with hope." It is often misused to mean "it is hoped": *We waited hopefully for our ship to come in* [not *Hopefully, our ship will come in,* but *We hope our ship will come in*].

if . . . then   Avoid using these words in tandem. Redundant: *If I get my license, then I can drive a cab.* Better: *If I get my license, I can drive a cab. Once I get my license, I can drive a cab.*

if, whether   Use *whether* instead of *if* when expressing options: *If we go to the movies, we don't know whether we'll see a comedy or a drama.*

illicit   *See* elicit, illicit.

immigrate   *See* emigrate, immigrate.

imminent   *See* eminent, imminent, immanent.

immoral   *See* amoral, immoral.

implicit   *See* explicit, implicit.

imply, infer   *Imply* means "to suggest something without stating it directly": *By putting his fingers in his ears, he implied that she should stop singing. Infer* means "to draw a conclusion from evidence": *When she dozed off in the middle of his declaration of eternal love, he inferred that she did not feel the same way about him.*

in, in to, into *In* refers to a location inside something: *Charles kept a snake in his room. In to* refers to motion with a purpose: *The resident manager came in to capture it. Into* refers to movement from outside to inside or from separation to contact: *The snake escaped by crawling into a drain.*

incredible, incredulous *Incredible* stories and events cannot be believed; *incredulous* people do not believe: *Kaitlyn told an incredible story of being abducted by a UFO over the weekend. We were all incredulous.*

infer *See* imply, infer.

inside of, outside of The "*of*" is unnecessary in these phrases: *He was outside the house.*

ironically *Ironically* means "contrary to what was or might have been expected" in a sense that implies the unintentional or foolish: *Ironically, the peace activists were planning a "War against Hate" campaign.* It should not be confused with *surprisingly* ("unexpectedly") or with *coincidentally* ("occurring at the same time or place").

irregardless This construction is a double negative because both the prefix *ir-* and the suffix *-less* are negatives. Use *regardless* instead.

it's, its *It's* is a contraction, usually for *it is* but sometimes for *it has: It's often been said that English is a difficult language to learn. Its* is a possessive pronoun: *The dog sat down and scratched its fleas.*

kind(s) *Kind* is singular: *This kind of house is easy to build. Kinds* is plural and should be used only to indicate more than one kind: *These three kinds of toys are better than those two kinds.*

kind of, sort of These constructions should not be used to mean *somewhat* or *a little: I was somewhat tired after the party.*

lay, lie *Lay* means "to place." Its main forms are *lay, laid,* and *laid.* It generally has a direct object, specifying what has been placed: *She laid her book on the steps and left it there. Lie* means "to recline" and does not take a direct object. Its main forms are *lie, lay,* and *lain: She often lay awake at night.*

less *See* fewer, less.

like *See* as, like.

literally *Literally* means "actually" or "exactly as written": *Literally thousands gathered along the parade route.* Do not use *literally* as an intensive adverb when it can be misleading or even ridiculous, as here: *His blood literally boiled.*

loose, lose   *Loose* is an adjective that means "not securely attached"; *lose* is a verb that means "to misplace": *Better tighten that loose screw before you lose the whole structure.*

may   *See* can, may.

maybe, may be   *Maybe* is an adverb meaning "perhaps": *Maybe he can get a summer job as a lifeguard. May be* is a verb phrase meaning "is possible": *It may be that I can get a job as a lifeguard, too.*

moral, morale   *Moral* means "lesson," especially a lesson about standards of behavior or the nature of life: *The moral of the story is do not drink and drive. Morale* means "attitude" or "mental condition": *Employee morale dropped sharply after the president of the company was arrested.*

more/more of   *See* all/all of . . .

more important, more importantly   Use *more important*.

most   *See* almost, most.

myself (himself, herself, and so on)   Pronouns ending with *-self* refer to or intensify other words: *Jack hurt himself. Standing in the doorway was the man himself.* When you are unsure whether to use *I* or *me, she* or *her,* or *he* or *him* in a compound subject or object, you may be tempted to substitute one of the *-self* pronouns. Don't do it: *The quarrel was between her and me* [not *myself*]. *(For more on pronouns, see Part 7, starting on p. 309.)*

neither   *See* either, neither.

nohow, nowheres   These words are nonstandard for *anyway, in no way, in any way, in any place,* and *in no place.* Do not use them in formal writing.

number   *See* amount, number.

off of   Omit the *of: She took the painting off the wall.*

one another   *See* each other, one another.

outside of   *See* inside of, outside of.

plus   Avoid using *plus* as a coordinating conjunction (use *and*) or a transitional expression (use *moreover*): *He had to walk the dog, do the dishes, empty the garbage, and* [not *plus*] *write a term paper.*

precede, proceed   *Precede* means "come before"; *proceed* means "go forward": *Despite the heavy snows that preceded us, we managed to proceed up the hiking trail.*

**36
usage**

previous to, prior to Avoid these wordy and somewhat pompous substitutions for *before*.

principal, principle *Principal* is an adjective meaning "most important" or a noun meaning "the head of an organization" or "a sum of money": *Our principal objections to the school's principal are that he is a liar and a cheat. Principle* is a noun meaning "a basic standard or law": *We believe in the principles of honesty and fair play.*

proceed *See* precede, proceed.

raise, rise *Raise* means "to lift or cause to move upward." It takes a direct object—someone raises something: *I raised the windows in the classroom. Rise* means "to go upward." It does not take a direct object—something rises by itself: *We watched the balloon rise to the ceiling.*

real, really Do not use the words *real* or *really* when you mean *very: The cake was very [*not *real* or *really*] good.*

reason . . . is because, reason why These are redundant expressions. Use either *the reason is that* or *because: The reason he fell on the ice is that he cannot skate. He fell on the ice because he cannot skate.*

refer to *See* allude, elude, refer to.

respectfully, respectively *Respectfully* means "with respect": *Treat your partners respectfully. Respectively* means "in the given order": *The three Williams she referred to were Shakespeare, Wordsworth, and Yeats, respectively.*

rise *See* raise, rise.

set, sit *Set* is usually a transitive verb meaning "to establish" or "to place." It takes a direct object, and its principal parts are *set, set,* and *set: DiMaggio set the standard of excellence in fielding. She set the box down in the corner. Sit* is usually intransitive, meaning "to place oneself in a sitting position." Its principal parts are *sit, sat,* and *sat: The dog sat on command.*

shall, will Today, most writers use *will* instead of *shall* in the ordinary future tense for the first person: *I will celebrate my birthday by throwing a big party. Shall* is still used in questions. *Shall we dance?*

should of *See* could of, should of, would of.

site *See* cite, sight, site.

some Avoid using the adjective *some* in place of the adverb *somewhat: He felt somewhat [*not *some] better after a good night's sleep.*

some of *See* all/all of . . .

somewheres Use *somewhere* or *someplace* instead.

sort of *See* kind of, sort of.

suppose *See* expect, suppose.

sure Avoid confusing the adjective *sure* with the adverb *surely: The dress she wore to the party was surely bizarre.*

sure and *Sure and* is often used colloquially. In formal writing, *sure to* is preferred: *Be sure to [not be sure and] get to the wedding on time.*

take *See* bring, take.

than, then *Than* is a conjunction used in comparisons: *I am taller than you. Then* is an adverb referring to a point in time: *We will sing and then dance.*

that, which Many writers use *that* for restrictive (that is, essential) clauses and *which* for nonrestrictive (that is, nonessential) clauses: *The bull that escaped from the ring ran through my china shop, which was located in the square. (Also see Chapter 44, pp. 342–45.)*

36
usage

their, there, they're *Their* is a possessive pronoun: *They gave their lives. There* is an adverb of place: *She was standing there. They're* is a contraction of *they are: They're reading more poetry this semester.*

this here, these here, that there, them there When writing, avoid these nonstandard forms.

to, too, two *To* is a preposition; *too* is an adverb; *two* is a number: *The two of us got lost too many times on our way to his house.*

try and *Try to* is the standard form: *Try to [not try and] understand.*

uninterested *See* disinterested, uninterested.

unique *Unique* means "one of a kind." Do not use any qualifiers with it.

use, utilize *Use* is preferable because it is simpler: *Use five sources in your project.*

verbally, orally To say something *orally* is to say it aloud: *We agreed orally to share credit for the work, but when I asked her to confirm it in writing, she refused.* To say something *verbally* is to use words: *His eyes flashed anger, but he did not express his feelings verbally.*

wait for, wait on People *wait for* those who are late; they *wait on* tables.

weather, whether The noun *weather* refers to the atmosphere: *She worried that the weather would not clear* *up in time for the victory celebration. Whether* is a conjunction referring to a choice between alternatives: *I can't decide whether to go now or next week.*

well   *See* good, well.

whether   *See* if, whether, *and* weather, whether.

which, who, whose   *Which* is used for things, and *who* and *whose* for people: *My fountain pen, which I had lost last week, was found by a child who had never seen one before, whose whole life had been spent with ballpoints.*

who, whom   Use *who* with subjects and their complements. Use *whom* with objects (of verbs). *The person who will fill the post is Janelle, whom you met last week.* (Also see Chapter 41, pp. 320–21.)

will   *See* shall, will.

36
usage

would of   *See* could of, should of, would of.

your, you're   *Your* is a possessive pronoun: *Is that your new car? You're* is a contraction of *you are: You're a lucky guy.*

There is a core simplicity
to the English language
and its American variant,
but it's a slippery core.

—STEPHEN KING

PART
7

Editing
for Grammar
Conventions

37 Fix sentence fragments.

A word group that begins with a capital letter and ends with a period may not be a complete sentence. A complete sentence meets all three of the following requirements:

- **A sentence names a *subject,*** the *who* or *what* that the sentence addresses.

- **A sentence has a complete *verb* that indicates tense, person, and number.**

- **A sentence includes at least one independent *clause.*** An independent clause has a subject and a complete verb and does not begin with a subordinating word such as *although, because, that,* or *which.*

In the following example, the first word group meets all three requirements and is a complete sentence. Although the second word group has a subject and a complete verb, they are part of a dependent clause that begins with the subordinating word *because.* Therefore, it is not a complete sentence.

> **POSSIBLE FRAGMENT** Many people feel threatened by globalization. *Because they think it will undermine their cultural traditions.*

You can fix fragments in one of two ways: either transform them into sentences, or attach them to a nearby independent clause.

▶ **Many people feel threatened by globalization. ~~Because they~~ They think it will undermine their cultural traditions.**

▶ **Many people feel threatened by globalization,/ ~~Because~~ because they think it will undermine their cultural traditions.**

37a Repairing dependent-clause fragments

Fragments that begin with a subordinating word such as *although, even though,* or *whenever* can usually be attached to a nearby independent clause.

► **None of the thirty-three subjects indicated any concern about the amount or kind of fruit the institution served. ~~Even~~ though all of them identified diet as an important issue for those with diabetes.**

even

It is sometimes better to transform such a fragment into a complete sentence by deleting the subordinating word.

► **The harmony of our group was disrupted in two ways. ~~When members~~ either disagreed about priorities or advocated different political strategies.**

Members

NAVIGATING THROUGH COLLEGE AND BEYOND

Intentional Fragments

Advertisers often use attention-getting fragments: "Hot deal! Big savings! Because you're worth it." Occasionally, you may want to use a sentence fragment for stylistic reasons. Keep in mind, however, that advertising and college writing have different contexts and purposes. In formal writing, use deliberate sentence fragments sparingly.

37a
frag

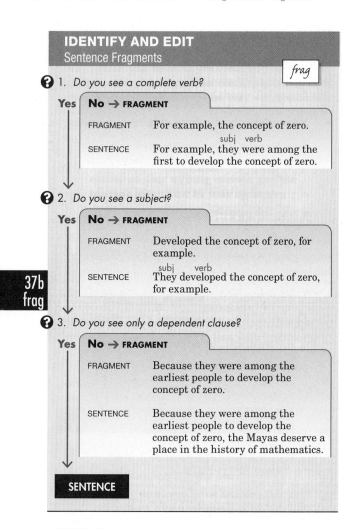

IDENTIFY AND EDIT
Sentence Fragments

frag

? 1. *Do you see a complete verb?*

Yes | **No → FRAGMENT**

FRAGMENT | For example, the concept of zero.
SENTENCE | subj   verb
For example, they were among the first to develop the concept of zero.

? 2. *Do you see a subject?*

Yes | **No → FRAGMENT**

FRAGMENT | Developed the concept of zero, for example.
SENTENCE | subj   verb
They developed the concept of zero, for example.

? 3. *Do you see only a dependent clause?*

Yes | **No → FRAGMENT**

FRAGMENT | Because they were among the earliest people to develop the concept of zero.

SENTENCE | Because they were among the earliest people to develop the concept of zero, the Mayas deserve a place in the history of mathematics.

SENTENCE

37b
frag

37b Repairing phrase fragments

Often unintentional fragments are **phrases,** word groups that lack a subject or a complete verb or both and usually function as modifiers or nouns. Phrase fragments frequently begin with **verbals**—words derived from verbs, such as *putting* or *to put.* They do not change form to reflect tense and number.

FRAGMENT That summer, we had the time of our lives. *Swimming in the mountain lake each day and exploring the nearby woods.*

One way to fix this fragment is to transform it into an independent clause with its own subject and verbs:

▶ **That summer, we had the time of our lives.**
We swam
~~**Swimming**~~ **in the mountain lake each day**
 ^
 explored
and ~~exploring~~ the nearby woods.
 ^

Another way to fix the problem is to attach the fragment to the part of the previous sentence that it modifies (in this case, *the time of our lives*).

▶ **That summer, we had the time of our lives,/**
 ^
 swimming
~~**Swimming**~~ **in the mountain lake each day**
 ^

and exploring the nearby woods.

Phrase fragments can also begin with one-word prepositions such as *as, at, by, for, from, in, of, on,* or *to.* Attach these fragments to a nearby sentence.

▶ **Impressionist painters often depicted**
 at
their subjects in everyday situations,/ ~~At~~ a
 ^ ^
restaurant, perhaps, or by the seashore.

37c Repairing other types of fragments

Word groups that start with transitions or with words that introduce examples, appositives, lists, and compound predicates can also cause problems.

1. Word groups that start with transitions
Some fragments start with two- or three-word prepositions that function as transitions, such as *as well as, as compared with,* or *in addition to.*

37c
frag

► For sixty-five years, the growth in consumer spending has been both steep and steady~~,~~ *in* ~~In~~ contrast to the growth in gross domestic product (GDP), which has fluctuated significantly.

2. Words and phrases that introduce examples
It is always a good idea to check word groups beginning with *for example, like, specifically,* or *such as.*

► Elizabeth I of England faced many dangers as a princess. For example, *she fell* ~~falling~~ out of favor with her sister, Queen Mary, and *was* ~~being~~ imprisoned in the Tower of London.

3. Appositives
An **appositive** is a noun or noun phrase that renames a noun or pronoun.

► In 1965, Lyndon Johnson increased the number of troops in Vietnam~~,~~ *a* ~~A~~ former French colony in Southeast Asia.

4. Lists
You can connect a list to the preceding sentence using a colon or a dash.

► In the 1930s, three great band leaders helped popularize jazz~~,~~: Louis Armstrong, Benny Goodman, and Duke Ellington.

5. Compound predicates
A **compound predicate** is made up of at least two verbs as well as their objects and modifiers, connected by a coordinating conjunction such as *and, but,* or *or.* The parts

of a compound predicate have the same subject and should be together in one sentence.

▶ **The group gathered at dawn at the base of the mountain,/ And assembled their gear in preparation for the morning's climb.**

and

38 Repair comma splices and run-ons sentences.

A **comma splice** is a sentence with at least two independent clauses joined by only a comma.

**38
cs/run-on**

> **COMMA SPLICE** The media influence people's political views, the family is another major source of ideas about the proper role of government.

A **run-on sentence,** sometimes called a **fused sentence,** does not even have a comma between the independent clauses, making it difficult for readers to tell where one clause ends and the next begins.

> **RUN-ON** Local news shows often focus on crime stories network and cable news broadcasts cover national politics in detail.

Comma splices and run-ons often occur when clauses are linked with a transitional expression such as *as a result, for example, in addition, in other words,* or *on the contrary* or a conjunctive adverb such as *however, consequently, moreover,* or *nevertheless. (See p. 287 for a list of familiar conjunctive adverbs and transitional expressions.)*

> **COMMA SPLICE** Rare books can be extremely valuable, *for example,* an original edition of Audubon's *Birds of America* is worth more than a million dollars.

> **RUN-ON**   Most students complied with the
> new policy *however* a few refused to
> do so.

Run-ons may also occur when a sentence's second clause either specifies or explains its first clause.

> **RUN-ON**   The economy is still recovering
> from the financial crisis that began
> in 2007 Bear Stearns was the first
> large investment bank to experi-
> ence problems that year.

You can repair comma splices and run-on sentences in one of five ways:

- Join the two clauses with a comma and a coordinating conjunction *(and, but, or, nor, for, so, yet).*
- Join the two clauses with a semicolon.
- Separate the clauses into two sentences.
- Turn one of the independent clauses into a dependent clause.
- Transform the two clauses into a single independent clause.

38a Joining two clauses with a comma and a coordinating conjunction such as *and* or *but*

Be sure to choose the coordinating conjunction that most clearly expresses the logical relationship between the clauses. A comma *must* precede the conjunction, or the sentence remains a run-on.

▶ **John is a very stubborn person, ⟨*so*⟩ I had a hard**

time convincing him to let me take the wheel.

38b Joining two clauses with a semicolon

A semicolon tells readers that two closely related clauses are logically connected. However, a semicolon does not spell out the logic of the connection.

► **Most students complied with the new**
  policy,/; a few refused.
      ^

To show the logic of the connection, you can add a conjunctive adverb or transitional expression.

► **Most students complied with the new**
      ; however,
  policy,/ a few refused to do so.
          ^

**Conjunctive Adverbs and
Transitional Expressions**

also	incidentally	now
as a result	indeed	nonetheless
besides	in fact	of course
certainly	in other words	on the contrary
consequently	instead	otherwise
finally	in the meantime	similarly
for example	likewise	still
for instance	meanwhile	then
furthermore	moreover	therefore
however	nevertheless	thus
in addition	next	undoubtedly

**38b
cs/run-on**

The conjunctive adverb or transitional expression is usually followed by a comma when it appears at the beginning of the second clause. It can also appear in the middle of a clause, set off by two commas, or at the end, preceded by a comma.

► **Most students complied with the new**
        , however,
  policy,/; a few refused.
      ^   ^
► **Most students complied with the new**
          , however
  policy,/; a few refused.
      ^   ^

When the first independent clause introduces or expands on the second one, you can use a colon instead of a semicolon.

► **Professor Kim then revealed his most**

  important point: the paper would count for
              ^

  half my grade.

IDENTIFY AND EDIT
Comma Splices and Run-ons

| cs | run-on |

These questions can help you spot comma splices and run-on sentences:

❓ 1. *Does the sentence contain only one independent clause?*

| No | Yes → **Not a run-on or comma splice** |

↓

❓ 2. *Does it contain two independent clauses joined by a comma and a coordinating conjunction (and, but, or, not, for, so, or yet)?*

| No | Yes → **Not a run-on or comma splice** |

↓

❓ 3. *Does it contain two independent clauses joined by a semi-colon, a semicolon and a transitional expression, a colon, or a dash?*

38b
cs/run-on

| No | Yes → **Not a run-on or comma splice** |

↓

RUN-ON	├──── independent clause ────┤ Football and most other team sports have a time limit ├──── independent clause ────┤ baseball has no time limit.
COMMA SPLICE	Football and most other team sports have a time limit, baseball has no time limit.
REVISED: COMMA AND COORDINATING CONJUNCTION	Football and most other team sports have a time limit, but baseball has no time limit. *[See 38a.]*
REVISED: SEMICOLON	Football and most other team sports have a time limit; baseball has no time limit. *[See 38b.]*
REVISED: TWO SENTENCES	Football and most other team sports have a time limit. Baseball has no time limit. *[See 38c.]*
REVISED: SUBORDINATION	Although football and most other team sports have a time limit, baseball has none. *[See 38d.]*
REVISED: ONE INDEPENDENT CLAUSE	Baseball, unlike football and most other team sports, has no time limit. *[See 38e.]*

38c Separating clauses into two sentences

The simplest way to correct comma splices and run-on sentences is to turn the clauses into separate sentences.

► I realized that it was time to choose,/ ~~either~~ *. Either*

I had to learn how to drive, or I had to move

back to the city.

When the two independent clauses are part of a quotation, with a phrase such as *he said* or *she noted* between them, each clause should be a separate sentence.

► "This was the longest day of my life," she
said,/ ~~"unfortunately,~~ it's not over yet." *"Unfortunately,*

38d Turning one of the independent clauses into a dependent clause

Remember that readers will expect subsequent sentences to tell them more about the subject of the main clause.

► ~~Most~~ students complied with the new policy, *Although most*

~~however~~ a few refused to do so.

38e Transforming two clauses into one independent clause

Transforming two clauses into one clear and correct independent clause is often worth the work.

► I realized that it was time ~~to choose,/~~ either
~~I had~~ to learn how to drive or ~~I had~~ to move
back to the city.

Sometimes you can change one of the clauses to a phrase and place it next to the word it modifies.

► Baseball cards are an obsession among
, *first printed in the nineteenth century,*
some collectors. ~~The cards were first~~
~~printed in the nineteenth century.~~

39 Maintain subject-verb agreement.

39
sv agr

Verbs must agree with their subjects in **person** (first, second, or third—*I, we; you; he, she, it, they*) and **number** (singular or plural). For regular verbs, the present tense -*s* or -*es* ending is added to the verb if its subject is third-person singular; otherwise, the verb has no ending.

Note, however, that the verb *be* has irregular forms in both the present and the past tense. The irregular verbs *be, have,* and *do* have the following forms in the present and past tenses.

Verb Tenses (Present and Past)

	READ (REGULAR)	BE	HAVE	DO
SINGULAR				
First person	read	am	have	do/don't
(I)	*(read)*	*(was)*	*(had)*	*(did/didn't)*
Second person	read	are	have	do/don't
(you)	*(read)*	*(were)*	*(had)*	*(did/didn't)*
Third person	reads	is	has	does/doesn't
(he, she, it)	*(reads)*	*(was)*	*(had)*	*(did/didn't)*
PLURAL				
First person	read	are	have	do/don't
(we)	*(read)*	*(were)*	*(had)*	*(did/didn't)*
Second person	read	are	have	do/don't
(you)	*(read)*	*(were)*	*(had)*	*(did/didn't)*
Third person	read	are	have	do/don't
(they)	*(read)*	*(were)*	*(had)*	*(did/didn't)*

IDENTIFY AND EDIT
Problems with Subject-Verb Agreement

agr

❋ 1. *Find the verb.*

	verb
PROBLEM SENTENCE	Hamlet and Claudius *brings* down the Danish royal family.

Verbs specify action, condition, or state of being.

❋ 2. *Ask the* who *or* what *question to identify the subject.*

	subject verb
PROBLEM SENTENCE	*Hamlet and Claudius brings* down the Danish royal family.

The answer to the question "What brings?" is *Hamlet and Claudius.*

❋ 3. *Determine the person (first, second, or third) and number (singular or plural) of the subject.*

	subject
PROBLEM SENTENCE	*Hamlet and Claudius* brings down the Danish royal family.

The subject of the sentence—*Hamlet and Claudius*—is a compound joined by *and* and is third-person plural.

❋ 4. *If necessary, change the verb to agree with the subject.*

	bring
EDITED PROBLEM SENTENCE	Hamlet and Claudius ~~brings~~ down the Danish royal family. ^

Bring is the third-person plural form of the verb.

39a
sv/agr

39a When a word group separates the subject from the verb

To locate the subject of a sentence, find the verb, and then ask the *who* or *what* question about it ("Who is?" "What is?"). Does that subject match the verb in number?

► The leaders of the trade union *opposes* the
oppose

new law.

The answer to the question "Who opposes?" is *leaders,* a plural noun, so the verb should be in the plural form: *oppose.*

If a word group beginning with *as well as, along with,* or *in addition to* follows a singular subject, the subject does not become plural.

► My teacher, as well as other faculty
members, *oppose* the new school policy.
opposes

39b Compound subjects

Compound subjects are made up of two or more parts joined by either a coordinating conjunction *(and, or, nor)* or a correlative conjunction *(both . . . and, either . . . or, neither . . . nor).*

1. **Most compound subjects are plural.**

   PLURAL   *The king and his advisers were*
   shocked by this turn of events.

   PLURAL   This poem's *first line and
   last word* have a powerful

   effect on the reader.

2. **Some compound subjects are singular.**
   Compound subjects should be treated as singular in the following circumstances:

   ■ When they are considered as a single unit:

   ► In some ways, *forty acres and
   a mule* continues to be what is

   needed.

- When they are preceded by the word *each* or *every:*

  ► *Each man and woman deserves* respect.

- When they refer to the same entity:

  ► *My best girlfriend and most dependable adviser is* my mother.

3. **Some compound subjects can be either plural or singular.** Compound subjects connected by *or, nor, either . . . or,* or *neither . . . nor* can take either a singular or a plural verb, depending on the subject that is closest to the verb.

   SINGULAR   **Either the children or *their mother* is to blame.**

   PLURAL   **Neither the experimenter nor *her subjects* were aware of the takeover.**

Sentences often sound less awkward with the plural subject closer to the verb.

39c   Collective subjects

A **collective noun** names a unit made up of many persons or things, treating it as an entity, such as *audience, family, group,* and *team.*

- **Most often, collective nouns are singular.** Words such as *news, athletics, physics,* and *statistics* are usually singular as well, despite their -*s* ending. Units of measurement used collectively, such as *six inches* or *20 percent,* are also treated as singular.

  ► The *audience is* restless.

39c
sv agr

► That *news leaves* me speechless.

► *One-fourth* of the liquid *was* poured
into test tube 1.

▪ **Some collective subjects are plural.**
When the members of a group are acting
as individuals, the collective subject can be
considered plural.

► The *group were* passing around a

bottle of beer.

You may want to add a modifying phrase that
contains a plural noun to make the sentence
clearer and avoid awkwardness.

► The *group of troublemakers were*
passing around a bottle of beer.

When units of measurement refer to people
or things, they are plural.

► *One-fourth* of the students *are* failing

the course.

39d Indefinite subjects

Indefinite pronouns do not refer to a specific person or item.

▪ **Most indefinite pronouns are singular.**
The following indefinite pronouns are always
singular: *anybody, anyone, anything, each, either, everybody, everyone, everything, neither,
nobody, no one, none, nothing, one, somebody,
someone,* and *something.*

► *Everyone* in my hiking club *is* an

experienced climber.

None and *neither* are always singular.

► In the movie, five men set out on an expedition, but *none returns.*

► *Neither sees* a way out of this predicament.

■ **Some indefinite pronouns are always plural.** A handful of indefinite pronouns that mean more than one by definition *(both, few, many, several)* are always plural.

► *Both* of us *want* to go to the rally for the environment.

■ **Some indefinite pronouns can be either plural or singular.** Some indefinite pronouns *(some, any, all, most)* can be either plural or singular, depending on whether they refer to a plural or singular noun in the sentence.

**39e
sv agr**

► *Some* of the *book is* missing, but *all* of the *papers are* here.

39e When the subject comes after the verb

In most English sentences, the verb comes after the subject. Sometimes, however, a writer will switch this order.

► Out back behind the lean-to *stand* *an old oak tree and a weeping willow.*

In sentences that begin with *there is* or *there are,* the subject always follows the verb.

► There *is* a worn wooden *bench* in the shade of the two trees.

39f Subject complement

A **subject complement** renames and specifies the sentence's subject. It follows a **linking verb**—a verb, often a form of *be,* that joins the subject to its description or definition: *children are innocent.* In the following sentence, the verb has been changed to agree with *gift,* the subject, instead of *books,* the subject complement.

▶   One gift that gives her pleasure ~~are~~ books.
         ^ *is*

39g Relative pronouns (who, which, or that)

39g sv agr

When a relative pronoun such as *who, which,* or *that* is the subject of a dependent clause, it is taking the place of a noun that appears earlier in the sentence—its **antecedent.** The verb that goes with *who, which,* or *that* must agree with this antecedent.

▶   **Measles is a childhood *disease that has* dangerous side effects.**

The phrase *one of the* implies more than one and so is plural. *Only one of the* implies just one, however, and is singular. Generally, use the plural form of the verb when the phrase *one of the* comes before the antecedent. Use the singular form of the verb when *only one of the* comes before the plural noun.

PLURAL

Tuberculosis is *one of the* diseases *that have* long, tragic histories in many parts of the world.

SINGULAR

Barbara is the *only one of the* scientists *who has* a degree in physics.

39h Phrases beginning with *-ing* verbs

A **gerund phrase** is an *-ing* verb form followed by objects, complements, or modifiers. When a gerund phrase is the subject in a sentence, it is singular.

► *Experimenting with drugs is* **a dangerous practice.**

39i Titles of works, names of companies, and words considered as words

► *The Two Gentlemen of Verona* ~~are~~ *is* **considered the weakest of Shakespeare's comedies.**

40a vb

► **Kraft Foods** ~~include~~ *includes* **many different brands.**

► **In today's highly partisan politics** *moderates* ~~have~~ *has* **come to mean "wishy-washy people."**

40 Check for problems with verbs.

Verbs report action and show time. They change form to indicate person and number, voice and mood.

40a Learning the forms of regular and irregular verbs

English verbs have five main forms, except for the verb *be,* which has eight:

- The **base form** is the form found in a dictionary. *(For irregular verbs, other forms are given as well. See pp. 299–300 for a list.)*
- The **present tense** form indicates an action occurring at the moment, habitually, or at a set future time and also introduces quotations, literary events, and scientific facts *(pp. 303–5 and pp. 306–7)*. The third-person singular present tense is the *-s* form.
- The **past tense** indicates an action completed at a specific time in the past *(pp. 303–5)*.
- The **past participle** is used with *have, has,* or *had* to form the perfect tenses *(pp. 303–5)*; with a form of the *be* verb to form the passive voice *(Chapter 33, pp. 256–57)*; and as an adjective (the *polished* silver).

- The **present participle** is used with a form of the *be* verb to form the progressive tenses *(pp. 303–5)*. It can also be used as a noun (the *writing* is finished) and as an adjective (the *smiling* man).

Regular verbs always add *-d* or *-ed* to the base verb to form the past tense and past participle. **Irregular verbs,** by contrast, do not form the past tense or past participle in a consistent way. Here are the five principal forms of the regular verb *walk* and the irregular verb *begin* as well as the eight forms of the verb *be.*

Principal Forms of *Walk* and *Begin*

BASE	PRESENT TENSE (THIRD PERSON)	PAST TENSE	PAST PARTICIPLE	PRESENT PARTICIPLE
walk	walks	walked	walked	walking
begin	begins	began	begun	beginning

Principal Forms of *Be*

BASE	PRESENT TENSE	PAST TENSE	PAST PARTICIPLE	PRESENT PARTICIPLE
be	I *am.* He, she, it *is.* We, you, they *are.*	I *was.* He, she, it *was.* We, you, they *were.*	I have *been.*	I am *being.*

1. A list of common irregular verbs You can also find the past tense and past participle forms of irregular verbs by looking up the base form in a standard dictionary.

Forms of Common Irregular Verbs

BASE	PAST TENSE	PAST PARTICIPLE
arise	arose	arisen
awake	awoke	awoke/awakened
be	was/were	been
beat	beat	beaten
become	became	become
begin	began	begun
blow	blew	blown
break	broke	broken
bring	brought	brought
buy	bought	bought
catch	caught	caught
choose	chose	chosen
cling	clung	clung
come	came	come
do	did	done
draw	drew	drawn
drink	drank	drunk
drive	drove	driven
eat	ate	eaten
fall	fell	fallen
fight	fought	fought
fly	flew	flown
forget	forgot	forgotten/forgot
forgive	forgave	forgiven
freeze	froze	frozen
get	got	gotten/got
give	gave	given
go	went	gone
grow	grew	grown
hang	hung	hung (for things)
hang	hanged	hanged (for people)
have	had	had
hear	heard	heard
know	knew	known
lay	laid	laid
lie	lay	lain
lose	lost	lost
pay	paid	paid
raise	raised	raised

**40a
vb**

BASE	PAST TENSE	PAST PARTICIPLE
ride	rode	ridden
ring	rang	rung
rise	rose	risen
say	said	said
see	saw	seen
set	set	set
shake	shook	shaken
sit	sat	sat
spin	spun	spun
steal	stole	stolen
spend	spent	spent
strive	strove/strived	striven/strived
swear	swore	sworn
swim	swam	swum
swing	swung	swung
take	took	taken
tear	tore	torn
tread	trod	trod/trodden
wear	wore	worn
weave	wove	woven
wring	wrung	wrung
write	wrote	written

**40a
vb**

2. *Went* and *gone*, *saw* and *seen*   *Went* and *saw* are the past tense forms of the irregular verbs *go* and *see*. *Gone* and *seen* are the past participle forms. These verb forms are sometimes confused.

► I had ~~went~~ there yesterday.
   ^gone^

► We ~~seen~~ the rabid dog and called for help.
   ^saw^

3. Irregular verbs such as *drink (drank/drunk)*
For a few irregular verbs, such as *swim (swam/ swum), drink (drank/drunk),* and *ring (rang/rung),* the difference between the past tense form and the past participle is only one letter. Be careful not to mix up these forms in your writing.

► I had ~~drank~~ more than eight bottles of
   ^drunk^

   water that day.

►   The church bell had ~~rang~~ *rung* five times before

she heard it.

40b   Distinguishing between *lay* and *lie,*
sit and *set,* and *rise* and *raise*

Even experienced writers confuse the verbs *lay* and
lie, sit and *set,* and *rise* and *raise.* The correct forms
are given in the following table.

Often-Confused Verbs and Their Principal Forms

BASE	-*S* FORM	PAST	PAST PARTICIPLE	PRESENT PARTICIPLE
lay (to place)	lays	laid	laid	laying
lie (to recline)	lies	lay	lain	lying
lie (to speak an untruth)	lies	lied	lied	lying
rise (to go/get up)	rises	rose	risen	rising
sit (to be seated)	sits	sat	sat	sitting
set (to put on a surface)	sets	sat	set	setting

40b vb

One verb in each of these groups *(lay, set, raise)* is
transitive, which means that an object receives the
action of the verb. The other verb *(lie, sit, rise)* is
intransitive and cannot take an object. You should
use a form of *lay, raise,* or *set* if you can replace the
verb with *place* or *put.*

►   The dog *lays a bone* at your feet, then *lies*

down and closes his eyes.

►   As the flames *rise,* the heat *raises*
direct object
the temperature of the room.

►   The technician *sits* down and *sets*
direct object
the samples in front of her.

Lay (to place) and *lie* (to recline) are also confusing because the past tense of the irregular verb *lie* is *lay (lie, lay, lain)*. Always double-check the verb *lay* when it appears in your writing.

► He washed the dishes carefully and ~~lay~~ *laid* them on a clean towel.

40d vb

40c   Adding an -s or -es ending

In the present tense, almost all verbs add an *-s* or *-es* ending if the subject is third-person singular. *(See Chapter 39, p. 290, for more on standard subject-verb combinations.)* Third-person singular subjects can be nouns *(woman, Benjamin, desk)*, pronouns *(he, she, it)*, or indefinite pronouns *(everyone)*.

► The stock market ~~rise~~ *rises* when economic news is good.

If the subject is in the first person *(I)*, the second person *(you)*, or the third-person plural *(people, they)*, the verb does *not* add an *-s* or *-es* ending.

► You invests your money wisely.

► People needs to learn about companies before buying their stock.

40d   Adding a -d or an -ed ending

These endings should be included on all regular verbs in the past tense and all past participles of regular verbs.

► The driving instructor ~~ask~~ *asked* the student driver to pull over to the curb.

► After we had ~~mix~~ *mixed* the formula, we let it cool.

Also check for missing *-d* or *-ed* endings on past participles used as adjectives.

concerned
► The ~~concern~~ parents met with the school
board. ^

40e Using tenses accurately

Tenses show the time of a verb's action. English
has three basic time frames—present, past, and
future—and each tense has simple, perfect, and
progressive verb forms to indicate the time span of
the actions taking place. *(For a review of the pres-*
ent tense forms of a typical verb and of the verbs be,
have, *and do, see p. 290; for a review of the principal*
forms of regular and irregular verbs, which are used
to form tenses, see pp. 297–300.)

40e
vb

1. The simple present and past tenses The
simple present tense describes actions occurring
at the moment, habitually, or at a set future time.
The **simple past tense** is used for actions completed at a specific time in the past.

SIMPLE PRESENT

Every May, she *plans* next year's marketing
strategy.

SIMPLE PAST

In the early morning hours before the office
opened, she *planned* her marketing strategy.

2. The simple future tense The **simple future**
tense takes *will* plus the verb. It is used for actions
that have not yet begun.

SIMPLE FUTURE

In May, I *will plan* next year's marketing
strategy.

3. The perfect tenses The **perfect tenses** take
a form of *have (has, had)* plus the past participle.

They indicate actions that were or will be completed by the time of another action or a specific time. The present perfect also describes actions that continue into the present.

> **PRESENT PERFECT**
>
> She *has* already *planned* next year's marketing strategy.

> **PAST PERFECT**
>
> By the time she resigned, Maria *had* already *planned* next year's marketing strategy.

> **FUTURE PERFECT**
>
> By May 31, she *will have planned* next year's marketing strategy.

**40e
vb**

When the verb in the past perfect is irregular, be sure to use the proper form of the past participle.

▶ **By the time the week was over, both plants
had ~~grew~~ five inches.**
  grown
  ∧

4. Progressive tenses The progressive tenses take a form of *be (am, are, was, were)* plus the present participle. The progressive forms of the simple and perfect tenses indicate ongoing action.

> **PRESENT PROGRESSIVE**
>
> She *is planning* next year's marketing strategy now.

> **PAST PROGRESSIVE**
>
> She *was planning* next year's marketing strategy when she started to look for another job.

> **FUTURE PROGRESSIVE**
>
> During the month of May, she *will be planning* next year's marketing strategy.

References to planned events that didn't happen take *was/were going to* plus the base form.

> She *was going to plan* the marketing strategy, but she left the company.

5. Perfect progressive tenses The **perfect progressive tenses** take *have* plus *be* plus the verb. These tenses indicate an action that takes place over a specific period of time. The present perfect progressive tense describes actions that start in the past and continue to the present; the past and future perfect progressive tenses are used for actions that ended or will end at a specified time or before another action.

PRESENT PERFECT PROGRESSIVE

She *has been planning* next year's marketing strategy since the beginning of May.

PAST PERFECT PROGRESSIVE

She *had been planning* next year's marketing strategy when she was offered another job.

FUTURE PERFECT PROGRESSIVE

By May 18, she *will have been planning* next year's marketing strategy for more than two weeks.

40f 40f vb

40f Using the past perfect tense

When a past event was ongoing but ended before a particular time or another past event, use the past perfect rather than the simple past.

▶ **Before the Johnstown Flood occurred in**
  had
  1889, people in the area ^expressed their

  concern about the safety of the dam on the

  Conemaugh River.

People expressed their concern before the flood occurred.

If two past events happened simultaneously, however, use the simple past, not the past perfect.

▶ **When the Conemaugh flooded, many people in the area ~~had~~ lost their lives.**

We think of research findings as having been collected at one time in the past. Use the past or present perfect tense to report the results of research:

► Three of the compounds (nos. 2, 3, and 6)
responded
~~respond~~ positively by turning purple.
 ^

has reviewed
► Clegg (1990) ~~reviews~~ studies of workplace
 ^

organization focused on struggles for

control of the labor process.

40g Using the present tense

If the conventions of a discipline require you to state what your paper does, do so in the present, not the future, tense.

► In this paper, I *describe* the effects of
increasing NaCl concentrations on the
germination of radish seeds.

Here are some other special uses of the present tense:

▪ By convention, events in a novel, short story, poem, or other literary work are described in the present tense.

► Even though Huck's journey down the
is
river ~~was~~ an escape from society, his
 ^
is
relationship with Jim ~~was~~ a form of
 ^
community.

▪ Like events in a literary work, scientific facts are considered to be perpetually present, even though they were discovered in the past. (Theories that have been disproved should appear in the past tense.)

have
► Mendel discovered that genes ~~had~~
different forms, or alleles. ^

- The present tense is also used to introduce a quotation, paraphrase, or summary of someone else's writing.

> ►   William Julius Wilson ~~wrote~~ *writes* that "the
>
>   disappearance of work has become
>
>   a characteristic feature of the inner-
>
>   city ghetto" (31).

Note: When using APA style, introduce others' writing or research findings with the past tense (for example, Wilson *wrote*) or past perfect tense (Johnson *has found*).

40h Using complete verbs

**40h
vb**

With only a few exceptions, all English sentences must contain a **complete verb,** which consists of the main verb along with any helping verbs that are needed to express the tense *(see pp. 303–5)* or voice *(see pp. 256–57).* **Helping verbs** include forms of *be, have,* and *do* and the modal verbs *can, could, may, might, shall, should, will, ought to, must,* and *would.* Helping verbs can be part of contractions *(he's running, we'd better go),* but they cannot be left out of the sentence entirely.

► They *will* be going on a field trip next week.

Do not use *of* in place of *have.*

► I could ~~of~~ *have* finished earlier.

A **linking verb,** often a form of *be,* connects the subject to a description or definition of it: *Cats are mammals.* Linking verbs can be part of contractions *(she's a student),* but they should not be left out entirely.

► Montreal *is* a major Canadian city.

40i Using the subjunctive mood

The **mood** of a verb indicates the writer's attitude. Use the **indicative mood** to state or to question facts, acts, and opinions *(Our collection is on display. Did you see it?).* Use the **imperative mood** for commands, directions, and entreaties. The subject of an imperative sentence is always *you,* but the *you* is usually understood, not written out *(Shut the door!).* Use the **subjunctive mood** to express a wish or a demand or to make a statement contrary to fact *(I wish I were a millionaire).* The mood that writers have the most trouble with is the subjunctive.

Verbs in the subjunctive mood may be in the present tense, past tense, or perfect tense. Present tense subjunctive verbs do not change form to signal person or number. The only form used is the verb's base form: *accompany* or *be,* not *accompanies* or *am, are, is.* Also, the verb *be* has only one past tense form in the subjunctive mood: *were.*

40i
vb

WISH

I wish I *were* more prepared for this test.

Words such as *ask, insist, recommend, request,* and *suggest* indicate the subjunctive mood; the verb in the *that* clause that follows should be in the subjunctive.

DEMAND

I insist that all applicants *find* their seats by 8:00 A.M.

CONTRARY-TO-FACT STATEMENT

He would not be so irresponsible if his father *were* [not *was*] still alive.

Contrary-to-fact statements often contain a subordinate clause that begins with *if;* the verb in the *if* clause should be in the subjunctive mood.

> ***Note:*** Some common expressions of conjecture are in the subjunctive mood, including *as it were, come rain or shine, far be it from me,* and *be that as it may.*

41 Check for problems with pronouns.

A **pronoun** *(he/him, it/its, they/their)* takes the place of a noun. The noun that the pronoun replaces is called its **antecedent.** In the following sentence, *snow* is the antecedent of the pronoun *it.*

▶ The *snow* fell all day long, and by nightfall *it* was three feet deep.

Like nouns, pronouns are singular or plural.

SINGULAR

▶ The *house* was dark and gloomy, and *it* sat in a grove of tall cedars.

PLURAL

▶ The *cars* swept by on the highway, all of *them* doing more than sixty-five miles per hour.

A pronoun needs an antecedent to refer to and agree with, and a pronoun must match its antecedent in number (plural/singular) and gender *(he/his, she/her, it/its).* A pronoun must also be in a form, or case, that matches its function in the sentence.

41a Making pronouns agree with their antecedents

Problems with pronoun-antecedent agreement tend to occur when a pronoun's antecedent is an indefinite pronoun, a collective noun, or a compound noun. Problems may also occur when writers are trying to avoid the generic use of *he.*

1. Indefinite pronouns Indefinite pronouns such as *someone, anybody,* and *nothing* refer to nonspecific people or things. They sometimes function as antecedents for other pronouns. Most indefinite pronouns are singular *(anybody, anyone, anything, each, either, everybody, everyone, everything, much, neither,*

41a
pn agr

nobody, none [meaning not one], no one, nothing, one, somebody, something).

ALWAYS SINGULAR   Did *either* of the boys lose *his* bicycle?

A few indefinite pronouns—*both, few, many,* and *several*—are plural.

ALWAYS PLURAL   *Both* of the boys lost *their* bicycles.

The indefinite pronouns *all, any, more, most,* and *some* can be either singular or plural, depending on the noun to which they refer.

PLURAL   The students debated, *some* arguing that *their* positions on the issue were in the mainstream.

SINGULAR   The bread is warm; *some* of *it* has already been eaten.

Problems arise when writers attempt to make indefinite pronouns agree with their antecedents without introducing gender bias. There are three ways to avoid gender bias when correcting a pronoun agreement problem such as the following.

FAULTY   None of the great Romantic writers believed that their achievements equaled their aspirations.

- If possible, change a singular indefinite pronoun to a plural pronoun, editing the sentence as necessary.

    ► ~~None~~ *All* of the great Romantic writers believed that their achievements ~~equaled~~ *fell short of* their aspirations.

IDENTIFY AND EDIT
Problems with Gender Bias and Pronoun-Antecedent Agreement

agr

Try these three strategies for avoiding gender bias when an indefinite pronoun or generic noun is the antecedent in a sentence:

✱ 1. *If possible, change the antecedent to a plural indefinite pronoun or a plural noun.*

> *All   our*
> - ~~Each~~ of us should decide ~~their~~ vote on issues,
> ^   ^
>   not personality.
>
> *Responsible citizens decide*
> - ~~The responsible citizen decides~~ their vote on
> ^
>   issues, not personality.

✱ 2. *Reword the sentence to eliminate the pronoun.*

> - Each of us should ~~decide their~~ vote on issues,
>
>   not personality.
>
> *votes*
> - The responsible citizen ~~decides their vote~~ on
> ^
>   issues, not personality.

✱ 3. *Substitute* he or she *or* his or her *(but never* his/her) *for the singular pronoun to maintain pronoun-antecedent agreement.*

> *his or her*
> - Each of us should decide ~~their~~ vote on issues,
> ^
>   not personality.
>
> *his or her*
> - The responsible citizen decides ~~their~~ vote on
> ^
>   issues, not personality.

> **Caution:** Use this strategy sparingly. Using *he or she* or *his or her* several times in quick succession makes for tedious reading.

41a
pn agr

- Reword the sentence to eliminate the indefinite pronoun.

  > *The*
  > ► ~~None of the~~ great Romantic writers
  >   ^
  >
  > believed that their achievements
  > *did not equal*
  > ~~equaled~~ their aspirations.
  >   ^

- Substitute *he or she* or *his or her* (but never *his/her*) for the singular pronoun. Change the sentence as necessary to avoid using this construction more than once.

  > ► **None of the great Romantic writers**
  >
  > **believed that ~~their achievements~~**
  >   *his or her*   *had been realized*
  > **~~equaled their~~ aspirations.**
  >   ^   ^

2. Generic nouns A **generic noun** represents anyone and everyone in a group—a typical doctor, the average voter. Because most groups consist of both males and females, using male pronouns to refer to generic nouns is usually considered sexist. To fix agreement problems with generic nouns, use one of the three options suggested in the preceding section.

> *College students*   *s*
> ► ~~A college student~~ should have **a** mind of
>   ^   ^
>
> their own.

> ► A college student should have ~~a mind of~~
>   *an independent point of view.*
>   ^
>
> ~~their own.~~

> ► A college student should have a mind of
>   *his or her*
>   ~~their~~ own.
>   ^

3. Collective nouns **Collective nouns** such as *team, family, jury, committee,* and *crowd* are singular unless the people in the group are acting as individuals.

▶ **All together, the crowd surged through the palace gates, trampling over everything in** *its*
~~**their**~~ **path.**

The phrase *all together* indicates that this crowd is acting as a collection of individuals.

▶ **The committee left the conference room and** *their*
returned to ~~its~~ offices.

In this case, the members of the committee are acting as individuals: each is returning to an office.

If you are using a collective noun that has a plural meaning, consider adding a plural noun to clarify the meaning: *The committee members returned to their offices.*

4. Compound antecedents Compound antecedents joined by *and* are almost always plural.

▶ **To remove all traces of the crime, James put the book and the magnifying glass back** *their places.*
in ~~its place.~~

When a compound antecedent is joined by *or* or *nor,* the pronoun should agree with the closest part of the compound antecedent. If one part is singular and the other is plural, the sentence will be smoother and more effective if the plural antecedent is closest to the pronoun.

PLURAL

Neither *the child nor the parents* shared *their* food.

When the two parts of the compound antecedent refer to the same person, or when the word *each* or *every* precedes the compound antecedent, use a singular pronoun.

SINGULAR

Being *a teacher and a mother* keeps *her* busy.

**41a
pn agr**

SINGULAR

Every poem and letter by Keats has *its* own

special power.

41b Making pronoun references clear

If a pronoun does not clearly refer to a specific antecedent, readers can become confused. Two common
problems are ambiguous references and implied
references.

1. Ambiguous references If a pronoun can refer to more than one noun in a sentence, the reference
is ambiguous. To clear up the ambiguity, eliminate
the pronoun, and use the appropriate noun.

**41b
ref**

▶ The friendly banter between Hamlet and
                                      Hamlet
   Horatio eventually provokes ~~him~~ to declare
                                           ^

   that his worldview has changed.

Sometimes the ambiguous reference can be
cleared up by rewriting the sentence.

  When   *was in London, she*
▶ Jane Austen ~~and Cassandra~~ corresponded
  ^   *with Cassandra.*   ^
  regularly ~~when she was in London.~~
          ^

2. Implied references The antecedent that a
pronoun refers to must be present in the sentence,
and it must be a noun or another pronoun, not a
word that modifies a noun. Possessives and verbs
cannot be antecedents in college writing.

    his
▶ In ~~Wilson's~~ essay "When Work Disappears,"
  Wilson ^
  ~~he~~ proposes a four-point plan for the
  ^

  revitalization of blighted inner-city

  communities.

▶ Every weekday afternoon, my brothers

skateboard home from school, and then they
their skateboards
leave ~~them~~ in the driveway.
^

3. *This, that,* and *which* The pronouns *this, that,* and *which* often refer vaguely to ideas expressed in preceding sentences. To make the sentence containing the pronoun clearer, either change the pronoun to a specific noun or add a specific antecedent or clarifying noun.

▶ As government funding for higher

education decreases, tuition increases. Are
these higher costs
we students supposed to accept ~~this~~ without
^

protest?

▶ As government funding for higher

education decreases, tuition increases. Are
situation
we students supposed to accept this without
^

protest?

**41b
ref**

4. *You, they,* and *it* The pronouns *you, they,* and *it* should refer to definite, explicitly stated antecedents. If the antecedent is unclear, replace the pronoun with an appropriately specific noun, or rewrite the sentence to eliminate the pronoun.

the government pays
▶ In some countries such as Canada, ~~they pay~~
^

for such medical procedures.
students
▶ According to college policy, ~~you~~ must have a
^

permit to park a car on campus.
The
▶ ~~In the~~ textbook, ~~it~~ states that borrowing to
^

fund the purchase of financial assets results

in a double-counting of debt.

In college writing, use *you* only to address the reader: *Turn left when you reach the corner.*

41c Choosing the correct pronoun case: for example, *I* vs. *me*

When a pronoun's form, or **case,** does not match its function in a sentence, readers will feel that something is wrong:

- Pronouns in the subjective case are used as subjects or subject complements: *I, you, he, she, it, we, they, who, whoever.*

- Pronouns in the objective case are used as objects of verbs or prepositions: *me, you, him, her, it, us, them, whom, whomever.*

- Pronouns in the possessive case show owner-ship: *my, mine, your, yours, his, hers, its, our, ours, their, theirs, whose.* Adjective forms (*her* room, *our* office) appear before nouns. Noun forms stand alone (that room is *hers; mine* is on the left). When noun forms act as subjects, the verb agrees with the antecedent *(room).*

1. Pronouns in compound structures **Compound structures** (words or phrases joined by *and, or,* or *nor*) can appear as subjects or objects. If you are not sure which form of a pronoun to use in a compound structure, treat the pronoun as the only subject or object, and note how the sentence sounds.

SUBJECT **Angela and *I* [not *me*] were cleaning up the kitchen.**

If you treat the pronoun as the only subject, the original sentence is clearly wrong: *Me [was] cleaning up the kitchen.*

OBJECT **My parents waited for an explanation from John and *me* [not *I*].**

41c case

If you treat the pronoun as the only object, the original sentence is clearly wrong: *My parents waited for an answer from I.*

2. Subject complements A **subject complement** renames and specifies the sentence's subject. It follows a **linking verb**—a verb, often a form of *be,* that links the subject to its description or definition: *Children are innocent.*

SUBJECT COMPLEMENT	**Mark's best friends are Jane and *I* [not *me*].**

You can also switch the order to make the pronoun into the subject: *Jane and I are Mark's best friends.*

3. Appositives Appositives are nouns or noun phrases that rename nouns or pronouns. They appear right after the word they rename and have the same function in the sentence that the word has.

SUBJECTIVE	**The two weary travelers, Ramon and *I* [not *me*], found shelter in an old cabin.**
OBJECTIVE	**The police arrested two protesters, Jane and *me* [not *I*].**

4. *We* or *us* When *we* or *us* comes before a noun, it has the same function in the sentence as the noun it precedes.

SUBJECTIVE	***We* [not *Us*] students never get to decide such things.**

We renames the subject: *students.*

OBJECTIVE	**Things were looking desperate for *us* [not *we*] campers.**

Us renames the object of the preposition *for: campers.*

41c case

**41c
case**

IDENTIFY AND EDIT
Problems with Pronoun Case

> *case*

Follow these steps to decide on the proper
form of pronouns in compound structures:

✱ 1. *Identify the compound structure (a pronoun and a noun or
other pronoun joined by and, but, or, or nor) in the problem sentence.*

> PROBLEM
> SENTENCE
>
> compound structure
> [Her or her roommate] should call the
> campus technical support office and
> sign up for broadband Internet service.
>
> PROBLEM
> SENTENCE
> The director gave the leading roles to
> compound structure
> [my brother and I].

✱ 2. *Isolate the pronoun that you are unsure about, then read
the sentence to yourself without the rest of the compound
structure. If the result sounds wrong, change the case of
the pronoun, and read the sentence again.*

> PROBLEM
> SENTENCE
> [Her ~~or her roommate~~] should call
> the campus technical support office
> and sign up for broadband Internet
> service.
>
> *Her should call the campus technical
> support office sounds wrong. The pronoun
> should be in the subjective case: she.*
>
> PROBLEM
> SENTENCE
> The director gave the leading roles to
> [~~my brother and~~ I].
>
> *The director gave the leading role[s] to I
> sounds wrong. The pronoun should be in
> the objective case: me.*

✱ 3. *If necessary, correct the original sentence.*

> *She*
> ▪ ~~Her~~ or her roommate should call the campus
> ^
> technical support office and sign up for broad-
> band Internet service.
>
> ▪ The director gave the leading roles to my
> *me*
> brother and ~~I~~.
> ^

5. Comparisons with *than* or *as* In comparisons, words are often left out of the sentence because the reader can guess what they would be. When a pronoun follows *than* or *as,* make sure you are using the correct form by mentally adding the missing word or words.

► Meg is quicker than she [is].

► We find ourselves remembering Maria as often as [we remember] her.

Sometimes the correct form depends on intended meaning:

► My brother likes our dog more than I [do].

► My brother likes our dog more than [he likes] me.

If a sentence with a comparison sounds too awkward or formal, add the missing words: *Meg is quicker than she is.*

41c
case

6. Pronouns as the subject or the object of an infinitive An **infinitive** is *to* plus the base verb *(to breathe, to sing, to dance)*. Whether a pronoun functions as the subject or the object of an infinitive, it should be in the objective case.

infinitive   infinitive
subject   object

► We wanted our lawyer and *her* to defend *us* against this unfair charge.

7. Pronouns in front of an *-ing* noun (a gerund)

- When a noun or pronoun appears before a **gerund** (an *-ing* verb form functioning as a noun), it should usually be treated as a possessive.

  animals'
  ► The ~~animals~~ fighting disturbed the
             ^
  entire neighborhood.

>   *their*
> ► **Because of ~~them~~ screeching, no one**
>   ^
>
> **could get any sleep.**

When the *-ing* word is functioning as a modifier, not a noun, use the subjective or objective case for the pronoun that precedes it. Consider these two sentences.

► **The teacher punished their cheating.**

Cheating is the object of the sentence, modified by the possessive pronoun *their*.

► **The teacher saw them cheating.**

Them is the object of the sentence, modified by *cheating*.

41d
case

41d Choosing between *who* and *whom*

The relative pronouns *who, whom, whoever,* and *whomever* are used to introduce dependent clauses and in questions. Their case depends on their function:

- **Subjective:** *who, whoever*
- **Objective:** *whom, whomever*

1. Pronouns in dependent clauses　If the pronoun is functioning as a subject and is performing an action, use *who* or *whoever*. If the pronoun is the object of a verb or preposition, use *whom* or *whomever*. (Note that *whom* usually appears at the beginning of the clause.)

SUBJECT　Henry Ford, *who* started the Ford Motor Company, was autocratic and stubborn.

OBJECT　Ford's son Edsel, *whom* the auto magnate treated cruelly, was a brilliant automobile designer.

2. Pronouns in questions To choose the correct form for the pronoun, answer the question with a personal pronoun.

SUBJECT ***Who* founded the General Motors Corporation?**

The answer could be *He founded it. He* is in the subjective case, so *who* is correct.

OBJECT ***Whom* did the Chrysler Corporation turn to for leadership in the 1980s?**

The answer could be *It turned to him. Him* is in the objective case, so *whom* is correct.

42 Check for problems with adjectives and adverbs.

Adjectives and **adverbs** are words that qualify—or modify—the meanings of other words. Adjectives modify nouns and pronouns. Adverbs modify verbs, adjectives, and other adverbs.

42a Using adverbs correctly

Adverbs modify verbs, adjectives, other adverbs, and even whole clauses. They tell where, when, why, how, how often, how much, or to what degree.

▶ The authenticity of the document is *hotly* contested.

▶ The water was *brilliant* blue and *icy* cold.

▶ Dickens mixed humor and pathos *better* than any other English writer after Shakespeare.

▶ *Consequently,* Dickens is still read by millions.

Do not substitute an adjective for an adverb. Watch especially for the adjectives *bad, good,* and *real,* which sometimes substitute for the adverbs *badly, well,* and *really* in casual speech.

▶ He plays the role so ~~bad~~ *badly* that it is an insult to Shakespeare.

▶ At times, he gets ~~real~~ *really* close to the edge of the stage.

▶ I've seen other actors play the role ~~good~~ *well,* but they were classically trained.

42b Using adjectives correctly

Adjectives modify nouns and pronouns; they do not modify any other kind of word. Adjectives tell what kind or how many and may come before or after the noun or pronoun they modify.

▶ The *looming* clouds, *ominous* and *gray,* frightened the children.

Some proper nouns have adjective forms. Proper adjectives, like the proper nouns they are derived from, are capitalized: *America/American.*

In some cases, a noun is used as an adjective without a change in form.

▶ *Cigarette* smoking harms the lungs and is banned in offices.

Occasionally, descriptive adjectives function as if they were nouns.

▶ The *unemployed* should not be equated with the *lazy*.

Watch out for some common problem areas with the use of adjectives:

■ **Adjectives treated as adverbs.** In common speech, we sometimes treat adjectives as adverbs. In writing, avoid this informal usage.

▶ He hit that ball ~~real good.~~ *really well*

Note that *well* can function as an adjective and subject complement with a linking verb to describe a person's health.

▶ Later that day, the patient felt *well* again.

▶ She ~~sure~~ *certainly* made me work hard for my grade.

■ **Adjectives with linking verbs.** Use adjectives after linking verbs to describe the subject. Descriptive adjectives that modify a sentence's subject but appear after a linking verb are called **subject complements.**

▶ During the winter, both Emily and Anne *were sick.*

Linking verbs are related to states of being and the five senses: *appear, become, feel, grow, look, smell, sound,* and *taste.* Verbs related to the senses can be either linking or action verbs, depending on the meaning of the sentence.

LINKING   The dog smelled *bad* [adjective].

ACTION   The dog smelled *badly* [adverb].

■ **Adjectives and adverbs that are spelled alike.** In most instances, -*ly* endings indicate adverbs; however, words with -*ly*

**42b
ad**

endings can sometimes be adjectives *(the lovely girl).* In standard English, many adverbs do not require the *-ly* ending, and some words are both adjectives and adverbs: *fast, only, hard, right,* and *straight.* Note that *right* also has an *-ly* form as an adverb: *rightly.* When in doubt, consult a dictionary.

42c Using positive, comparative, and superlative adjectives and adverbs

Most adjectives and adverbs have three forms: positive *(dumb),* comparative *(dumber),* and superlative *(dumbest).* The simplest form of the adjective is the positive form.

**42c
ad**

1. Comparatives and superlatives Use the comparative form to compare two things and the superlative form to compare three or more things.

▶ **In total area, New York is a *larger* state than Pennsylvania.**

▶ **Texas is the *largest* state in the Southwest.**

2. *-er/-est* endings and *more/most* To form comparatives and superlatives of short adjectives, add the suffixes *-er* and *-est* *(brighter/brightest).* With longer adjectives (three or more syllables), use *more* or *less* and *most* or *least (more dangerous/most dangerous).*

▶ **Mercury is the ~~most near~~ planet to the sun.**
                          nearest

A few short adverbs have *-er* and *-est* endings in their comparative and superlative forms *(harder/hardest).* Most adverbs, however, including all adverbs that end in *-ly,* use *more* or *less* and *most* or *least* in their comparative and superlative forms.

▶ **She sings *more loudly* than we expected.**

Two common adjectives—*good* and *bad*—form the comparative and superlative in an irregular way: *good, better, best* and *bad, worse, worst.*

▶ He felt ~~badder~~ as his illness progressed.
        worse

3. Double comparatives and superlatives

Use either an *-er* or an *-est* ending or *more/most* to form the comparative or superlative, as appropriate; do not use both.

▶ Since World War II, Britain has been the ~~most~~ closest ally of the United States.

4. Concepts that cannot be compared

Do not use comparative or superlative forms with adjectives such as *unique, infinite, impossible, perfect, round, square,* and *destroyed.* These concepts are *absolutes.* If something is unique, for example, it is the only one of its kind, making comparison impossible.

▶ You will never find ~~a more unique~~ *another*
   restaurant ~~than~~ this one.
                 like

42d   Avoiding double negatives

The words *no, not,* and *never* can modify the meaning of nouns and pronouns as well as other sentence elements.

NOUN	You are *no* friend of mine.
ADJECTIVE	The red house was *not* large.
VERB	He *never* ran in a marathon.

However, it takes only one negative word to change the meaning of a sentence from positive to negative. When two negatives are used together, they cancel each other, resulting in a positive meaning. Unless you want your sentence to have a positive meaning

(I am not unaware of your feelings in this matter), edit by changing or eliminating one of the negative words.

► They don't have ~~no~~ *any* reason to go there.
      ^

► He ~~can't~~ *can* hardly do that assignment.
      ^

Note that *hardly* has a negative meaning and cannot be used with *no, not,* or *never.*

43 Watch for problems with English grammar of special concern to multilingual writers.

43a art

Your native language or even the language of your ancestors may influence the way you use English. The following sections will help you with some common problems encountered by writers whose first language is not English. These sections might help native speakers as well.

43a Using articles *(a, an,* and *the)* appropriately

Some languages do not use articles at all, and most languages do not use articles in the same way as English. Therefore, articles often cause problems for multilingual writers. In English, there are only three articles: *a, an,* and *the.*

1. Using *a* or *an* A or *an* refers to one nonspecific person, place, or thing. *A* is used before words that begin with consonant sounds, whether or not the first letter is a vowel *(a European vacation, a country)*, and *an* is used before words that begin with vowel sounds, whether or not the first letter is a consonant *(an hour, an opener).*

Count nouns that are singular and refer to a nonspecific person, place, or thing take *a* or *an.* Noncount nouns and plural nouns do not take *a* or *an.* For a list of count and noncount nouns, see the box on page 328.

► The manager needs to hire ^*an*^ assistant.

► We needed to buy ~~a~~ furniture for our apartment.

2. Using *the* *The* refers to a specific person, place, or thing and can be used with singular or plural nouns. A person, place, or thing is specific if it has already been referred to in a preceding sentence, if it is specified within the sentence itself, or if it is commonly known.

**43a
art**

► We are trying to solve a difficult problem.

► ^*The problem*^ ~~Problem~~ started when we planned two

 meetings for the same day.

► ^*The girl*^ ~~Girl~~ you have been waiting for is here.

► ^*The moon*^ ~~Moon~~ is shining brightly this evening.

Exception: When a noun represents all examples of something, *the* should be omitted.

► ^*Dogs*^ ~~The dogs~~ were first domesticated long

 before recorded history.

Common nouns that refer to a specific person, place, or thing take *the.* Most proper nouns do not use articles unless they are plural, in which case they take the article *the.* There are some exceptions, however:

■ Proper nouns that include a common noun and *of* as part of the title: *the Museum of Modern Art, the Fourth of July, the Statue of Liberty*

COUNT and NONCOUNT NOUNS

A common noun that refers to something specific that can be counted is a **count noun.** Count nouns can be singular or plural, like *cup* or *suggestion (four cups, several suggestions).* **Noncount nouns** are nonspecific; these common nouns refer to categories of people, places, or things and cannot be counted. They do not have a plural form *(the pottery is beautiful, his advice was useful).*

Count Nouns	Noncount Nouns
cars	transportation
computers	Internet
facts	information
clouds	rain
stars	sunshine
tools	equipment
machines	machinery
suggestions	advice
earrings	jewelry
tables	furniture
smiles	happiness

43a
art

Following is a list of some quantifiers (words that tell how much or how many) for count nouns and for noncount nouns, as well as a few quantifiers that can be used with both:

■ **With count nouns only:** *several, many, a couple of, a number of, a few, few*

■ **With noncount nouns only:** *a great deal of, much, not much, little, a little, less,* a word that indicates a unit *(a bag of sugar)*

■ **With either count or noncount nouns:** *all, any, some, a lot of*

- Parts of the globe, names of oceans and seas, deserts, land and water formations: *the West, the Equator, the North Pole, the Mediterranean, the Sahara, the Bering Strait*
- Countries with more than one word in their names: *the Dominican Republic*
- Names of highways: *the Santa Monica Freeway*
- Landmark buildings: *the Eiffel Tower*
- Hotels: *the Marriott Hotel*
- Cultural and political institutions: *the Metropolitan Opera, the Pentagon*

43b Using helping verbs with main verbs

43b vb

Verbs change form to indicate person, number, tense, voice, and mood. *(For a detailed discussion of verbs, see Chapter 40.)* To do all this, a **main verb** is often accompanied by one or more **helping verbs** in a **verb phrase.** Helping verbs include forms of *do, have,* and *be* as well as modal verbs, such as *may, must, should,* and *would.*

1. *Do, Does, Did*   The helping verb *do* and its forms *does* and *did* combine with the base form of a verb to ask a question or to emphasize something. It can also combine with the word *not* to create an emphatic negative statement.

QUESTION	*Do* you hear those dogs barking?
EMPHATIC STATEMENT	I *do* hear them barking.
EMPHATIC NEGATIVE	I *do not* want to have to call the police about those dogs.

2. *Have, Has, Had*   The helping verb *have* and its forms *has* and *had* combine with a past participle (usually ending in *-d, -t,* or *-n*) to form the *perfect tenses.* Do not confuse the simple past tense with the present perfect tense (formed with *have* or *has*), which is distinct from the simple past because the action can continue in the present. *(For a review of perfect tense forms, see Chapter 40, pp. 303–4.)*

SIMPLE PAST	Those dogs *barked* all day.
PRESENT PERFECT	Those dogs *have barked* all day.
PAST PERFECT	Those dogs *had barked* all day.

3. *Be* Forms of *be* combine with a present participle (ending in *-ing*) to form the **progressive tenses,** which express continuing action. Do not confuse the simple present tense or the present perfect with these progressive forms. Unlike the simple present, which indicates an action that occurs frequently and might include the present moment, the present progressive form indicates an action that is going on right now. In its past form, the progressive tense indicates actions that are going on simultaneously. *(For a review of progressive tense forms, see Chapter 40, pp. 304–5.)*

SIMPLE PRESENT	Those dogs *bark* all the time.
PRESENT PROGRESSIVE	Those dogs *are barking* all the time.
PAST PROGRESSIVE	Those dogs *were barking* all day while I *was trying* to study.

Note: A number of verbs that are related to thoughts, preferences, and ownership are seldom used in the progressive tense in English. These include *appear, believe, know, like, need, own, seem, understand,* and *want.*

Forms of *be* combine with the past participle (which usually ends in *-d, -t,* or *-n*) to form the passive voice, which is often used to express a state of being instead of an action.

43b vb

BE + PAST PARTICIPLE

PASSIVE   The dogs *were scolded* by their owner.

PASSIVE   I *was satisfied* by her answer.

Intransitive verbs such as *happen* and *occur* cannot appear in the passive voice because they do not take direct objects.

▶   **The accident ~~was~~ happened after he returned from his trip.**

4. Modals   Other helping verbs, called **modals,** signify the manner, or mode, of an action. Unlike *be, have,* and *do,* one-word modals such as *may, must,* and *will* are almost never used alone as main verbs, nor do they change form to show person or number. Modals do not add *-s* endings, two modals are never used together (such as *might could*), and modals are always followed by the base form of the verb without *to.*

▶   **We must ~~to~~ study now.**

The one-word modals are *can, could, may, might, will, would, shall, should,* and *must.*

▶   **Contrary to press reports, she *will* not *run* for political office.**

Note that a negative word such as *not* may come between the helping and the main verb.

Phrasal modals, however, do change form to show time, person, and number. Here are some phrasal modals: *have to, have got to, used to, be supposed to, be going to, be allowed to, be able to.*

▶   **Yesterday, I *was going to* study for three hours.**

▶   **Next week, I *am going to* study three hours a day.**

43b
vb

43c Using verbs followed by gerunds or infinitives

Verbs in English differ as to whether they can be followed by a gerund, an infinitive, or either. The following verbs can be followed by a gerund but not an infinitive: *admit, advise, avoid, consider, defend, deny, discuss, enjoy, feel like, finish, forgive, imagine, mention, mind, practice, propose, quit, recommend, regret, resist, risk, suggest, support, tolerate, understand, urge.*

► We avoided ~~to climb~~ ^{climbing} the mountain during the storm.

Other verbs, such as the following, can be followed by an infinitive but not a gerund: *afford, appear, attempt, choose, claim, decide, expect, fail, hope, hurry, intend, learn, manage, mean, need, offer, plan, prepare, promise, refuse, request, seem, tend, threaten, want, wish, would like.*

► We attempted ~~reaching~~ ^{to reach} the summit when the weather cleared.

These verbs can be followed by either a gerund or an infinitive with no change in meaning: *begin, continue, hate, like, love, prefer, start.*

► We began climbing.

► We began to climb.

Other verbs, however, have a different meaning when followed by a gerund than they do when followed by an infinitive *(remember, stop, try)*. Compare these examples.

► She stopped eating.

    She was eating but she stopped.

► She stopped to eat.

    She stopped what she was doing before in order to eat.

Note: For some verbs, such as *allow, cause, encourage, have, persuade, remind,* and *tell,* a noun or pronoun must precede the infinitive: *I reminded my sister to return my sweater.* For a few verbs, such as *ask, expect, need,* and *want,* the noun may either precede or follow the infinitive, depending on the meaning you want to express: *I want to return my sweater to my sister. I want my sister to return my sweater.*

Make, let, and *have* are followed by a noun or pronoun plus the base form without *to: Make that boy come home on time.*

43d Using complete subjects and verbs

1. Using a complete subject Every clause in English has a subject, even if it is only a stand-in subject like *there* or *it.* Check your clauses to make sure that each one has a subject.

▶ No one thought the party could end, but
　it
　ended abruptly when the stock market
　^

　crashed.

　There is
▶ ~~Is~~ general agreement that the crash helped
　^

　bring on the Great Depression.

2. Including a complete verb Verb structure, as well as where the verb is placed within a sentence, varies dramatically across languages, but in English each sentence needs to include at least one complete verb. The verb cannot be an infinitive—the *to* form of the verb—or an *-ing* form without a helping verb.

NOT COMPLETE	The caterer *to bring* dinner.
COMPLETE VERBS	The caterer *brings* dinner.
	The caterer *will bring* dinner.
	The caterer *is bringing* dinner.

43d
inc

NOT COMPLETE	Children *running* in the park.
COMPLETE VERBS	Children *are running* in the park.
	Children *have been running* in the park.
	Children *will be running* in the park.

43e Using only one subject or object

Watch out for repeated subjects in your clauses.

▶ The celebrity ~~he~~ signed my program.

Watch out as well for repeated objects in clauses that begin with relative pronouns *(that, which, who, whom, whose)* or relative adverbs *(where, when, how).*

**43f
ad**

▶ Our dog guards the house where we live ~~there.~~

Even if the relative pronoun does not appear in the sentence but is only implied, you should still omit repeated objects.

▶ He is the man I need to talk to ~~him.~~

The relative pronoun *whom* (he is the man *whom* I need to talk to) is implied, so *him* is not needed.

43f Using adjectives correctly

English adjectives do not change form to agree with the form of the nouns they modify. They stay the same whatever the number or gender of the noun. *(For more on adjectives, see Chapter 42, pp. 322–24.)*

▶ Juan is an *attentive* father. Alyssa is an *attentive* mother. They are *attentive* parents.

Adjectives usually come before a noun, but they can also occur after a linking verb.

▶ The food at the restaurant was *delicious.*

The position of an adjective can affect its meaning, however. The phrase *my old friend,* for example, can refer to a long friendship *(a friend I have known for a long time)* or an elderly friend *(my friend who is eighty years old).* In the sentence *My friend is old,* by contrast, *old* has only one meaning—elderly.

1. Adjective order When two or more adjectives modify a noun cumulatively, they follow a sequence—determined by their meaning—that is particular to English logic:

1. Size and shape: *big, small, huge, tiny*
2. Evaluation: *cozy, intelligent, outrageous, elegant*
3. Color: *yellow, green, pale*
4. Origin and type: *African, Czech, gothic*
5. Nouns used as adjectives: *brick, plastic, glass, stone*
6. NOUN

43f
ad

▶ **the tall, African, stone statues**

2. Present and past participles used as adjectives Both the present and past participle forms of verbs can function as adjectives. To use them properly, keep the following in mind:

▪ Present participle adjectives usually modify nouns that are the agent of an action.

▪ Past participle adjectives usually modify nouns that are the recipient of an action.

▶ **This problem is *confusing*.**

The present participle *confusing* modifies *problem,* which is the agent, or cause of the confusion.

▶ **The students are *confused* by the problem.**

The past participle *confused* modifies *students,* who are the recipients of the confusion the problem is causing.

The following are some other present and past participle pairs that often cause problems: *amazing/amazed, annoying/annoyed, boring/bored, depressing/depressed, embarrassing/embarrassed, exciting/excited, fascinating/fascinated, frightening/frightened, interesting/interested, satisfying/satisfied, shocking/shocked, surprising/surprised, tiring/tired.*

43g Putting adverbs in the correct place

Although adverbs can appear in almost any position within a sentence, they should not separate a verb from its direct object. *(For more on adverbs, see Chapter 42, pp. 321–22.)*

> quickly
> ► Juan found ~~quickly~~ his cat.

The negative word *not* usually precedes the main verb and follows the first helping verb in a verb phrase.

> not
> ► I have been ~~not~~ sick lately.

43h Using prepositions

Every language uses prepositions idiomatically in ways that do not match their literal meaning, which is why prepositional phrases can be difficult for multilingual writers. In English, prepositions combine with other words in such a variety of ways that the combinations can be learned only with repetition and over time. A good dictionary can help you choose the correct preposition to use with the verb *throw,* for example, depending on whether you are *throwing something at someone, throwing something away,* or *throwing out an idea for a group to consider.*

The prepositions that indicate time and location are often the most idiosyncratic in a language. The following are some common ways in which the prepositions *at, by, in,* and *on* are used.

TIME

AT The wedding ceremony starts *at two o'clock.* [a specific clock time]

BY   Our honeymoon plans should be ready *by next week.* [a particular time]

IN   The reception will start *in the evening.* [a portion of the day]

ON   The wedding will take place *on May 1.* The rehearsal is *on* Tuesday. [a particular date or day of the week]

LOCATION

AT   I will meet you *at the zoo.* [a particular place]

You need to turn right *at the light.* [a corner or an intersection]

We took a seat *at the table.* [near a piece of furniture]

BY   Meet me *by the fountain.* [a familiar place]

IN   Park your car *in the parking lot,* and give the money to the attendant *in the booth.* [on a space of some kind or inside a structure]

I enjoyed the bratwurst *in Chicago.* [a city, state, or other geographic location]

I found that article *in this book.* [a print medium]

ON   An excellent restaurant is located *on Mulberry Street.* [a street, avenue, or other thoroughfare]

I spilled milk *on the floor.* [a surface]

I watched the report *on television.* [an electronic medium]

43i Using direct objects with two-word verbs

A two-word verb, or **phrasal verb,** combines with a preposition to make its meaning complete and often has an idiomatic meaning that changes when the preposition changes: *look out, look for.* If a two-word verb has a direct object, the preposition (also called a particle) may be either separable *(I filled the form out)* or inseparable *(I got over the shock)*. If the verb is separable, the direct object can also follow the preposition if it is a noun *(I filled out the form)*. If the direct object is a pronoun, however, it must appear between the verb and preposition.

          it
►   **I filled out it.**
           ^

Here is a list of common phrasal verbs. An asterisk (*) indicates a separable particle:

break down: stop functioning
*call off: cancel
*fill out: complete
*find out: discover
get over: recover
*give up: surrender; stop work on
*leave out: omit
look forward to: anticipate
look into: research
*look up: check a fact
look up to: admire
put up with: endure
run across: meet unexpectedly
run out: use up
stand up for: defend
turn down: reject

43i

It wasn't a matter of
rewriting but simply of
tightening up all the bolts.

—Marguerite Yourcenar

PART

8

Editing
for Correctness
Punctuation, Mechanics, and Spelling

You may have been told that commas are used to mark pauses, but that is not an accurate general principle. To clarify meaning, commas are used in the following situations:

- Following introductory elements *(pp. 340–41)*
- After each item in a series and between coordinate adjectives *(pp. 341 and 342)*
- Between coordinated independent clauses *(pp. 341–42)*
- To set off interruptions or nonessential information *(pp. 342–47)*
- To set off direct quotations *(pp. 347–348)*
- In dates, addresses, people's titles, and numbers *(pp. 348–49)*
- To replace an omitted word or phrase or to prevent misreading *(pp. 349–50)*

44a Using a comma after an introductory word group

A comma both attaches an introductory word, phrase, or clause to and distinguishes it from the rest of the sentence.

▶ **Finally, the car careened to the right.**

▶ **Reflecting on her life experiences, Washburn attributed her successes to her own efforts.**

▶ **Until he noticed the handprint on the wall, the detective was frustrated by the lack of clues.**

When the introductory phrase is shorter than five words and there is no danger of confusion without a comma, the comma can be omitted.

▶ **For several hours we rode on in silence.**

Do not add a comma after a word group that functions as the subject of the sentence.

▶ **Persuading constituents/ is one of a
politician's most important tasks.**

44b Using commas between items in
a series

A comma should appear after each item in a series.

▶ **Three industries that have been important
to New England are shipbuilding, tourism,
and commercial fishing.**

Commas clarify which items are part of the series.

| CONFUSING | For the hiking trip, we needed to pack lunch, chocolate and trail mix. |
| CLEAR | For the hiking trip, we needed to pack lunch, chocolate, and trail mix. |

Note: If you are writing for a journalism course,
you may be required to leave out the final comma
that precedes *and* in a series, just as magazines and
newspapers usually do. Follow the convention that
your instructor prefers.

44c Using a comma in front of a
coordinating conjunction that joins
independent clauses

When a coordinating conjunction *(and, but, for, nor,
or, so,* or *yet)* is used to join clauses that could each
stand alone as a sentence, put a comma before the
coordinating conjunction.

▶ **Injuries were so frequent that he began to**

worry, and his style of play became more

cautious.

If the word groups you are joining are not independent clauses, do not add a comma *(see p. 350).*

Exception: If you are joining two short clauses, you may leave out the comma unless it is needed for clarity.

▶ **The running back caught the ball and the fans cheered.**

44d Adding a comma between coordinate adjectives

A comma is used between **coordinate adjectives** because these adjectives modify a noun independently.

▶ **This brave, intelligent, persistent woman was the first female to earn a PhD in psychology.**

If you cannot add *and* between the adjectives or change their order, they are **cumulative adjectives,** with each one modifying the ones that follow it, and should not be separated with a comma or commas *(see pp. 335 and 351).*

▶ **Andrea Boccelli, the world-famous Italian tenor, has performed in concerts and operas.**

> *World-famous* modifies *Italian tenor,* not just the noun *tenor.* You could not add *and* between the adjectives (world-famous *and* Italian tenor) or change their order (*Italian world-famous tenor*).

44e Using commas to set off nonessential elements

Nonessential, or **nonrestrictive,** words, phrases, and clauses add information to a sentence but are not required for its basic meaning to be understood. Nonrestrictive additions are set off with commas.

▶ **Mary Shelley's best-known novel,**

Frankenstein or the Modern Prometheus,

was first published in 1818.

The sentence would have the same basic meaning without the title.

Restrictive words, phrases, and clauses are essential to a sentence because they identify exactly who or what the writer is talking about. Restrictive additions are not set off with commas.

► **Mary Shelley's novel *Frankenstein or the Modern Prometheus* was first published in 1818.**

Without the title, the reader would not know which novel the sentence is referring to.

Three types of additions to sentences often cause problems: adjective clauses, adjective phrases, and appositives.

1. Adjective clauses Adjective clauses begin with a relative pronoun or an adverb—*who, whom, whose, which, that, where,* or *when*—and modify a noun or pronoun within the sentence.

44e
^
,

NONRESTRICTIVE

With his tale of Odysseus, *whose journey can be traced on modern maps,* Homer brought accounts of alien and strange creatures to the ancient Greeks.

RESTRICTIVE

The contestant *whom he most wanted to beat* was his father.

Note: Use *that* only with restrictive clauses. *Which* can introduce either restrictive or nonrestrictive clauses. Some writers prefer to use *which* only with nonrestrictive clauses.

2. Adjective phrases Like an adjective clause, an adjective phrase also modifies a noun or pronoun in a sentence. Adjective phrases begin with a preposition (for example, *with, by, at,* or *for*) or a verbal (a word formed from a verb). Adjective phrases can be either restrictive or nonrestrictive.

IDENTIFY AND EDIT
Commas with Nonrestrictive Words or Word Groups

Follow these steps if you have trouble determining whether a word or word group should be set off with a comma or commas:

❋ 1. *Identify the word or word group that may require commas. Pay special attention to words that appear between the subject and verb.*

> PROBLEM SENTENCE
> subj
> Joan Didion [a native of California]
> verb
> has written essays and screenplays
>
> as well as novels.

> PROBLEM SENTENCE
> subj
> Her book *[The Year of Magical Thinking]*
> verb
> is a description of the experience of grief.

❋ 2. *Read the sentence to yourself without the word or word group. Does the basic meaning stay the same, or does it change? Can you tell what person, place, or thing the sentence is about?*

> SENTENCE WITHOUT THE WORD GROUP
> Joan Didion has written essays and screenplays as well as novels.
>
> The subject of the sentence is identified by name, and the basic meaning of the sentence does not change.

> SENTENCE WITHOUT THE WORD GROUP
> Her book is a description of the experience of grief.
>
> Without the words *The Year of Magical Thinking*, we cannot tell what book the sentence is describing.

❋ 3. *If the meaning of the sentence stays the same without the word or word group, set it off with commas. If the meaning changes, the word or word group should not be set off with commas.*

> - Joan Didion, a native of California, has written essays and screenplays as well as novels.
>
> - Her book *The Year of Magical Thinking* is a description of the experience of grief.
>
>   The sentence is correct. Commas are not needed to enclose *The Year of Magical Thinking*.

44e
^,

NONRESTRICTIVE

Some people, *by their faith in human nature or their general good will,* bring out the best in others.

The phrase is nonessential because it does not specify which people are being discussed.

RESTRICTIVE

People *fighting passionately for their rights* can inspire others to join a cause.

The phrase indicates which people the writer is talking about.

3. Appositives Appositives are nouns or noun phrases that rename nouns or pronouns and appear right after the word they rename.

NONRESTRICTIVE

One researcher, *the widely respected R. S. Smith,* has shown that a child's performance on IQ tests can be inconsistent.

Because the word *one* already restricts the word *researcher,* the researcher's name is not essential to the meaning of the sentence.

RESTRICTIVE

The researcher *R. S. Smith* has shown that a child's performance on IQ tests can be inconsistent.

The name *R. S. Smith* tells readers which researcher is meant.

44f
^
,

44f Using a comma or commas with transitional and parenthetical expressions, contrasting comments, and absolute phrases

1. Transitional expressions Conjunctive adverbs *(however, therefore, moreover)* and other transitional phrases *(for example, on the other hand)* are usually set off by commas. *(For a list of transitional expressions, see Chapter 38, p. 287.)*

► **Brian Wilson, for example, was unable to cope with the pressures of touring with the Beach Boys.**

When a transitional expression connects two independent clauses, use a semicolon before and a comma after it.

► **The Beatles were a phenomenon when they toured the United States in 1964; subsequently, they became the most successful rock band of all time.**

Short expressions such as *also, at least, certainly, instead, of course, then, perhaps,* and *therefore* do not always need to be set off with commas.

► **I found my notes and *also* got my story in on time.**

2. Parenthetical expressions   The information that parenthetical expressions provide is relatively insignificant and could easily be left out. Therefore, they are set off with a comma or commas.

► **Human cloning, so they say, will be possible within a decade.**

3. Contrasting comments   Contrasting comments beginning with words such as *not, unlike,* or *in contrast to* should be set off with commas.

► **Adam Sandler is famous as a comedian, not a tragedian.**

4. Absolute phrases   Absolute phrases usually include a noun *(sunlight)* followed by a participle *(shining)* and are used to modify whole sentences.

► **The snake slithered through the tall grass,
the sunlight shining now and then on its
green skin.**

44g Using a comma or commas to set off words of direct address, *yes* and *no*, mild interjections, and tag questions

► **Thank you, Mr. Rao, for your help.**
► **Yes, I will meet you at noon.**
► **Of course, if that's what you want, we'll do it.**
► **We can do better, don't you think?**

44h Using a comma or commas to separate a direct quotation from the rest of the sentence

44h
,

► **Irving Howe declares, "Whitman is quite
realistic about the place of the self in an
urban world" (261).**
► **"Whitman is quite realistic about the place
of the self in an urban world," declares
Irving Howe (261).**

If the quoted sentence is interrupted, use commas
to set off the interrupting words.

► **"When we interpret a poem," DiYanni says,
"we explain it to ourselves in order to
understand it."**

If you are quoting more than one sentence and
interrupting the quotation between sentences, the
interrupting words should end with a period.

▶ **"But it is not possible to give to each department an equal power of self defense," James Madison writes in *The Federalist No. 51*. "In republican government the legislative authority, necessarily, predominates."**

A comma is not needed to separate an indirect quotation or a paraphrase from the words that identify its source.

▶ **Irving Howe notes/ that Whitman realistically depicts the urban self as free to wander (261).**

Note: A comma is not needed if the quotation ends with a question mark or an exclamation point: *"Where is my sun screen?" she asked in a panic.*

(For more on using quotations, see Chapter 48, pp. 361–62.)

44i

44i Using commas with dates, addresses, titles and numbers

■ **Dates.** Use paired commas in dates when the month, day, and year are included. Do not use commas when the day of the month is omitted or when the day appears before the month.

▶ **On March 4, 1931, she traveled to New York.**

▶ **She traveled to New York in March 1931.**

▶ **She traveled to New York on 4 March 1931.**

■ **Addresses.** Use commas to set off the parts of an address or the name of a state, but do not use a comma preceding a zip code.

> ► **At Cleveland, Ohio, the river changes direction.**

> ► **My address is 63 Oceanside Drive, Apt. 2A, Surf City, New Jersey 08008.**

■ **People's titles or degrees.** Put a comma between the person's name and the title or degree when it comes after the name, followed by another comma.

> ► **Luis Mendez, MD, gave her the green light to resume her exercise regimen.**

■ **Numbers.** When a number has more than four digits, use commas to mark off the numerals by hundreds—that is, by groups of three beginning at the right.

> ► **Andrew Jackson received 647,276 votes in the 1828 presidential election.**

■ If the number is four digits long, the comma is optional.

> ► **The survey had 1856 [or 1,856] respondents.**

Exceptions: Street numbers, zip codes, telephone numbers, page numbers (p. 2304), and years (1828) do not include commas.

44j Using a comma to take the place of an omitted word or phrase or to prevent misreading

When a writer omits one or more words from a sentence to create an effect, a comma is often needed to make the meaning of the sentence clear for readers.

> ► **Under the tree he found his puppy, and under the car, his cat.**

Commas are also used to keep readers from misunderstanding a writer's meaning when words are repeated or might be misread.

► **Many birds that sing, sing first thing in the morning.**

It is often better, however, to revise the sentence to avoid the need for the clarifying comma: *Many songbirds sing first thing in the morning.*

44k Common errors in using commas

A comma used incorrectly can confuse readers. Commas should *not* be used in the following situations:

▪ To separate major elements in an independent clause.

► **Reflecting on your life/ is necessary for emotional growth.**

The subject, *reflecting on your life,* should not be separated from the verb, *is.*

► **Clarkson decided/ that her own efforts were the key to her success.**

The verb *decided* should not be separated from its direct object, the subordinate clause *that her own efforts were the key to her success.*

▪ Before the first or after the final item in a series.

► **Americans work longer hours than/ German, French, or British workers/ are expected to work.**

Note: Commas should never be used after *such as* or *like (see p. 352).*

▪ To separate compound word groups that are not independent clauses.

► **Injuries were so frequent that he became worried/ and started to play more cautiously.**

▪ To set off restrictive elements.

▶ **The applicants/ who had studied for the admissions test/ were restless and eager for the exam to begin.**

▶ **The director/ Alfred Hitchcock/ was responsible for many classic thrillers and horror films, including *Psycho.***

Adverb clauses beginning with *after, as soon as, before, because, if, since, unless, until,* or *when* are usually essential to a sentence's meaning and therefore are not usually set off with commas when they appear at the end of a sentence.

RESTRICTIVE	I am eager to test the children's IQ again *because significant variations in a child's test score indicate that the test itself may be flawed.*

**44k
no ,**

Clauses beginning with *although, even though, though,* or *whereas* present a contrasting thought and are usually nonrestrictive.

NONRESTRICTIVE	IQ tests can be useful indicators of a child's abilities, *although they should not be taken as the definitive measurement of a child's intelligence.*

■ Between cumulative adjectives (*see p. 342*).

▶ **Three/ well-known/ U.S. writers visited the artist's studio.**

■ Between adjectives and nouns.

▶ **An art review by a celebrated, powerful/ writer would be guaranteed publication.**

■ Between adverbs and adjectives.

▶ **The artist's studio was delightfully/ chaotic.**

■ After coordinating conjunctions *(and, but, or, nor, for, so, yet).*

▶ The *duomo* in Siena was begun in the thirteenth century, and⁄ it was used as a model for other Italian cathedrals.

■ After *although, such as,* or *like.*

▶ Stage designers can achieve many unusual effects, such as⁄ the helicopter that landed onstage in *Miss Saigon.*

■ Before a parenthesis.

▶ When in office cubicles⁄ (a recent invention), workers need to be considerate of others.

45a
;

■ With a question mark or an exclamation point.

▶ "Where are my glasses?⁄" she asked.

45 Semicolons

Semicolons are used to join ideas that are closely related and grammatically equivalent.

45a Using a semicolon to join independent clauses

A semicolon should join two related independent clauses when they are not joined by a comma and a coordinating conjunction *(and, but, or, nor, for, so, yet).*

▶ **Before 8000 BCE wheat was not the luxuriant plant it is today; it was merely a wild grass that spread throughout the Middle East.**

Sometimes, the close relationship is a contrast.

▶ **Philip had completed the assignment; Lucy had not.**

Note: If a comma is used between two clauses without a coordinating conjunction, the sentence is a comma splice, a serious error. If no punctuation appears between the two clauses, the sentence is a run-on. One way to correct a comma splice or a run-on is with a semicolon. *(For more on comma splices and run-on sentences, see Chapter 38, pp. 285–90.)*

45b Using semicolons with transitional expressions that connect independent clauses

Transitional expressions, including transitional phrases *(for example, in addition, on the contrary)* and conjunctive adverbs *(consequently, however),* indicate the relationship between two clauses. When a transitional expression appears between two clauses, it is preceded by a semicolon and usually followed by a comma. Using a comma instead of a semicolon creates a comma splice. *(For a list of transitional expressions, see Chapter 38, p. 287. For help with correcting comma splices, see pp. 285–90.)*

▶ **Sheila had to wait until the plumber arrived; consequently, she was late for the exam.**

The semicolon always appears between the two clauses, even when the transitional expression appears in another position within the second clause. Wherever it appears, the transitional expression is usually set off with a comma or commas.

▶ **My friends are all taking golf lessons;**
my roommate and I, however, are more
interested in tennis.

45c Using a semicolon to separate items or clauses in a series when the items or clauses contain commas

Because the following sentence contains a series with internal commas, the semicolons are needed for clarity.

▶ **The committee included Dr. Curtis**
Youngblood, the county medical examiner;
Roberta Collingwood, the director of the
bureau's criminal division; and Darcy
Coolidge, the chief of police.

If two independent clauses are joined by a co-ordinating conjunction *(and, but, for, nor, or, so, yet)* and at least one of them already contains several internal commas, a semicolon can help readers locate the point where the clauses are separated.

▶ **The closing scenes return to the English**
countryside, recalling the opening; but
these scenes are bathed in a different,
cooler light, suggesting that memories of
her marriage still haunt her.

45d Common errors in using semicolons

Watch out for and correct common errors in using the semicolon:

45d
;

- To join a dependent clause or a phrase to an independent clause.

  ► **Professional writers need to devote time every day to their writing⨯ although doing so takes discipline.**

  ► **Seemingly tame and lovable⨯ housecats can actually be fierce hunters.**

- To join most independent clauses linked by a coordinating conjunction *(and, but, or, nor, for, so,* or *yet).*

  ► **Nineteenth-century women wore colorful clothes⨯ but their attire looks drab in the black-and-white photographs of the era.**

  45d
;

- To introduce a series, an explanation, or a quotation.

  ► **My day was planned⨯ a morning walk, an afternoon in the library, dinner with friends, and a great horror movie.**

  ► **The doctor finally diagnosed the problem⨯ a severe sinus infection.**

  ► **Boyd warns of the difficulty in describing Bach⨯ "Even his physical appearance largely eludes us."**

A colon draws attention to what it is introducing. It also has other conventional uses.

46a Using colons to introduce lists, appositives, or quotations

Colons are almost always preceded by complete sentences (independent clauses).

LIST	**Several majors interest me: biology, chemistry, and art.**
APPOSITIVE	**She shared with me her favorite toys: a spatula and a pot lid.**
QUOTATION	**He said the dreaded words: "Let's just be friends."**

46b Using a colon when a second independent clause elaborates on the first one

The colon can be used to link independent clauses when the second clause restates or elaborates on the first. Use it when you want to emphasize the second clause.

▶ **I can predict tonight's sequence of events:**

   My brother will arrive late, talk loudly, and

   eat too much.

Note: When a complete sentence follows a colon, the first word may begin with either a capital or a lowercase letter. Be consistent throughout your document.

46c Using colons in business letters and memos, in ratios and expressions of times of day, for city and publisher citations in bibliographies, and between titles and subtitles

► **Dear Mr. Worth: To:**

► **The ratio of armed to unarmed members of the gang was 3:1.**

► **He woke up at 6:30 in the morning.**

► **New York: McGraw, 2010**

► ***Possible Lives: The Promise of Public Education in America***

Note: Colons are often used to separate biblical chapters and verses (John 3:16), but the Modern Language Association (MLA) recommends using a period instead (John 3.16).

46d
:

46d Common errors in using the colon

■ Between a verb and its object or complement.

► **The elements in a good smoothie are:/ yogurt, fresh fruit, and honey.**

■ Between a preposition and its object or objects.

► **Many feel that cancer can be prevented by a diet of:/ fruit, nuts, and vegetables.**

■ After *such as, for example,* or *including.*

► **I am ready for a change, such as:/ a vacation.**

Apostrophes show possession and indicate omitted letters in contractions. Apostrophes are used in such a variety of ways that they can be confusing. The most common confusion is between plurals and possessives.

47a Using apostrophes to indicate possession

For a noun to be possessive, two elements are usually required: someone or something is the possessor and someone, something, or some attribute or quality is possessed.

1. Forming the possessive of singular nouns
To form the possessive of all singular nouns, add an apostrophe plus -*s* to the noun: *baby's*. Even singular nouns that end in -*s* form the possessive by adding -*'s: bus's.*

 If a singular noun with more than two syllables ends in -*s,* and adding -*'s* would make the word sound awkward, it is acceptable to use only an apostrophe to form the possessive: *Socrates'.* Be consistent.

2. Forming the possessive of plural nouns
- To form the possessive of a plural noun that ends in -*s,* add only an apostrophe: *subjects', babies'.*
- To form the possessive of a plural noun that does not end in -*s,* add an apostrophe plus -*s: men's, cattle's.*

3. Showing joint possession   To express joint ownership by two or more people, use the possessive form for the last name only; to express individual ownership, use the possessive form for each name.

► **Felicia and Elias's report**

► **The city's and the state's finances**

47a
v

4. Forming the possessive of compound nouns For compound words, add an apostrophe plus -*s* to the last word in the compound to form the possessive: *my father-in-law's job.*

47b Using an apostrophe and -*s* with indefinite pronouns

Indefinite pronouns such as *no one, everyone, everything,* and *something* do not refer to a specific person or a specific item. Use -*'s* to form the possessive.

▶ **Well, it is anybody's guess.**

47c Using apostrophes to mark contractions

In a contraction, the apostrophe substitutes for omitted letters:

| it's | for *it is* or *it has* |
| weren't | for *were not* |

Apostrophes can also substitute for omitted numbers in a year *(the class of '11).*

Note: Although the MLA and APA style manuals allow contractions in academic writing, some instructors think they are too informal. Check with your instructor before using contractions.

47d Forming plural letters, words used as words, numbers, and abbreviations

An apostrophe plus -*s* (*'s*) can be used to show the plural of a letter. Underline or italicize single letters but not the apostrophe or the -*s*.

▶ *Committee* has two *m*'s, two *t*'s, and two *e*'s.

47d
ν

If a word is used as a word rather than as a symbol of the meaning it conveys, it can be made plural by adding an apostrophe plus -*s*. The word should be italicized or underlined, but the -*s* should not be.

► **There are twelve *no*'s in the first paragraph.**

MLA and APA style now recommend against using an apostrophe to form plurals of numbers and abbreviations.

► **He makes his 2s look like 5s.**

► **Professor Morris has two PhDs.**

47e   Common errors in using apostrophes

Do not use an apostrophe in the following situations:

- **With a plural noun.** Most often, writers misuse the apostrophe by adding it to a plural noun that is not possessive. The plurals of most nouns are formed by adding -*s: boy/ boys, girl/girls, teacher/teachers.* Possessives are formed by adding an apostrophe plus -*s* (*'s*): *boy/boy's, girl/girl's, teacher/teacher's.* The possessive form and the plural form are not interchangeable.

  ► The tea~~cher's~~ asked the gir~~l's~~ and
    teachers   *girls*
    bo~~y's~~ for their attention.
    boys

- **With possessive pronouns and contractions.** Be careful not to use a contraction when a possessive is called for, and vice versa. Personal pronouns and the relative pronoun *who* have special possessive forms, which never require apostrophes (*my/mine, your/yours, his, her/hers, it/its, our/ours, their/theirs,* and *whose*). When an apostrophe appears with a pronoun, the apostrophe usually marks omissions in a contraction, unless the pronoun is indefinite (*see p. 359*).

> That cat of ~~our's~~ *ours* is always sleeping!
> The dog sat down and scratched ~~it's~~ *its* fleas.

Its is a possessive pronoun. *It's* is a contraction for *it is* or *it has: It's [It + is] too hot.*

> They gave ~~they're~~ *their* lives.

Their is a possessive pronoun; *they're* is a contraction of *they are.* Both are also confused with the adverb *there: She was standing there.*

48 Quotation marks

48a
" "

Quotation marks enclose words, phrases, and sentences that are quoted directly; titles of short works such as poems, articles, songs, and short stories; and words and phrases used in a special sense.

Note: Citations in this chapter follow MLA style. See Part 4 for examples of APA style and Part 5 for examples of Chicago style.

48a Using quotation marks to indicate direct quotations

Direct quotations from written material may include whole sentences or only a few words or phrases.

> In *Angela's Ashes,* Frank McCourt writes, "Worse than the ordinary miserable childhood is the miserable Irish childhood" (11).

> Frank McCourt believes that being Irish worsens what is all too "ordinary"—a "miserable childhood" (11).

Use quotation marks to enclose everything a speaker says in written dialogue. If the quoted sentence is interrupted by a phrase like *he said,* enclose just the quotation in quotation marks.

Do not use quotation marks to set off an indirect quotation, which reports what a speaker said but does not use the exact words.

▶ **He said that ⁀he didn't know what I was talking about.⁀**

Exception: If you are using a quotation that is longer than four typed lines, set it off from the text as a **block quotation.** A block quotation is *not* surrounded by quotation marks. The following long quotes follow MLA style. *(For examples of APA style, see Part 4.)*

> As Carl Schorske points out, the young Freud was passionately interested in classical archeology:
>
>> He cultivated a new friendship in the Viennese professional elite—especially rare in those days of withdrawal— with Emanuel Loewy, a professor of archeology. "He keeps me up till three o'clock in the morning," Freud wrote appreciatively to Fliess. "He tells me about Rome." (273)

48a
" "

Longer verse quotations (four lines or more) are indented block style, like long prose quotations. If you cannot fit an entire line of poetry on a single line of your typescript, you may indent the turned line an extra quarter inch (three spaces).

Use single quotation marks to set off a quotation within a quotation.

▶ **In response to alumni, the president of the university said, "I know you're saying to me, 'We want a winning football team.' But I'm telling you that I want an honest football team."**

48b Using quotation marks to enclose titles of short works

The titles of long works, such as books, are usually put in italics or underlined *(see Chapter 53, pp. 383–84)*. The titles of book chapters, essays, most poems, and other short works are usually put in quotation marks. Quotation marks are also used for titles of unpublished works, including student papers, theses, and dissertations.

▶ **"The Girl in Conflict" is Chapter 11 of *Coming of Age in Samoa.***

Note: If quotation marks are needed within the title of a short work, use single quotation marks: "The 'Animal Rights' War on Medicine."

48c Using quotation marks to indicate that a word or phrase is being used in a special way

Put quotation marks around a word or phrase that someone else has used in a way that you or your readers may not agree with. These quotation marks function as raised eyebrows do in conversation and should be used sparingly.

▶ **The "worker's paradise" of Stalinist Russia included slave-labor camps.**

Words cited as words can also be put in quotation marks, although the more common practice is to italicize them.

▶ **The words "compliment" and "complement" sound alike but have different meanings.**

48d Other punctuation with quotation marks

As you edit, check all closing quotation marks and the marks of punctuation that appear next to them to make sure that you have placed them in the right order.

48d
" "

1. Periods and commas   Always place the period or comma before the final quotation mark even when the quotation is brief.

► **"Instead of sharing an experience the spectator must come to grips with things," Brecht writes in "The Epic Theatre and Its Difficulties."**

Exception: A parenthetical citation in either MLA or APA style always appears between the closing quotation mark and the period: *Brecht wants the spectator to "come to grips with things" (23).*

2. Question marks and exclamation points
Place a question mark or an exclamation point after the final quotation mark unless the quoted material is itself a question or an exclamation.

► **How does epic theater make us "come to grips with things"?**

► **Brecht was asked, "Are we to see science in the theatre?"**

3. Colons and semicolons   Place colons and semicolons after the final quotation mark.

► **Dean Wilcox cited the items he called his "daily delights": a free parking space for his scooter at the faculty club, a special table in the club itself, and friends to laugh with after a day's work.**

4. Dashes   Place a dash outside either an opening or a closing quotation mark if the dash precedes or follows the quotation or outside both if two dashes are used to set off the quotation.

► **One phrase—"time is running out"— haunted me throughout my dream.**

Place a dash inside either an opening or a closing quotation mark if it is part of the quotation.

► **"Where is the—" she called. "Oh, here it is. Never mind."**

(For more on integrating quotations into your sentences, see Chapter 13, Write the Paper, pp. 93–96.)

48e Common errors in using quotation marks

Watch out for and correct common errors in using quotation marks:

■ **To distance yourself from slang, clichés, or trite expressions.** It is best to avoid overused or slang expressions altogether in college writing. If your writing situation permits slang, however, do not enclose it in quotation marks.

WEAK   Californians are so "laid back."

REVISED   Many Californians have a carefree style.

48e
" "

■ **For indirect quotations.** Do not use quotation marks for indirect quotations. Watch out for errors in pronoun reference as well. *(See Chapter 41, pp. 314–16.)*

INCORRECT   He wanted to tell his boss that "he needed a vacation."

CORRECT   He told his boss that his boss needed a vacation.

CORRECT   He said to his boss, "You need a vacation."

■ **In quotations that end with a question.** Only the question mark that ends the quoted sentence is needed, even when the entire sentence that includes the quotation is also a question.

► **What did Juliet mean when she cried, "O Romeo, Romeo! Wherefore art thou Romeo?"?**

- **To enclose the title of your own paper.**
  Do not use quotation marks around the title of your own essay at the beginning of your paper.

  ► "Edgar Allan Poe and the Paradox of the Gothic"

49 Other punctuation marks

49a The period

Use a period to end all sentences except direct questions or exclamations. Statements that ask questions indirectly end in a period.

► **She asked me where I had gone to college.**

A period is conventionally used with the following common abbreviations, which end in lowercase letters:

Mr.	Mrs.	i.e.	Mass.
Ms.	Dr.	e.g.	Jan.

If the abbreviation is made up of capital letters, however, the periods are optional:

RN (or R.N.)	BA (or B.A.)
MD (or M.D.)	PhD (or Ph.D.)

Periods are omitted in abbreviations for organizations, famous people, states in mailing addresses, and acronyms (words made up of initials):

FBI	JFK	MA	NATO
CIA	LBJ	TX	NAFTA

When in doubt, consult a dictionary.

49b The question mark

Use a question mark after a direct question.

▶ **Who wrote *The Old Man and the Sea*?**

Occasionally, a question mark changes a statement into a question.

▶ **You expect me to believe a story like that?**

Do not use a question mark after an indirect quotation, even if the words being indirectly quoted were originally a question.

▶ **He asked her if she would be at home later?.**

Note: When questions follow one another in a series, each one can be followed by a question mark even if the questions are not complete sentences. Each question in the series can begin with either a capital or a lowercase letter.

▶ **What will you contribute? Your time? Your talent? Your money? [*or* your time? your talent? your money?]**

49c
.?!

49c The exclamation point

Use exclamation points sparingly to convey shock, surprise, or some other strong emotion.

▶ **Stolen! The money was stolen! Right before our eyes, somebody snatched my purse and ran off with it.**

Using numerous exclamation points throughout a document actually weakens their force. Try to convey emotion with your choice of words and your sentence structure instead.

▶ **Jefferson and Adams both died on the same day in 1826, exactly fifty years after the signing of the Declaration of Independence!.**

The fact that the sentence reports is surprising enough without the addition of an exclamation point.

49d Dashes

Use a dash or dashes to set off words, phrases, or clauses that deserve special attention. A typeset dash, sometimes called an *em dash,* is a single, unbroken line about as wide as a capital *M.* Most word-processing programs provide the em dash as a special character or will convert two hyphens to an em dash as an automatic function. Otherwise, you can make a dash by typing two hyphens in a row with no space between them (--). Do not put a space before or after the dash.

1. To set off parenthetical material, a series, or an explanation

► **All finite creations—including humans—are incomplete and contradictory.**

► **Coca-Cola, potato chips, and brevity—these are the marks of a good study session in the dorm.**

► **I think the Comets will win the tournament for one reason—their goalie.**

Sometimes, a dash is used to set off an independent clause within a sentence. In such sentences, the set-off clause provides interesting information but is not essential to the main assertion.

► **The first rotary gasoline engine—it was made by Mazda—burned 15 percent more fuel than conventional engines.**

2. To indicate a sudden change in tone or idea

► **Breathing heavily, the archaeologist opened the old chest in wild anticipation and found— an old pair of socks and an empty soda can.**

Note: Used sparingly, the dash can be an effective mark of punctuation, but if it is overused, it can make your writing disjointed.

▶ **After we found the puppy—shivering under the porch—, we brought her into the house— into the entryway, actually—and wrapped her in an old towel—to warm her up.**

49e Parentheses

Parentheses should be used infrequently and only to set off supplementary information, a digression, or a comment that interrupts the flow of thought within a sentence or paragraph.

▶ **The tickets (ranging in price from $10 to $50) go on sale Monday.**

When parentheses enclose a whole sentence, the sentence begins with a capital letter and ends with a period before the final parenthesis. A sentence that appears inside parentheses *within a sentence* should neither begin with a capital letter nor end with a period.

▶ **Folktales and urban legends often reflect the concerns of a particular era. (The familiar tale of a cat accidentally caught in a microwave oven is an example of this phenomenon.)**

▶ **Angela Merkel (she is the first female chancellor of Germany) formed a coalition government following her election in 2005.**

If the material in parentheses is at the end of an introductory or nonessential word group followed by a comma, place the comma after the closing parenthesis. A comma should never appear before the opening parenthesis.

▶ **As the soloist walked onstage (carrying her famous violin), the audience rose to its feet.**

Parentheses enclose numbers or letters that label items in a list.

**49e
( )**

▶ **He says the argument is nonsense because
(1) university presidents don't work as well
as machines, (2) university presidents don't
do any real work at all, and (3) universities
should be run by faculty committees.**

Parentheses also enclose in-text citations in
many systems of documenting sources. *(For more on
documenting sources, see Parts 3, 4, and 5.)*

Note: Too many parentheses are distracting to
readers. If you find that you have used a large number of parentheses in a draft, go over it carefully to
see if any of the material within parentheses really
deserves more emphasis.

49f Brackets

Brackets set off information you add to a quotation
that is not part of the quotation itself.

▶ **Samuel Eliot Morison has written, "This
passage has attracted a good deal of scorn
to the Florentine mariner [Verrazano], but
without justice."**

Morison's sentence does not include the name of the
"Florentine mariner," so the writer places the name
in brackets.

Use brackets to enclose the word *sic* (Latin for
"thus") after a word in a quotation that was incorrect in the original. If you are following MLA style,
the word *sic* should not be underlined or italicized.

▶ **The critic noted that "the battle scenes in
The Patriot are realistic, but the rest of the
film is historically inaccurate [sic]."**

49g Ellipses

Use three spaced periods, called ellipses or an ellipsis mark, to show readers that you have omitted
words from a passage you are quoting.

FULL QUOTATION FROM A WORK BY WILKINS

In the nineteenth century, railroads, lacing their way across continents, reaching into the heart of every major city in Europe and America, and bringing a new romance to travel, added to the unity of nations and fueled the nationalist fires already set burning by the French Revolution and the wars of Napoleon.

EDITED QUOTATION

In his account of nineteenth-century society, Wilkins argues that "railroads . . . added to the unity of nations and fueled the nationalist fires already set burning by the French Revolution and the wars of Napoleon."

If you are omitting the end of a quoted sentence, the three ellipsis points are preceded by a period to end the sentence.

49g
. . .

EDITED QUOTATION

In describing the growth of railroads, Wilkins pictures them "lacing their way across continents, reaching into the heart of every major city in Europe and America. . . ."

When you need to add a parenthetical reference after the ellipses at the end of a sentence, place it after the quotation mark but before the final period: . . ." (253).

Ellipses are usually not needed to indicate an omission when only a word or phrase is being quoted.

▶ **Railroads brought "a new romance to travel," according to Wilkins.**

To indicate the omission of an entire line or more from the middle of a poem, insert a line of spaced periods.

Note: Ellipses should be used only as a means of shortening a quotation, never as a device for changing its fundamental meaning or emphasis.

49h Slashes

Use the slash to show divisions between lines of poetry when you quote more than one line of a poem as part of a sentence. Add a space on either side of the slash. When you are quoting four or more lines of poetry, use a block quotation instead *(see p. 363)*.

► **In "The Tower," Yeats makes his peace with "All those things whereof / Man makes a superhuman / Mirror-resembling dream" (163–165).**

The slash is sometimes used between two words that represent choices or combinations. Do not add spaces around the slash when you use it in this way.

► **The college offers three credit/noncredit courses.**

50 cap

Slashes mark divisions in online addresses (URLs): *http://www.georgetown.edu/crossroads/navigate.html.*

Some writers use the slash as a marker between the words *and* and *or* or between *he* and *she* or *his* and *her* to avoid sexism. Most writers, however, consider such usage awkward. It is usually better to rephrase the sentence.

50 Capitalization

Many rules for the use of capital letters have been fixed by custom, such as the convention of beginning each sentence with a capital letter, but the rules change all the time. A recent dictionary is a good guide to capitalization.

50a Proper nouns

Proper nouns are the names of specific people, places, or things. Capitalize proper nouns, words derived from proper nouns, brand names, abbreviations of capitalized words, and call letters of radio and television stations:

> Ronald Reagan
> Reaganomics
> Apple computer
> FBI (government agency)
> WNBC (television station)

Note: Although holidays and the names of months and days of the week are capitalized, seasons, such as *summer,* are not. Neither ordinary the days of the month when they are spelled out *(the seventh of March).*

50a
cap

TYPES and EXAMPLES of PROPER NOUNS

- **People:** Helena Bonham Carter, Sonia Sotomayor, Bill Gates
- **Nationalities, ethnic groups, and languages:** English, Swiss, African Americans, Arabs, Chinese, Turkish
- **Places:** the United States of America, Tennessee, the Irunia Restaurant, the Great Lakes, *but* my state, the lake
- **Organizations and institutions:** Phi Beta Kappa, Republican Party (Republicans), Department of Defense, Cumberland College, the North Carolina Tarheels, *but* the department, this college, our hockey team
- **Religious bodies, books, and figures:** Jews, Christians, Baptists, Hindus, Roman Catholic Church, the Bible, the Koran or Qur'an, the Torah, God, Holy Spirit, Allah, *but* a Greek goddess, a biblical reference

PROPER NOUNS *(continued)*

- **Scientific names and terms:** *Homo sapiens, H. sapiens, Acer rubrum, A. rubrum,* Addison's disease *(or* Addison disease*),* Cenozoic era, Newton's first law, *but* the law of gravity
- **Names of planets, stars, and other astronomical bodies:** Earth (as a planet) *but* the earth, Mercury, Polaris *or* the North Star, Whirlpool Galaxy, *but* a star, that galaxy, the solar system
- **Computer terms:** the Internet, the World Wide Web *or* the Web, *but* search engine, a network, my browser
- **Days and months:** Monday, Veterans Day, August, the Fourth of July, *but* yesterday, spring and summer, the winter term, second-quarter earnings
- **Historical events, movements, and periods:** World War II, Impressionism, the Renaissance, the Jazz Age, the Declaration of Independence, the Magna Carta, *but* the last war, a golden age, the twentieth century, the amendment
- **Academic subjects and courses:** English 101, Psychology 221, a course in Italian, *but* a physics course, my art history class

50b cap

50b Personal titles

Family members: Aunt Lou, *but* my aunt, Father (name used alone) *or* my father

Political figures: Governor Andrew Cuomo, Senator Olympia Snowe, *but* the governor, my senator

Most writers do not capitalize the title *president* unless they are referring to the President of the United States: *The* president *of this university has seventeen honorary degrees.*

50c Titles of creative works

Capitalize the important words in titles and subtitles. Do not capitalize articles *(a, an, the),* the *to* in infinitives, or prepositions and conjunctions unless they begin or end the title or subtitle. Capitalize both parts of a hyphenated word. In MLA style, capitalize subordinating conjunctions *(because).* Capitalize the first word after a colon or semicolon in a title. Capitalize titles of major divisions of a work, such as chapters:

- **Book:** *Water for Elephants*
- **Play:** *The Importance of Being Earnest*
- **Building:** the Eiffel Tower
- **Ship or aircraft:** *Titanic* or *Concorde*
- **Painting:** the *Mona Lisa*
- **Article or essay:** "Next-Generation Scientists"
- **Poem:** "Stopping by Woods on a Snowy Evening"
- **Music:** "The Star-Spangled Banner"
- **Document:** the Bill of Rights
- **Course:** Economics 206: Macroeconomic Analysis
- **Chapter:** "Capitalization" in *Writing Intensive*

50d cap

50d Names of areas and regions

Names of geographical regions are generally capitalized if they are well established, like *the Midwest* and *Central Europe.* Names of directions, as in the sentence *Turn south,* are not capitalized.

CORRECT	*East* meets *West* at the summit.
CORRECT	You will need to go *west* on Sunset.

The word *western,* when used as a general direction or the name of a genre, is not capitalized *(the western High Noon).* It is capitalized when it is part of the name of a specific region: *I visited* <u>Western</u> *Europe last year.*

50e Names of races, ethnic groups, and sacred things

The words *black* and *white* are usually not capitalized when they are used to refer to members of racial groups because they are adjectives that substitute for the implied common nouns *black person* and *white person.* However, names of ethnic groups and races are capitalized: *African Americans, Italians, Asians, Caucasians.*

Note: In accordance with current APA guidelines, most social scientists capitalize the terms *Black* and *White,* treating them as proper nouns.

Many religious terms, such as *sacrament, altar,* and *rabbi,* are not capitalized. The word *Bible* is capitalized (though *biblical* is not), but it is never capitalized when it is used as a metaphor for an essential book.

▶ His book ***Winning at Stud Poker*** used to be the *bible* of gamblers.

50f First word of a sentence or quoted sentence

A capital letter is used to signal the beginning of a new sentence. Capitalize the first word of a quoted sentence but not the first word of a quoted phrase.

▶ Jim, the narrator of *My Ántonia,* concludes, "Whatever we had missed, we possessed together the precious, the incommunicable past" (324).

▶ Jim took comfort in sharing with Ántonia "the precious, the incommunicable past" (324).

If you need to change the first letter of a quotation to fit your sentence, enclose the letter in brackets.

► **The lawyer noted that "[t]he man seen leaving the area after the blast was not the same height as the defendant."**

If you interrupt the sentence you are quoting with an expression such as *he said,* the first word of the rest of the quotation should not be capitalized.

► **"When I come home an hour later," she explained, "the trains are usually less crowded."**

50g First word after a colon

If the word group that follows a colon is not a complete sentence, do not capitalize it. If it is a complete sentence, you may capitalize it or not, but be consistent throughout your document. (See whether your instructor or style guide prefers one option.)

► **The question is serious: do you think peace is possible?**

   or

► **The question is serious: Do you think peace is possible?**

51 Abbreviations and symbols

Unless you are writing a scientific or technical report, spell out most terms and titles, except in the following cases.

51a Titles that always precede or follow a person's name

Some abbreviations appear before a person's name *(Mr., Mrs., Dr.),* and some follow a proper name *(Jr., Sr., MD, Esq., PhD).* When an abbreviation follows a person's name, a comma is placed between the name and the abbreviation:

> Mrs. Jean Bascom
> Elaine Less, CPA, LL.D.

Many writers consider the comma before *Jr.* and *Sr.* to be optional.

Do not use two abbreviations that represent the same thing: *Dr. Peter Joyce, MD.* Use either *Dr. Peter Joyce* or *Peter Joyce, MD.*

Spell out titles used without proper names.

> ► **Mr. Carew asked if she had seen the** ~~dr.~~ *doctor*

51b Familiar abbreviations

If you use a technical term or the name of an organization in a report, you may abbreviate it as long as your readers are likely to be familiar with the abbreviation. Abbreviations of three or more capital letters generally do not use periods.

FAMILIAR ABBREVIATION	**The *EPA* has had a lasting impact on the air quality in this country.**
UNFAMILIAR ABBREVIATION	**After you have completed them, take these forms to the *Human Resources and Education Center* [not *HREC*].**

Write out an unfamiliar term or name the first time you use it, and give the abbreviation in parentheses.

> ► **The Student Nonviolent Coordinating Committee (SNCC) was far to the left of other civil rights organizations. However,**

SNCC quickly burned itself out and disappeared.

Abbreviations or symbols associated with numbers should be used only when accompanying a number: *3 p.m.,* not *in the p.m.; $500,* not *How many $ do you have?* The abbreviation *BC* ("Before Christ") follows a date; *AD* ("in the year of our Lord") precedes the date. The alternative abbreviations *BCE* ("Before the Common Era") and *CE* ("Common Era") can be used instead of *BC* or *AD,* respectively; both of these follow the date.

> 6:00 p.m. or 6:00 P.M. or 6:00 P.M. or 6:00 PM
> 9:45 a.m. or 9:45 A.M. or 9:45 A.M. or 9:45 AM
> 498 BC or 498 B.C. or 498 BCE or 498 BCE or 498 B.C. or 498 B.C.E.
> AD 275 or 275 CE or 275 CE or A.D. 275 or 275 C.E.
> 6,000 rpm
> 271 cm

51b
abbr

Note: Be consistent. If you use A.M. in one sentence, do not switch to *A.M.* in the next sentence. If an abbreviation is made up of capital letters, the periods are optional: *B.C. or BC. (For more on using periods with abbreviations, see Chapter 49, p. 366.)*

In charts and graphs, abbreviations and symbols such as = for *equals, in.* for *inches, %* for *percent,* and $ with numbers are acceptable because they save space.

NAVIGATING THROUGH COLLEGE AND BEYOND

Scientific Abbreviations

Most abbreviations used in scientific or technical writing, such as those related to measurement, should be given without periods: *mph, lb, dc, rpm.* If an abbreviation looks like an actual word, however, you can use a period to prevent confusion: *in., Fig.*

51c Latin abbreviations

Latin abbreviations can be used in notes or works-cited lists, but in formal writing, it is usually a good idea to avoid even common Latin abbreviations *(e.g., et al., etc.,* and *i.e.)*. Instead of *e.g.,* use *such as* or *for example.* Reword or omit constructions that use *etc.*

> *cf.* compare *(confer)*
> *e.g.* for example, such as *(exempli gratia)*
> *et al.* and others *(et alia)*
> *etc.* and so forth, and so on *(et cetera)*
> *i.e.* that is *(id est)*
> *N.B.* note well *(nota bene)*
> *viz.* namely *(videlicet)*

51d Inappropriate abbreviations and symbols

**51d
abbr**

Days of the week *(Sat.),* places *(TX* or *Tex.),* the word *company (Co.),* people's names *(Wm.),* disciplines and professions *(econ.),* parts of speech *(v.),* parts of written works *(ch., p.),* symbols *(@),* and units of measurement *(lb.)* are all spelled out in formal writing.

> ► The *environmental* [not *env.*] engineers
> from the Paramus Water *Company* [not *Co.*]
> are arriving in *New York City* [not *NYC*]
> this *Thursday* [not *Thurs.*] to correct the
> problems in the *physical education* [not
> *phys. ed.*] building in time for *Christmas*
> [not *Xmas*].

Exceptions: If an abbreviation such as *Inc., Co.,* or *Corp.* is part of a company's official name, then it can be included in formal writing: *Apple Inc. announced these changes in late December.* The ampersand symbol *(&)* can also be used, but only if it is part of an official name: *Church & Dwight.* Symbols such as @ may also appear within a URL.

52 Numbers

52a Numbers versus words

In nontechnical writing, spell out numbers up to one hundred, and round numbers greater than one hundred.

► Approximately *two hundred fifty* students passed the exam, but *twenty-five* students failed.

When you are using a great many numbers or when a spelled-out number would require more than three or four words, use numerals.

► This regulation affects nearly *10,500* taxpayers, substantially more than the *200* originally projected. Of those affected, *2,325* filled out the papers incorrectly, and another *743* called the office for help.

Round numbers larger than one million are expressed in numerals and words: *8 million, 2.4 trillion.* Use all numerals rather than mixing numerals and spelled-out words for the same type of item in a passage.

► We wrote to 132 people, but only 16 responded.

Exception: When two numbers appear together, spell out one and use numerals for the other: *two 20-pound bags.*

Punctuation tip: Use a hyphen with two-word numbers from twenty-one through ninety-nine, whether they appear alone or within a larger number: *fifty-six, one hundred twenty-eight.* A hyphen also appears in two-word fractions *(one-third, five-eighths)* and in compound words made up of a spelled-out number or numeral and another word *(forty-hour work week, 5-page paper).*

In technical and business writing, use numerals for exact measurements and all numbers greater than ten.

► The endosperm halves were placed in each of 14 small glass test tubes.

► Sample solutions with GA_3 concentrations ranging from 0 g/mL to 10^5 g/mL were added, one to each test tube.

Note: In nontechnical writing, spell out the names of units of measurement *(inches, liters)* in text. Use abbreviations *(in., L)* and symbols *(%)* in charts and graphs to save space.

52b Numbers that begin sentences

If a number begins a sentence, reword the sentence or spell out the numeral.

► ***Three hundred twelve*** students are in each elementary grade.

52c Conventional uses of numerals

- **Dates:** October 9, 2002; AD 1066 (*or* A.D. 1066); *but* October ninth, May first
- **Time of day:** 6 AM (*or* A.M. *or* a.m.), a quarter past eight in the evening, three o'clock in the morning
- **Addresses:** 21 Meadow Road, Apt. 6J; Grand Island, NY 14072
- **Percentages:** 73 percent, 73%
- **Fractions and decimals:** 21.84, 6½, two-thirds, a fourth
- **Measurements:** 100 miles per hour (*or* 100 mph), 9 kilograms (*or* 9 kg), 38°F, 15°Celsius, 3 tablespoons (*or* 3 T), 4 liters (*or* 4 L), 18 inches (*or* 18 in.)
- **Volume, page, chapter:** volume 4, chapter 8, page 44
- **Scenes in a play:** *Hamlet,* act 2, scene 1, lines 77–84

- **Scores and statistics:** 0 to 3, 98–92, an average age of 35
- **Amounts of money:** 10¢ (*or* 10 cents), $125, $2.25, $2.8 million
- **Serial or identification numbers:** batch number 4875, 105.5 on the AM dial
- **Surveys:** 9 of 10
- **Telephone numbers:** (716) 555-2174

To make a number plural, add -*s*.

53 Italics (underlining)

Italics, characters in a typeface that slants to the right, are used to set off certain words and phrases. If italics are not available, you may underline words that would be typeset in italics. MLA style, however, requires italics.

53a ital

53a Titles of works or separate publications

Italicize (or underline) titles of books, magazines, journals, newspapers, comic strips, plays, films, television series, musical compositions, choreographic works, artworks, Web sites, software, long poems, pamphlets, and other long works. In titles of lengthy works, *a, an,* or *the* is capitalized and italicized (underlined) if it is the first word, but *the* is not generally treated as part of the title in names of newspapers and periodicals: the *New York Times.*

▶ **Picasso's *Guernica* captures the anguish and despair of violence.**

▶ **Plays by Shakespeare provide details and story lines for Verdi's opera *Falstaff,* Cole Porter's musical comedy *Kiss Me, Kate,* and Baz Luhrmann's film *Romeo and Juliet.***

Court cases may also be italicized or underlined.

▶ **In *Brown v. Board of Education of Topeka* (1954), the U.S. Supreme Court ruled that segregation in public schools is unconstitutional.**

Exception: Do not use italics or underlining when referring to the Bible and other sacred books.

Quotation marks are used for the titles of short works—essays, newspaper and magazine articles and columns, short stories, individual episodes of television and radio programs, short poems, songs, and chapters or other book subdivisions. Quotation marks are also used for titles of unpublished works, including student papers, theses, and dissertations. *(See Chapter 48, p. 363, for more on quotation marks with titles.)*

53b Names of ships, trains, aircraft, and spaceships

▶ **The commentators were stunned into silence when the space shuttle *Challenger* exploded.**

53c Foreign terms

▶ **In the Paris airport, we recognized the familiar no smoking sign: *Défense de fumer.***

Many foreign words have become accepted as part of the English language—rigor mortis, pasta, and sombrero, for example—and therefore require no italics or underlining. (These words appear in English dictionaries.)

53d Scientific names

The scientific (Latin) names of organisms are always italicized.

53d
ital

▶ **Most chicks are infected with**
Cryptosporidium baileyi, a parasite
typical of young animals.

Note: Although the whole name is italicized, only the genus part of the name is capitalized.

53e Words, letters, and numbers referred to as themselves

For clarity, italicize words or phrases used as words rather than for the meaning they convey. (You may also use quotation marks for this purpose.) Letters and numbers used alone should also be italicized.

▶ **The term _romantic_ does not mean the same**
thing to the Shelley scholar that it does to
the fan of Danielle Steel's novels.

▶ **Add a _3_ to that column.**

53f
ital

53f For emphasis

An occasional word in italics helps you make a point. Too much emphasis, however, may mean no emphasis at all.

WEAK   You don't *mean* that your *teacher*
        told the whole *class* that *he* did not
        know the answer *himself?*

REVISED Your teacher admitted that he
        did not know the answer? That is
        amazing.

If you add italics or underlining to a quotation, indicate the change in parentheses following the quotation.

▶ **Instead of promising that no harm will**
come to us, Blake only assures us that we
"need not _fear_ harm" (emphasis added).

54 Hyphens

54a To form compound words

A hyphen joins two nouns to make one compound word. Scientists speak of a *kilogram-meter* as a measure of force, and professors of literature talk about the *scholar-poet*. The hyphen lets us know that the two nouns work together as one.

A dictionary is the best resource when you are unsure about whether to use a hyphen. If you cannot find a compound word in the dictionary, spell it as two separate words.

54b To create compound adjective or noun forms

A noun can also be linked with an adjective, an adverb, or another part of speech to form a compound adjective:

54b
hyph

> accident-prone
> quick-witted

Hyphens are also used in nouns designating family relationships and compounds of more than two words:

> brother-in-law
> stay-at-home

Compound nouns with hyphens generally form plurals by adding *-s* or *-es* to the most important word: *mother-in-law/mothers-in-law*.

Some proper nouns that are joined to make an adjective are hyphenated: the *Franco-Prussian war*.

Hyphens often help clarify adjectives that come before the word they modify. Modifiers that are hyphenated when they are placed *before* the word they modify are usually not hyphenated when they are placed *after* the word they modify.

► It was a *bad-mannered* reply.

► The reply was *bad mannered*.

Do not use a hyphen to connect *-ly* adverbs to the words they modify.

▶ **They explored the newly/discovered territories.**

In a pair or series of compound nouns or adjectives, add suspended hyphens after the first word of each item.

▶ **The child care center accepted three-, four-, and five-year-olds.**

54c To spell out fractions and compound numbers

Use a hyphen when writing out fractions or compound numbers from twenty-one to ninety-nine:

> three-fourths of a gallon
> thirty-two

Note: In MLA style, use a hyphen to show inclusive numbers: *pages 101-40.*

54d To attach some prefixes and suffixes

Use a hyphen to join a prefix and a capitalized word.

▶ **Skipping the parade on the Fourth of July is positively *un-American!***

A hyphen is sometimes used to join a capital letter and a word: *T-shirt, V-six engine.*

The prefixes *ex-, self-,* and *all-* and the suffixes *-elect, -odd,* and *-something* generally take hyphens. However, most prefixes are not attached by hyphens, unless a hyphen is needed to show pronunciation or to reveal a special meaning that distinguishes the word from the same word without a hyphen: *recreate* versus *re-create.* Check a dictionary to be certain you are using the standard spelling.

**54d
hyph**

▶ **Because he was an *ex-convict,* he was a *nonjudgmental coworker.***

▶ **They were *self-sufficient, antisocial* neighbors.**

54e To divide words at the ends of lines

When you must divide words, do so between syllables. However, pronunciation alone cannot always tell you where to divide a word. If you are unsure about how to break a word into syllables, consult your dictionary.

▶ **My writing group had a very fruitful *collaboration* [not *colla-boration*].**

Note: Never leave just one or two letters on a line.

55 Spelling

Proofread your writing carefully. Misspellings creep into the prose of even the best writers. Use the following strategies to help you improve your spelling:

- Use your computer software's spell checker. Remember, however, that a spell checker cannot tell *how* you are using a particular word. If you write *their* but mean *there,* a spell checker cannot point out your mistake. Spell checkers also cannot point out many misspelled proper nouns.
- Become familiar with major spelling rules and commonly misspelled words.
- Use your dictionary whenever you are unsure about the spelling of a specific word.

The basic spelling rules that follow will help you become a stronger speller.

1. Use *i* before *e* except after *c* or when sounded like *a,* as in *neighbor* and *weigh.*

- **_i_ before _e:_** believe, relieve, chief, grief, wield, yield
- **Except after _c:_** receive, deceive, ceiling, conceit

    Exceptions: seize, caffeine, codeine, weird, height

2. Prefixes do not change a word's spelling when attached.   Examples include *preview, reconnect, unwind, deemphasize.*

3. Suffixes change a word's spelling depending on the suffix or the final letter(s) of the root word.

- **Final silent _e_**

    Drop it if the suffix begins with a vowel: *force/forcing, remove/removable, surprise/surprising*

    Keep it if the suffix begins with a consonant: *care/careful.*

    Exceptions: argue/argument, true/truly, change/changeable, judge/judgment, acknowledge/acknowledgment

    Note: Keep the silent *e* if it is needed to clarify the pronunciation or if the word would be confused with another word without the *e:*

    dye/dyeing (to avoid confusion with *dying*)
    hoe/hoeing (to avoid mispronunciation)

- **Final _y:_**

    Keep it when adding the suffix *-ing: enjoy/enjoying, cry/crying*

    Keep or change it when adding other suffixes:

    - **When _y_ follows a consonant, change to _i_ or _ie_:** happy/happier, marry/married

55
sp

- **When *y* follows a vowel, keep it:**
  defray/defrayed, enjoy/enjoying

▪ **Final consonant:**

Double it if the root word ends in a single vowel + a consonant and is only one syllable long or has an accent on the final syllable: *grip/gripping, refer/referred*

For other types of root words, do not double the consonant: *crack/cracking, laundering*

Exceptions: bus/busing, focus/focused

▪ **-*ly* with words that end in -*ic*:**

Add -*ally*: logic/logically, terrific/terrifically

Exception: public/publicly

▪ **Words ending in -*able*/-*ible*, -*ant*/-*ent*, and -*ify*/-*efy*:**

**55
sp**

Consult a dictionary for the correct spelling of words ending in these frequently confused suffixes.

4. Form most plurals according to standard rules, with some exceptions. Most plurals are formed by adding -*s*. Some are formed by adding -*es*.

- **Words ending in -*s*, -*sh*, -*x*, -*z*, "soft" -*ch* (add -*es*):** bus/buses, bush/bushes, fox/foxes, buzz/buzzes, peach/peaches
- **Words ending in a consonant + *o* (add -*es*):** hero/heroes, tomato/tomatoes, *but* solo/solos
- **Words ending in a consonant + *y* (change *y* to *i* and add -*es*):** beauty/beauties, city/cities, *but* the Kirbys (a family's name)
- **Words ending in -*f* or -*fe* (change *f* to *v* and add -*s* or -*es*):** leaf/leaves, knife/knives, wife/wives, *but* staff/staffs, roof/roofs

Most plurals follow standard rules, but some have irregular forms *(child/children, tooth/teeth)*, and some words with foreign roots create plurals in the pattern of the language they come from, as do these words:

> analysis/analyses
> crisis/crises
> datum/data
> medium/media
> stimulus/stimuli
> thesis/theses

Some nouns with foreign roots have regular and irregular plural forms *(appendix/appendices/appendixes)*. Be consistent in the spelling you choose.

Note: Some writers now treat *data* as though it were singular, but the preferred practice is still to recognize that *data* is plural and takes a plural verb: *The data are clear on this point: the pass/fail course has become outdated by events.* Scientists are particularly strict about plural usage.

**55
sp**

Compound nouns with or without hyphens generally form plurals by adding *-s* or *-es* to the most important word: *sister-in-law/sisters-in-law, attorney general/attorneys general.*

For some compound words that appear as one word, the same rule applies *(passersby)*; for others, it does not *(cupfuls)*. Consult a dictionary if you are not sure.

If both words in the compound are equally important, add *-s* to the second word: *singer-songwriters.*

A few words such as *fish* and *sheep* have the same forms for singular and plural.

 For MULTILINGUAL WRITERS

American and British Spelling

Standard British spelling differs from American spelling for some words—among them *analyze/analyse, color/colour, canceled/ cancelled, defense/defence, theater/theatre, realize/realise,* and *judgment/judgement.*

Discipline-Specific Resources

The list that follows will help you get started doing research in specific disciplines. Print sources appear before electronic sources. Remember that Web addresses change frequently, so if you cannot access a site, try using a search engine.

Anthropology
Abstracts in Anthropology
Annual Review of Anthropology
Dictionary of Anthropology
Encyclopedia of World Cultures
American Anthropology Association
    <http://www.aaanet.org>
National Anthropological Archives
    <http://www.nmnh.si.edu/naa/>
Anthropology Resources on the Internet
    <http://www.anthropologie.net>

Art and Architecture
Art Abstracts
Art Index
BHA: Bibliography of the History of Art
Encyclopedia of World Art
McGraw-Hill Dictionary of Art
Artcyclopedia
    <http://www.artcyclopedia.com>
The Louvre
    <http://www.louvre.fr/>
The Metropolitan Museum of Art (New York)
    <http://www.metmuseum.org>
Voice of the Shuttle Art History and Architecture
    <http://vos.ucsb.edu/index.asp>

Biology
Biological Abstracts
Biological and Agricultural Index
Encyclopedia of the Biological Sciences
Henderson's Dictionary of Biological Terms
Zoological Record
Biology Online
    <http://www.biology-online.org/>
Harvard University Biology Links
    <http://mcb.harvard.edu/BioLinks.html>
National Science Foundation: Biology
    <http://www.nsf.gov/news/overviews/biology/index.jsp>

Business
ABI/Inform
Accounting and Tax Index
Business and Industry
Business Periodicals
Encyclopedia of Business Information Sources
Newslink Business Newspapers
    <http://newslink.org/biznews.html>

Chemistry
Chemical Abstracts (CASEARCH)
McGraw-Hill Dictionary of Chemistry
Van Nostrand Reinhold Encyclopedia of Chemistry

American Chemical
  Society
  <http://www.chemistry
  .org>
Sheffield ChemDex
  <http://www.chemdex
  .org>
WWW Virtual Library:
  Chemistry
  <http://www.liv.ac
  .uk/chemistry/links
  /links.html>

Classics
Oxford Classical
  Dictionary
Princeton Encyclopedia of
  Classical Sites
Perseus Digital Library
  <http://www.perseus
  .tufts.edu>

Communications
  and Journalism
Communication Abstracts
  International
Encyclopedia of
  Communications
Journalism Abstracts
Journalism and Mass
  Communications
Mass Media Bibliography
American Communication
  Association
  <http://www.american
  comm.org>
The Poynter Institute
  <http://www.poynter
  .org>

Computer Science
  and Technology
Computer Abstracts
Dictionary of Computing
Encyclopedia of Computer
  Science
McGraw-Hill Encyclopedia
  of Science and
  Technology

FOLDOC (Free Online
  Dictionary of
  Computing)
  <http://foldoc.org/>
MIT Computer Science and
  Artificial Intelligence
  Laboratory
  <http://www.csail.mit
  .edu/>

Cultural Studies,
  American and Ethnic
  Studies
Dictionary of American
  Negro Biography
Encyclopedia of World
  Cultures
Gale Encyclopedia of
  Multicultural America
Mexican American
  Biographies
National Museum of the
  American Indian
  <http://www.nmai.si
  .edu>
Schomburg Center for
  Research in Black
  Culture
  <http://www.nypl
  .org/research/sc/sc
  .html>
Smithsonian Center for
  Folklife and Cultural
  Heritage
  <http://www.folklife
  .si.edu/>

Economics
EconLit
PAIS: Public Affairs
  Information Service
Internet Resources for
  Economists
  <http://www.oswego
  .edu/~economic
  /econweb.htm>
Resources for Economists
  on the Internet
  <http://www.rfe.org>

Education
Dictionary of Education
Education Index
Encyclopedia of
Educational Research
International Encyclopedia
of Education
Resources in Education
The Educator's Reference
Desk
<http://www.eduref.org>
EdWeb
<http://edwebproject
.org>
U.S. Department of
Education
<http://www.ed.gov>

Engineering
Applied Science and
Technology Index
Engineering Index
McGraw-Hill Encyclopedia
of Engineering
IEEE Spectrum
<http://www.spectrum
.ieee.org>

Environmental
Sciences
Dictionary of the
Environment
Encyclopedia of Energy,
Technology, and the
Environment
Encyclopedia of the
Environment
Environment Abstracts
Environment Index
Envirolink
<http://envirolink.org>
U.S. Environmental
Protection Agency
<http://www.epa.gov>

Film
Dictionary of Film Terms
The Film Encyclopedia
Film Index International
Film Literature Index
Internet Movie Database
<http://www.imdb.com>

Geography
Geographical Abstracts
Longman Dictionary of
Geography
Modern Geography: An
Encyclopedic Survey
CIA World Factbook
<https://www.cia.gov
/library/publications
/the-world-factbook
/index.html>

Geology
Bibliography and Index of
Geology
Challinor's Dictionary of
Geology
The Encyclopedia of Field
and General Geology
American Geological
Institute
<http://www.agiweb
.org>
U.S. Geological Survey
<http://www.usgs.gov>

Health and Medicine
American Medical
Association
Encyclopedia of
Medicine
Cumulated Index Medicus
Medical and Health
Information Directory
Nutrition Abstracts and
Reviews
U.S. National Library of
Medicine
<http://www.nlm.nih
.gov>
World Health Organization
<http://www.who.int>

History
America: History and Life
Dictionary of Historical
Terms
Encyclopedia of American
History
An Encyclopedia of World
History
Historical Abstracts

Electronic Documents in History
<http://www2.tntech.edu/history/edocs.html>

History Cooperative
<http://www.historycooperative.org/>

History World
<http://www.historyworld.net/>

NARA Archival Research Catalog
<http://www.archives.gov/research_room/arc/index.html>

Languages, Linguistics, and Rhetoric

Cambridge Encyclopedia of Language

International Encyclopedia of Linguistics

LLBA: Linguistics and Language Behavior Abstracts

MLA International Bibliography

Center for Applied Linguistics
<http://www.cal.org>

CompPile
<http://comppile.org>

SIL International Linguistics
<http://www.sil.org/linguistics>

Silva Rhetoricoe
<http://humanities.byu.edu/rhetoric/Silva.htm>

Literature

Concise Oxford Dictionary of Literary Terms

MLA International Bibliography

The New Princeton Encyclopedia of Poetry and Poetics

Project Gutenberg
<http://www.gutenberg.org>

Mathematics

American Statistics Index

Facts on File Dictionary of Mathematics

International Dictionary of Applied Mathematics

Mathematical Reviews (MathSciNet)

American Mathematical Society
<http://www.ams.org>

Math Forum
<http://mathforum.org>

Music

Music Index

New Grove Dictionary of Music and Musicians

New Oxford Companion to Music

New Oxford Dictionary of Music

RILM Abstracts of Musical Literature

All Music
<http://allmusic.com>

Philosophy

Dictionary of Philosophy

Philosopher's Index

Routledge Encyclopedia of Philosophy

American Philosophical Association
<http://www.apaonline.org>

EpistemeLinks.com
<http://www.epistemelinks.com>

Physics

Dictionary of Physics

McGraw-Hill Encyclopedia of Physics

Physics Abstracts

American Institute of Physics
<http://aip.org>

American Physical Society
<http://www.aps.org>

Physics World
<http://physicsworld.com>

Political Science
Almanac of American Politics
Congressional Quarterly Almanac
Encyclopedia of Government and Politics
International Political Science Abstracts
Public Affairs Information Service (PAIS)
Political Resources on the Web
<http://www.political resources.net>
Thomas: Legislative Information on the Internet
<http://thomas.loc.gov>
United Nations
<http://www.un.org>

Psychology
International Dictionary of Psychology
Psychological Abstracts
American Psychological Association
<http://www.apa.org>
American Psychological Society
<http://www.psychologicalscience.org>
Encyclopedia of Psychology
<http://www.psychology.org/>
PsychWeb
<http://www.psywww.com>

Religion
ATLA Religion

Dictionary of Bible and Religion
Encyclopedia of Religion
Religion Index
Religions and Scriptures
<http://www.wright-house.com/religions>

Sociology
Annual Review of Sociology
Encyclopedia of Social Work
Encyclopedia of Sociology
Sociological Abstracts
American Sociological Association
<http://asanet.org>
The SocioWeb
<http://www.socioweb.com/>

Theater and Dance
International Encyclopedia of the Dance
McGraw-Hill Encyclopedia of World Drama
The WWW Virtual Library: Theater and Drama
<http://vl-theatre.com>

Women's Studies
Women Studies Abstracts
Women's Studies: A Guide to Information Sources
Women's Studies Encyclopedia
Feminist Majority Foundation Online
<http://www.feminist.org>
National Women's History Project
<http://www.nwhp.org>

Glossary
of Grammatical Terms

This glossary defines key terms used in this handbook to discuss editing for style, for grammar conventions, and for punctuation and mechanics. References in parentheses following most of the terms indicate the chapters or chapter sections in which those terms are discussed.

absolute phrase (44f) A phrase made up of a noun or pronoun and a participle that modifies an entire sentence: *Their heads hanging, the boys walked off the field.*

abstract noun See *noun.*

active voice (28c; 33b) The form of a transitive verb in which the subject of the sentence is doing the acting. See *voice.*

adjective (42b, c; 43f) A word that modifies a noun or pronoun with information specifying, for example, which one, what kind, or how many: *a delicious orange.*

adjective clause or **relative clause** (44e) A dependent clause that begins with a relative pronoun or adverb (such as *who, whom, whose, which, that,* or *where*) and modifies a noun or pronoun (see *adjective*): *The house that I grew up in eventually sold for a million dollars.*

adjective phrase (44e) A phrase that begins with a preposition or verbal and modifies a noun or pronoun: *The game, by far the longest of the season, lasted twenty-one innings.*

adverb (42a, c) A word that modifies a verb, an adjective, or another adverb with information specifying, for example, when, where, how, how often, how much, to what degree, or why: *She was terribly unhappy.*

adverb clause (44k) A dependent clause, usually introduced by a subordinating word (such as *after, because,* or *when*), that modifies a verb, an adjective, or another adverb (see *adverb*): *After he lost the tennis match, Rodrigo went straight to the gym.*

agreement (39; 41a) The appropriate pairing in number, person, and gender of one word with another. See *pronoun agreement* and *subject-verb agreement.*

antecedent (39g; 41) The noun that a pronoun replaces. In the sentence *Katya, who was at the concert, saw her picture in the paper,* the antecedent of the pronouns *who* and *her* is *Katya.* See *pronoun reference.*

appositive (37c; 41c; 44e.3) A noun or noun phrase that appears next to a noun or pronoun and renames it: *My friend Max, the best dancer on campus, is a chemistry major.*

articles (43a) The words *a, an,* and *the. A* and *an* are **indefinite articles;** *the* is a **definite article.**

auxiliary verb (43b) See *helping verb.*

block quotation (48a) A long direct quotation that is not enclosed by quotation marks but is set off from the text.

case (41c) The form of a noun or pronoun, determined by the grammatical role it plays in a sentence. See *pronoun case.*

clause (37, 44c) A group of related words containing a subject and a predicate. An **independent (main) clause** can stand on its own as a sentence: *We can have a picnic.* A **dependent (subordinate) clause** cannot stand on its own as a sentence: *We can have a picnic if it doesn't rain.*

cliché (35d) An overworked expression or figure of speech.

collective noun (39c; 41a.3) See *noun.*

comma splice (38) An error in which two independent clauses are joined by a comma without a coordinating conjunction.

common noun See *noun.*

comparison (42c) The form of an adjective or adverb that indicates its degree or amount. The positive degree is the simple form and involves no comparison: *large, difficult* (adjectives); *far, confidently* (adverbs). The comparative degree compares two things: *larger, more difficult; farther, more/less confidently.* The superlative degree compares three or more things, indicating which is the greatest or the least: *largest, most difficult; farthest, most/least confidently.*

complement See *subject complement* and *object complement.*

complete predicate See *predicate.*

complete subject See *subject.*

complete verb (37; 40h) A main verb and any helping verbs needed to indicate tense, person, and number.

complex sentence See *sentence.*

compound predicate (37c) Two or more predicates connected by a conjunction.

compound sentence See *sentence.*

compound-complex sentence See *sentence.*

compound structures (41c.1) Words or phrases joined by *and, or,* or *nor.*

compound subject (39b) See *subject*.

concise (25) Of writing, employing as few words as needed to be clear and engaging.

concrete noun See *noun*.

concrete word (35b) A **concrete** word names things that can be perceived with the senses, such as *chocolate* or *jacket*.

conjunction (31; 39b) A word that joins words, phrases, or clauses and indicates their relation to each other. **Coordinating conjunctions** (such as *and, but, or, nor, for, so,* or *yet*) join words or ideas of equal weight or function: *The night grew colder, but the boys and girls kept trick or treating.* **Correlative conjunctions** (such as *both . . . and, neither . . . nor, not only . . . but also*) link sentence elements of equal value, always in pairs: *She knew that either her mother or her father would drive her to the airport.* **Subordinating conjunctions** (such as *after, although, as if, because, if,* or *when*) introduce dependent or subordinate clauses, linking sentence elements that are not of equal importance: *They waltzed while the band played on.*

conjunctive adverb (38b; 45b) A word or expression such as *for example, however,* or *therefore* that indicates the relation between two clauses. Unlike conjunctions, conjunctive adverbs are not grammatically strong enough on their own to hold the two clauses together, requiring the clauses to be separated by a period or semicolon: *The night grew colder; however, the boys and girls kept trick or treating.*

connotation (35a) The secondary, or implicit, meaning of a word that derives from the feelings and images it evokes.

contraction (47c) A shortened word formed when two words are combined and letters are replaced with an apostrophe: *doesn't* for *does not*.

coordinate adjectives (44d) Two or more adjectives that act individually to modify a noun or pronoun: *It was a dark and stormy night.* Coordinate adjectives are separated by a comma: *It was a dark, stormy night.*

coordinating conjunction or **coordinator** See *conjunction*.

coordination (31a) In a sentence, the joining of elements of equal weight. See also *subordination*.

correlative conjunction See *conjunction*.

count noun (43a) See *noun*.

cumulative adjectives (44d) Adjectives that act as a set and should not be separated by a comma. The first adjective modifies the following adjective or adjectives as well as the noun or pronoun: *world-famous American sculptor.*

cumulative sentence (32c) A sentence that begins with a subject and verb and then accumulates information in a series of descriptive modifiers: *The reporters ran after the film star, calling out questions and shoving each other aside.*

dangling modifier (30e) A modifier that confusingly implies an actor different from the sentence's subject: *Being so valuable, thousands of people flooded into California during the Gold Rush.*

definite article See *articles.*

demonstrative pronoun A pronoun such as *this, that, these,* and *those* that points out nouns and pronouns that come later: *This is the house that Jack built.*

denotation (35a) The primary, or dictionary, definition of a word.

dependent or **subordinate clause** See *clause.*

dialect A variant of a language that is used by a particular social, geographical, or ethnic group.

diction (35) Word choice.

direct address (44g) A construction that includes a word or phrase that names the person or group being spoken to: *Are you coming, Vinny?*

direct object See *object.*

direct question (49b) A sentence that asks a question and concludes with a question mark. Contrast with *indirect question.*

direct quotation (48a) The reproduction of the exact words someone else has spoken or written. In academic writing, direct quotations are enclosed in quotation marks or, if long, set off in a separate block of text.

doublespeak (34d) The deceitful use of language to obscure facts and mislead readers.

euphemism (34d) An innocuous word or phrase that substitutes for a harsh, blunt, or offensive alternative: *pass away* for *die.*

excessive coordination The use of coordination to string together too many ideas at once.

excessive subordination (31c) The use of subordination to string together too many subordinate expressions at once.

exclamatory sentence (32d; 49c) A sentence that expresses strong emotion and ends with an exclamation point.

expletive construction (25c) The use of *there, here,* or *it* in the subject position of a sentence, followed by a form of *be: Here are the directions.* The subject follows the verb.

faulty coordination (31a) The use of coordination to join sentence elements that aren't logically equivalent, or elements joined with an inappropriate coordinating word.

faulty parallelism (29) An error that results when items in a series, paired ideas, or items in a list do not have the same grammatical form.

faulty predication (27b) An illogical, ungrammatical combination of subject and predicate.

figure of speech or **figurative language** (35e) An imaginative expression, usually a comparison, that amplifies the literal meaning of other words. See also *metaphor* and *simile*.

fused sentence (38) See *run-on sentence*.

gender (41a) The classification of nouns and pronouns as masculine (*he, father*), feminine (*she, mother*), or neuter (*it, painter*).

generic noun (41a.2) A noun used to represent anyone and everyone in a group: *the average voter; the modern university.*

gerund (39h; 41c.7) The present participle (*-ing*) form of a verb used as a noun: *Most college courses require writing.* See *verbal*.

gerund phrase (39h) A word group consisting of a gerund followed by objects, complements, or modifiers: *Walking to the mailbox was my grandmother's only exercise.*

helping or **auxiliary verb** (40h; 43b) Verbs that combine with main verbs to indicate a variety of meanings, including tense, mood, voice, and manner. Helping verbs include forms of *be, have,* and *do* and the modal verbs *can, could, may, might, shall, should,* and *will.* See *modal verb*.

idiom (35c) An expression whose meaning is established by custom and cannot be determined from the dictionary definition of the words that compose it: *Boston Red Sox fans were in seventh heaven when their team finally won the World Series in 2004.*

imperative mood (28c; 40i) Of verbs, the mood that expresses commands, directions, and entreaties: *Please don't leave.* See *mood*.

indefinite article See *articles*.

indefinite pronoun (39d; 41a.1) A pronoun such as *someone, anybody, nothing,* and *few* that does not refer to a specific person or item.

independent or **main clause** See *clause*.

indicative mood (28c; 40i) Of verbs, the most common mood, used to make statements (*We are going to the beach*) or ask questions (*Do you want to come along?*). See *mood*.

indirect object See *object*.

indirect question (49b) A sentence that reports a question and ends with a period: *My mother often wonders if I'll ever settle down.* Contrast with *direct question*.

indirect quotation (48a) A sentence that reports, as opposed to repeating verbatim, what someone else has said or written. Indirect quotations are not enclosed in quotation marks.

infinitive (30d; 41c) A verbal consisting of the base form of a verb preceded by *to: to run, to eat.* See *verbal.*

infinitive phrase An infinitive, plus any subject, objects, or modifiers, that functions as an adverb, adjective, or noun: *When I was a child, I longed <u>to be a famous soprano</u>.*

intensive pronoun A pronoun ending with the suffix *-self* or *-selves* that adds emphasis to the noun or pronoun it follows. It is grammatically optional: *I <u>myself</u> couldn't care less.*

interjection A forceful expression, usually written with an exclamation point: *Hey! Beat it!*

interrogative pronoun A pronoun (*who, whose, whom, which, what, whatever*) used to ask questions.

interrogative sentence A sentence that poses a direct question.

intransitive verb (40b) A verb that describes an action or a state of being and does not take a direct object: *The tree <u>fell</u>.*

inversion (32d) In sentences, a reversal of standard word order, as when the verb comes before the subject: *Up jumped the cheerleaders.*

irregular verb (40a) A verb that forms the past tense and past participle other than by adding *-ed* or *-d.*

jargon (34c) One group's specialized, technical language used in an inappropriate context; that is, used with people outside the group or when it does not suit a writer's purpose.

limiting modifier (30b) A word such as *only, even, almost, really,* and *just* that qualifies the meaning of another word or word group.

linking verb (39f; 40h; 41c.2) A verb that joins a subject to its subject complement. Forms of *be* are the most common linking verbs: *They <u>are</u> happy.* Others include *look, appear, feel, become, smell, sound,* and *taste: The cloth <u>feels</u> soft.*

main verb The part of a verb phrase that carries the principal meaning.

mechanics (50–54) Conventions regarding the use of capital letters, italics, abbreviations, numbers, and hyphens.

metaphor (35e) An implied comparison between two unlike things: *Your harsh words <u>stung</u> my pride.* See *figure of speech.* Compare to *simile.*

misplaced modifier (30a–c) A modifier placed confusingly far from the expression it modifies, that ambiguously modifies more than one expression, or that awkwardly disrupts the relationships among the grammatical elements of a sentence.

mixed construction (27) A sentence with parts that do not fit together logically or grammatically.

mixed metaphor (35e) A confusing combination of two or more incompatible or incongruous metaphoric comparisons: *His fortune burned a hole in his pocket and trickled away.*

modal verb (43b.4) A helping verb that signifies the manner, or mode, of an action: *You should get ready for your guests.*

modifier (30; 42) A word or group of words functioning as an adjective or adverb to describe or limit another word or group of words.

mood (40i) The form of a verb that reveals the speaker's or writer's attitude toward the action of a sentence. The **indicative mood** is used to state or question facts, acts, and opinions: *The wedding is this weekend. Did you get your suit pressed?* The **imperative mood** is used for commands, directions, and entreaties: *Take your dirty dishes to the kitchen.* The **subjunctive mood** is used to express a wish or a demand or to make a statement contrary to fact: *If I were rich, I would travel the world by boat.*

noncount noun (43a) See *noun.*

nonrestrictive element (44e) A nonessential element that adds information to a sentence but is not required for understanding its basic meaning.

noun A word that names a person, place, thing, or idea: *David, Yosemite, baseball, democracy.* **Common nouns** name a general class and are not capitalized: *teenager, dorm, street.* **Proper nouns** name specific people, places, or things and are capitalized: *Shakespeare, London, Globe Theater.* **Count nouns** name specific items that can be counted: *muscle, movie, bridge.* **Noncount nouns** name nonspecific things that cannot be counted: *advice, air, time.* **Concrete nouns** name things that can be perceived by the senses: *wind, song, man.* **Abstract nouns** name qualities and concepts that do not have physical properties: *love, courage, hope.* **Collective nouns** are singular in form but name groups of people or things: *crew, family, audience.*

noun clause A dependent clause that functions as a noun: *They told me where to meet them.*

noun phrase A noun plus all of its modifiers.

number (39) The form of a verb, noun, or pronoun that indicates whether it is singular or plural.

object A noun or pronoun that receives or is influenced by the action reported by a transitive verb, a preposition, or a verbal. A **direct object** receives the action of a transitive verb or verbal and usually follows it in a sentence: *Tom and I watched the sunrise together.* An **indirect object** names for or to whom something is done: *Tom promised me a pancake breakfast afterward.* The **object of a preposition** usually follows a preposition and completes its meaning: *We drove into <u>town</u> together.*

object complement A word or group of words that follows an object in a sentence and describes or renames it: *I call my cousin <u>Mr. Big</u>.*

object of a preposition See *object*.

objective case See *pronoun case*.

parallelism (29) The presentation of equal ideas in the same grammatical form: individual terms with individual terms, phrases with phrases, and clauses with clauses.

participial phrase (32a) A word group that consists of a participle and any objects or modifiers and functions as an adjective: *<u>Jumping the fence</u>, the dog ran down the street.*

participle (40a) The *-ing* (present participle) or *-ed* (past participle) form of a verb. (In regular verbs, the past tense and the past participle are the same.) Participles are used with helping verbs in verb phrases (*They <u>are walking</u> slowly*), as verbals (*<u>Walking</u> is good exercise*), and as adjectives (*The <u>walking</u> dead haunt his dreams*). See *verb phrase* and *verbal*.

parts of speech The eight primary categories to which all English words belong: verbs, nouns, pronouns, adjectives, adverbs, prepositions, conjunctions, and interjections.

passive voice (28c; 33b) The form of a transitive verb in which the subject of the sentence is acted upon. See *voice*.

perfect tense See *tense*.

periodic sentence (32c) A sentence in which the key word, phrase, or idea appears at the end: *Despite a massive investment, the assembling of a stellar cast, and months of marketing hype, the movie flopped.*

person (39) The form of a verb or pronoun that indicates whether the subject of a sentence is speaking or writing (*first person*), is spoken or written to (*second person*), or is spoken or written about (*third person*).

personal pronoun (41) A pronoun that stands for a specific person or thing. The personal pronouns are *I, me, you, he, his, she, her, it, we, us, they,* and *them*.

phrasal verb (35c, 43i) A verb that combines with a preposition to make its meaning complete and often has an idiomatic meaning that changes when the preposition changes: *look out, dig into.*

phrase (37b) A group of related words that lacks either a subject or a predicate or both and cannot stand alone as an independent sentence. Phrases function within sentences as nouns, verbs, and modifiers.

plural Referring to more than one. See *number*.

possessive case See *pronoun case*.

possessive noun A noun that indicates possession or ownership: *Jesse's, America's.*

possessive pronoun A pronoun that indicates ownership: *mine, ours.*

predicate (27b) In a sentence, the verb and its objects, complements, or modifiers. The predicate reports or declares (*predicates*) something about the subject. The verb itself, including any helping verbs, constitutes the **simple predicate.** The simple predicate together with its objects, complements, and modifiers constitutes the **complete predicate.**

preposition (43h) A word that precedes a noun, pronoun, or noun phrase (the *object of the preposition*) and allows the resulting *prepositional phrase* to modify another word or word group in the sentence.

prepositional phrase A preposition and its object: *We went to the movies after completing our exams.*

present tense See *tense.*

pretentious language (34b) Language that is overly formal or full of fancy phrases, making it inappropriate for academic writing.

progressive tense See *tense.*

pronoun (41) A word that takes the place of a noun.

pronoun agreement (41a) The appropriate pairing in number, person, and gender of a pronoun with its antecedent: *Judi loved her tiny apartment.*

pronoun case (41c) The form of a pronoun that reflects its function in a sentence. Most pronouns have three cases: **subjective** (*I, she*), **objective** (*me, her*), and **possessive** (*my, hers*).

pronoun reference (41b) The nature of the relationship—clear or ambiguous—between a pronoun and the word it replaces, its **antecedent.**

proper adjective (42b) An adjective formed from a proper noun, such as *Britain/British.*

proper noun (50a) See *noun.*

quotation (48a, d, e) A restatement, either directly (verbatim) or indirectly, of what someone has said or written. See *direct quotation* and *indirect quotation.*

reciprocal pronoun A pronoun such as *each other* or *one another* that refers to the separate parts of its plural antecedent: *They helped one another escape from the flooded city.*

redundancy (25a) Unnecessary repetition.

reflexive pronoun A pronoun ending in *-self* or *-selves* that refers to the sentence subject: *They asked themselves if they were doing the right thing.* Reflexive pronouns, unlike intensive pronouns, are grammatically necessary. See *intensive pronoun*.

regionalism (34a) An expression common to the people in a particular region.

regular verb (40a) A verb that forms its past tense and past participle by adding *-d* or *-ed* to the base form.

relative clause See *adjective clause*.

relative pronoun A pronoun such as *who, whom, which,* or *that* used to relate a relative (adjective) clause to an antecedent noun or pronoun: *The woman who came in second is a friend of ours.*

restrictive element (44e) A word, phrase, or clause with essential information about the noun or pronoun it describes. Restrictive elements are not set off by commas: *The house that Jack built is sturdy.*

rhetorical question (32d) A question asked for effect, with no expectation of an answer.

run-on sentence or **fused sentence** (38) An error in which two independent clauses are joined together without punctuation or a connecting word.

sentence A subject and predicate not introduced by a subordinating word that fit together to make a statement, ask a question, give a command, or express an emotion. A **simple sentence** is composed of only one independent clause: *I am studying.* A **compound sentence** contains two or more coordinated independent clauses: *I would like to go to the movies, but I am studying.* A **complex sentence** contains one independent clause and one or more dependent clauses: *If you try to make me go to the movies, I'll be really annoyed.* A **compound-complex sentence** contains two or more coordinated independent clauses and at least one dependent clause: *I'm staying home to study because I'm failing the course, but I'd much rather go to a movie.*

sentence fragment (37) An incomplete sentence that is treated as if it were complete, with a capital letter at the beginning and a closing mark of punctuation.

sexist language (34e) Language that demeans or stereotypes women or men based on their sex.

simile (35e) A comparison, using *like* or *as,* of two unlike things: *His eyes were like saucers.* See *figure of speech*.

simple predicate See *predicate*.

simple sentence See *sentence*.

simple subject See *subject*.

simple tense See *tense*.

singular Referring to one. See *number*.

slang (34a) An informal and playful type of language used within a social group or discourse community and generally not appropriate for academic writing.

specific word (35b) A word that names a particular kind of thing or item, such as *pines* or *college senior.*

split infinitive (30d) One or more words interposed between the two words of an infinitive: *The team hoped to immediately rebound from its defeat.*

subject (37; 39b) The words that name the topic of a sentence, which the predicate makes a statement about. The **simple subject** is the pronoun or noun that identifies the topic of a sentence: *The dog was in the yard.* The **complete subject** includes the simple subject and its modifiers: *The big black dog was in the yard.* A **compound subject** contains two or more subjects connected by a conjunction: *The dog and cat faced each other across the fence.*

subject complement (39f; 41c.2; 42b) A word or word group that follows a linking verb and renames or specifies the sentence's subject. It can be a noun or an adjective.

subject-verb agreement (39) The appropriate pairing, in number and person, of a subject and a verb: *The student looks confused. The students look confused.*

subjective case See *pronoun case.*

subjunctive mood (28c; 40) Of verbs, the mood used to express a wish or a request or to state a condition contrary to fact: *I wish I were home.* See *mood.*

subordinating conjunction or **subordinator** See *conjunction.*

subordination (31b, c) In a sentence, the joining of a secondary (subordinate) element to the main element in a way that shows the logical relationship between the two: *Although we shopped for hours, we didn't find a dress for the party.*

synonyms (35a) Words with similar meanings, such as *scowl* and *frown.*

syntax The rules for forming grammatical sentences in a language.

tag question (44g) A question attached at the end of a sentence. *It's hot today, isn't it?*

tense (40e) The form of a verb that indicates its time of action, whether present, past, or future. There are three **simple tenses:** present (*I laugh*), past (*I laughed*), and future (*I will laugh*). The **perfect tenses** indicate actions that were or will be completed by the time of another action or time: *I have spoken* (present perfect), *I had spoken* (past perfect), *I will have spoken* (future perfect). The **progressive forms** of the simple and perfect tenses indicate ongoing action: *I am laughing* (present progressive), *I was laughing* (past progressive), *I will* *be laughing* (future progressive), *I have been laughing* (present perfect progressive), *I had been laughing* (past perfect progressive), *I will have been laughing* (future progressive).

transitive verb (40b) A verb that takes a direct object. *He bought a new bike last week.*

verb (37) A word that reports an action, a condition, or a state of being. Verbs change form to indicate person, number, tense, voice, and mood.

verb phrase A main verb plus its helping verbs: *Louie is helping with the party preparations.*

verbal (37b) A word formed from a verb that functions as a noun, an adjective, or an adverb, not as a verb.

verbal phrase A verbal plus an object, a complement, or a modifier.

voice (33b) The form of a verb used to indicate whether the subject of a sentence does the acting or is acted upon. In the **active voice,** the subject acts: *The crowd sang "Take Me Out to the Ballgame."* In the **passive voice,** the subject is acted upon: *"Take Me Out to the Ballgame" was sung by the crowd.*

wordy phrase (25b) A phrase that provides little or no information: *The fact is, the planets revolve around the sun.*

Credits

Index

Index for Multilingual Writers

Abbreviations and Symbols for Editing and Proofreading

abbr	Faulty abbreviation **51**	*p*	Punctuation error
ad	Misused adjective or adverb **42**		⌢ Comma **44a–j**
agr	Problem with subject-verb or pronoun agreement **39, 41a**	*no ,*	Unnecessary comma **44k**
appr	Inappropriate word or phrase **34**		; Semicolon **45**
art	Incorrect or missing article **26d, 43a**		: Colon **46**
awk	Awkward		⌄ Apostrophe **47**
cap	Faulty capitalization **50**		" " Quotation marks **48**
case	Error in pronoun case **41c**		. ?! Period, question mark, exclamation point **49a–c**
cliché	Overused expression **35d**		— ( ) [ ] Dash, parentheses, brackets,
com	Incomplete comparison **26c**		. . . / ellipses, slash **49d–h**
coord	Problem with coordination **31**	*para*	Problem with a paraphrase **12d**
cs	Comma splice **38**	*pass*	Ineffective use of passive voice **33b**
d	Diction problem **34, 35**	*pn agr*	Problem with pronoun agreement **41a**
dev	More development needed	*quote*	Problem with a quotation **12d, 13b, 48a**
dm	Dangling modifier **30e**	*ref*	Problem with pronoun reference **41b**
doc	Documentation problem		
	APA **19, 20, 21, 22**	*rep*	Repetitious words or phrases **25a**
	Chicago **23, 24**	*run-on*	Run-on (or fused) sentence **38**
	MLA **14, 15, 16, 17, 18**	*sexist*	Sexist language **34e, 41a**
emph	Problem with emphasis **31**	*shift*	Shift in point of view, tense, mood, or voice **28**
exact	Inexact word **35**	*sl*	Slang **34a**
frag	Sentence fragment **37**	*sp*	Misspelled word **55**
fs	Fused (or run-on) sentence **38**	*sub*	Problem with subordination **31**
hyph	Problem with hyphen **54**	*sv agr*	Problem with subject-verb agreement **39**
inc	Incomplete construction **26**	*t*	Verb tense error **40e**
ital	Italics or underlining needed **53**	*usage*	See Glossary of Usage **36**
jarg	Jargon **34c**	*var*	Vary your sentence structure **32**
lc	Lowercase letter needed **50**	*vb*	Verb problem **40**
mix	Mixed construction **27**	*w*	Wordy **25**
mm	Misplaced modifier **30a–d**	*ww*	Wrong word **35f**
mng	Meaning not clear	*//*	Parallelism needed **29**
mood	Error in mood **40i**	*#*	Add space
ms	Error in manuscript form **6**	*^*	Insert
	APA **21**	*◠*	Close up space
	Chicago **24**	*x*	Obvious error
	MLA **17**	*??*	Unclear
num	Error in number style **52**		
¶	Paragraph		

Contents